The Mooring of Starting Out

Also by John Ashbery

THE MOORING OF STARTING OUT

JOHN ASHBERY

The

First

Five

Books

of

Poetry

THE ECCO PRESS

THE ECCO PRESS
100 West Broad Street
Hopewell, New Jersey 08525

Published simultaneously in Canada by
Penguin Books Canada Ltd., Ontario
Printed in the United States of America

Library of Congress Cataloging-in-Publication Data
Ashbery, John.
    The mooring of starting out : the first five books of poetry / by John Ashbery.—1st
Ecco ed.
            p.   cm.
    Contents: Some trees—The tennis court oath—Rivers and mountains—The double
dream of spring—Three poems.
    ISBN 0-88001-527-6
    ISBN 0-88001-547-0 (paperback)
    I. Title.
  PS3501.S475A6   1997
  811'.54—dc 21   96-36982

Designed by Angela Foote Design
The text of this book is set in Caslon
9 8 7 6 5 4 3 2 1
FIRST EDITION 1997

Contents

THREE POEMS   **307**

TITLE INDEX   385

SOME TREES

TO MY PARENTS

Two Scenes

We see us as we truly behave:
From every corner comes a distinctive offering.
The train comes bearing joy;
The sparks it strikes illuminate the table.
Destiny guides the water-pilot, and it is destiny.
For long we hadn't heard so much news, such noise.
The day was warm and pleasant.
"We see you in your hair,
Air resting around the tips of mountains."

2.

A fine rain anoints the canal machinery.
This is perhaps a day of general honesty
Without example in the world's history
Though the fumes are not of a singular authority
And indeed are dry as poverty.
Terrific units are on an old man
In the blue shadow of some paint cans
As laughing cadets say, "In the evening
Everything has a schedule, if you can find out what it is."

Popular Songs

He continued to consult her for her beauty
(The host gone to a longing grave).
The story then resumed in day coaches
Both bravely eyed the finer dust on the blue. That summer
("The worst ever") she stayed in the car with the cur.
That was something between her legs.
Alton had been getting letters from his mother
About the payments—half the flood
Over and what about the net rest of the year?
Who cares? Anyway (you know how thirsty they were)
The extra worry began it—on the
Blue blue mountain—she never set foot
And then and there. Meanwhile the host
Mourned her quiet tenure. They all stayed chatting.
No one did much about eating.
The tears came and stopped, came and stopped, until
Becoming the guano-lightened summer night landscape,
All one glow, one mild laugh lasting ages.
Some precision, he fumed into his soup.

You laugh. There is no peace in the fountain.
The footmen smile and shift. The mountain
Rises nightly to disappointed stands
Dining in "The Gardens of the Moon."
There is no way to prevent this
Or the expectation of disappointment.
All are aware, some carry a secret
Better, of hands emulating deeds

Of days untrustworthy. But these may decide.
The face extended its sorrowing light
Far out over them. And now silent as a group
The actors prepare their first decline.

Eclogue

Cuddie: Slowly all your secret is had
               In the empty day. People and sticks go down to the water.
               How can we be so silent? Only shivers
               Are bred in this land of whistling goats.

Colin: Father, I have long dreamed your whitened
               Face and sides to accost me in dull play.
               If you in your bush indeed know her
               Where shall my heart's vagrant tides place her?

Cuddie: A wish is induced by a sudden change
               In the wind's decay. Shall we to the water's edge,
               O prince? The peons rant in a light fume.
               Madness will gaze at its reflection.

Colin: What is this pain come near me?
               Now I thought my heart would burst,
               And there, spiked like some cadenza's head,
               A tiny crippled heart was born.

Cuddie: I tell you good will imitate this.
               Now we must dip in raw water
               These few thoughts and fleshy members.
               So evil may refresh our days.

Colin: She has descended part way!
               Now father cut me down with tears.
               Plant me far in my mother's image
               To do cold work of books and stones.

Cuddie: I need not raise my hand

Colin: *She burns the flying peoples*

Cuddie: To hear its old advice

Colin: *And spears my heart's two beasts*

Cuddie: Or cover with its mauves.

Colin: *And I depart unhurt.*

The Instruction Manual

As I sit looking out of a window of the building
I wish I did not have to write the instruction manual on the uses of a new
    metal.
I look down into the street and see people, each walking with an inner peace,
And envy them—they are so far away from me!
Not one of them has to worry about getting out this manual on schedule.
And, as my way is, I begin to dream, resting my elbows on the desk and
    leaning out of the window a little,
Of dim Guadalajara! City of rose-colored flowers!
City I wanted most to see, and most did not see, in Mexico!
But I fancy I see, under the press of having to write the instruction manual,
Your public square, city, with its elaborate little bandstand!
The band is playing *Scheherazade* by Rimsky-Korsakov.
Around stand the flower girls, handing out rose- and lemon-colored flowers,
Each attractive in her rose-and-blue striped dress (Oh! such shades of rose
    and blue),
And nearby is the little white booth where women in green serve you green
    and yellow fruit.
The couples are parading; everyone is in a holiday mood.
First, leading the parade, is a dapper fellow
Clothed in deep blue. On his head sits a white hat
And he wears a mustache, which has been trimmed for the occasion.
His dear one, his wife, is young and pretty; her shawl is rose, pink, and white.
Her slippers are patent leather, in the American fashion,
And she carries a fan, for she is modest, and does not want the crowd to see
    her face too often.
But everybody is so busy with his wife or loved one
I doubt they would notice the mustachioed man's wife.
Here come the boys! They are skipping and throwing little things on the
    sidewalk

Which is made of gray tile. One of them, a little older, has a toothpick in his
    teeth.
He is silenter than the rest, and affects not to notice the pretty young girls in
    white.
But his friends notice them, and shout their jeers at the laughing girls.
Yet soon all this will cease, with the deepening of their years,
And love bring each to the parade grounds for another reason.
But I have lost sight of the young fellow with the toothpick.
Wait—there he is—on the other side of the bandstand,
Secluded from his friends, in earnest talk with a young girl
Of fourteen or fifteen. I try to hear what they are saying
But it seems they are just mumbling something—shy words of love,
    probably.
She is slightly taller than he, and looks quietly down into his sincere eyes.
She is wearing white. The breeze ruffles her long fine black hair against her
    olive cheek.
Obviously she is in love. The boy, the young boy with the toothpick, he is in
    love too;
His eyes show it. Turning from this couple,
I see there is an intermission in the concert.
The paraders are resting and sipping drinks through straws
(The drinks are dispensed from a large glass crock by a lady in dark blue),
And the musicians mingle among them, in their creamy white uniforms, and
    talk
About the weather, perhaps, or how their kids are doing at school.

Let us take this opportunity to tiptoe into one of the side streets.
Here you may see one of those white houses with green trim
That are so popular here. Look—I told you!
It is cool and dim inside, but the patio is sunny.
An old woman in gray sits there, fanning herself with a palm leaf fan.
She welcomes us to her patio, and offers us a cooling drink.
"My son is in Mexico City," she says. "He would welcome you too
If he were here. But his job is with a bank there.
Look, here is a photograph of him."

And a dark-skinned lad with pearly teeth grins out at us from the worn
   leather frame.
We thank her for her hospitality, for it is getting late
And we must catch a view of the city, before we leave, from a good high
   place.
That church tower will do—the faded pink one, there against the fierce blue
   of the sky. Slowly we enter.
The caretaker, an old man dressed in brown and gray, asks us how long we
   have been in the city, and how we like it here.
His daughter is scrubbing the steps—she nods to us as we pass into the
   tower.
Soon we have reached the top, and the whole network of the city extends
   before us.
There is the rich quarter, with its houses of pink and white, and its
   crumbling, leafy terraces.
There is the poorer quarter, its homes a deep blue.
There is the market, where men are selling hats and swatting flies
And there is the public library, painted several shades of pale green and
   beige.
Look! There is the square we just came from, with the promenaders.
There are fewer of them, now that the heat of the day has increased,
But the young boy and girl still lurk in the shadows of the bandstand.
And there is the home of the little old lady—
She is still sitting in the patio, fanning herself.
How limited, but how complete withal, has been our experience of
   Guadalajara!
We have seen young love, married love, and the love of an aged mother for
   her son.
We have heard the music, tasted the drinks, and looked at colored houses.
What more is there to do, except stay? And that we cannot do.
And as a last breeze freshens the top of the weathered old tower, I turn my
   gaze
Back to the instruction manual which has made me dream of Guadalajara.

The Grapevine

Of who we and all they are
You all now know. But you know
After they began to find us out we grew
Before they died thinking us the causes

Of their acts. Now we'll not know
The truth of some still at the piano, though
They often date from us, causing
These changes we think we are. We don't care

Though, so tall up there
In young air. But things get darker as we move
To ask them: Whom must we get to know
To die, so you live and we know?

A Boy

I'll do what the raids suggest,
Dad, and that other livid window,
But the tide pushes an awful lot of monsters
And I think it's my true fate.

It had been raining but
It had not been raining.

No one could begin to mop up this particular mess.
Thunder lay down in the heart.
"My child, I love any vast electrical disturbance."
Disturbance! Could the old man, face in the rainweed,

Ask more smuttily? By night it charged over plains,
Driven from Dallas and Oregon, always *whither,*
Why not now? The boy seemed to have fallen
From shelf to shelf of someone's rage.

That night it rained on the boxcars, explaining
The thought of the pensive cabbage roses near the boxcars.
My boy. Isn't there something I asked you once?
What happened? It's also farther to the corner
Aboard the maple furniture. *He*
Couldn't lie. He'd tell 'em by their syntax.
But listen now in the flood.
They're throwing up behind the lines.
Dry fields of lightning rise to receive
The observer, the mincing flag. *An unendurable age.*

Glazunoviana

The man with the red hat
And the polar bear, is he here too?
The window giving on shade,
Is that here too?
And all the little helps,
My initials in the sky,
The hay of an arctic summer night?

The bear
Drops dead in sight of the window.
Lovely tribes have just moved to the north.
In the flickering evening the martins grow denser.
Rivers of wings surround us and vast tribulation.

The Hero

Whose face is this
So stiff against the blue trees,

Lifted to the future
Because there is no end?

But that has faded
Like flowers, like the first days

Of good conduct. Visit
The strong man. Pinch him—

There is no end to his
Dislike, the accurate one.

Poem

While we were walking under the top
The road so strangely lit by lamps
And I wanting only peace
From the tradesmen who tried cutting my hair
Under their lips a white word is waiting
Hanging from a cliff like the sky

It is because of the sky
We ever reached the top
On that day of waiting
For the hand and the lamps
I moisten my crystal hair
Never so calmly as when at peace

With the broken sky of peace
Peace means it to the sky
Let down your hair
Through peaceful air the top
Of ruins because what are lamps
When night is waiting

A roomful of people waiting
To die in peace
Then strike the procession of lamps
They brought more than sky
Lungs back to the top
Means to doom your hair

Those bright pads of hair
Before the sea held back waiting

And you cannot speak to the top
It moves toward peace
And know the day of sky
Only by falling lamps

Beyond the desert lamps
Mount enslaved crystal mountains of hair
Into the day of sky
Silence is waiting
For anything peace
And you find the top

The top is lamps
Peace to the fragrant hair
Waiting for a tropical sky

Album Leaf

The other marigolds and the cloths
Are crimes invented for history.
What can we achieve, aspiring?
And what, aspiring, can we achieve?

What can the rain that fell
All day on the grounds
And on the bingo tables?
Even though it is clearing,

The statue turned to a sweeter light,
The nearest patrons are black.
Then there is a storm of receipts: night,
Sand the bowl did not let fall.

The other marigolds are scattered like dust.
Sweet peas in dark gardens
Squirt false melancholy over history.
If a bug fell from so high, would it land?

The Picture of Little J. A. in a Prospect of Flowers

He was spoilt from childhood
by the future, which he mastered
rather early and apparently
without great difficulty.
BORIS PASTERNAK

1.

Darkness falls like a wet sponge
And Dick gives Genevieve a swift punch
In the pajamas. "Aroint thee, witch."
Her tongue from previous ecstasy
Releases thoughts like little hats.

"He clap'd me first during the eclipse.
Afterwards I noted his manner
Much altered. But he sending
At that time certain handsome jewels
I durst not seem to take offence."

In a far recess of summer
Monks are playing soccer.

2.

So far is goodness a mere memory
Or naming of recent scenes of badness
That even these lives, children,
You may pass through to be blessed,
So fair does each invent his virtue.

And coming from a white world, music
Will sparkle at the lips of many who are
Beloved. Then these, as dirty handmaidens
To some transparent witch, will dream

Of a white hero's subtle wooing,
And time shall force a gift on each.

That beggar to whom you gave no cent
Striped the night with his strange descant.

3.

Yet I cannot escape the picture
Of my small self in that bank of flowers:
My head among the blazing phlox
Seemed a pale and gigantic fungus.
I had a hard stare, accepting
Everything, taking nothing,
As though the rolled-up future might stink
As loud as stood the sick moment
The shutter clicked. Though I was wrong,
Still, as the loveliest feelings

Must soon find words, and these, yes,
Displace them, so I am not wrong
In calling this comic version of myself
The true one. For as change is horror,
Virtue is really stubbornness

And only in the light of lost words
Can we imagine our rewards.

Pantoum

Eyes shining without mystery,
Footprints eager for the past
Through the vague snow of many clay pipes,
And what is in store?

Footprints eager for the past,
The usual obtuse blanket.
And what is in store
For those dearest to the king?

The usual obtuse blanket
Of legless regrets and amplifications
For those dearest to the king.
Yes, sirs, connoisseurs of oblivion,

Of legless regrets and amplifications,
That is why a watchdog is shy.
Yes, sirs, connoisseurs of oblivion,
These days are short, brittle; there is only one night.

That is why a watchdog is shy,
Why the court, trapped in a silver storm, is dying.
These days are short, brittle; there is only one night
And that soon gotten over.

Why, the court, trapped in a silver storm, is dying!
Some blunt pretense to safety we have
And that soon gotten over
For they must have motion.

Some blunt pretense to safety we have:
Eyes shining without mystery
For they must have motion
Through the vague snow of many clay pipes.

Grand Abacus

Perhaps this valley too leads into the head of long-ago days.

What, if not its commercial and etiolated visage, could break through the
meadow wires?

It placed a chair in the meadow and then went far away.

People come to visit in summer, they do not think about the head.

Soldiers come down to see the head. The stick hides from them.

The heavens say, "Here I am, boys and girls!"

The stick tries to hide in the noise. The leaves, happy, drift over the dusty
meadow.

"I'd like to see it," someone said about the head, which has stopped
pretending to be a town.

Look! A ghastly change has come over it. The ears fall off—they are
laughing people.

The skin is perhaps children, they say, "We children," and are vague near the
sea. The eyes—

Wait! What large raindrops! The eyes—

Wait, can't you see them pattering, in the meadow, like a dog?

The eyes are all glorious! And now the river comes to sweep away the last of
us.

Who knew it, at the beginning of the day?

It is best to travel like a comet, with the others, though one does not see
them.

How far that bridle flashed! "Hurry up, children!" The birds fly back, they
say, "We were lying,

We do not want to fly away." But it is already too late. The children have
vanished.

The Mythological Poet

The music brought us what it seemed
We had long desired, but in a form
So rarefied there was no emptiness
Of sensation, as if pleasure
Might persist, like a dear friend
Walking toward one in a dream.
It was the toothless murmuring
Of ancient willows, who kept their trouble
In a stage of music. Without tumult
Snow-capped mountains and heart-shaped
Cathedral windows were contained
There, until only infinity
Remained of beauty. Then lighter than the air
We rose and packed the picnic basket.

But there is beside us, they said,
Whom we do not sustain, the world
Of things, that rages like a virgin
Next to our silken thoughts. It can
Be touched, they said. It cannot harm.

But suddenly their green sides
Foundered, as if the virgin beat
Their airy trellis from within.
Over her furious sighs, a new
Music, innocent and monstrous
As the ocean's bright display of teeth
Fell on the jousting willows.

We are sick, they said. It is a warning
We were not meant to understand.

2.

The mythological poet, his face
Fabulous and fastidious, accepts
Beauty before it arrives. The heavenly
Moment in the heaviness of arrival
Deplores him. He is merely
An ornament, a kind of lewd
Cloud placed on the horizon.

Close to the zoo, acquiescing
To dust, candy, perverts; inserted in
The panting forest, or openly
Walking in the great and sullen square
He has eloped with all music
And does not care. For isn't there,
He says, a final diversion, greater
Because it can be given, a gift
Too simple even to be despised?
And oh beside the roaring
Centurion of the lion's hunger
Might not child and pervert
Join hands, in the instant
Of their interest, in the shadow
Of a million boats; their hunger
From loss grown merely a gesture?

Sonnet

Each servant stamps the reader with a look.
After many years he has been brought nothing.
The servant's frown is the reader's patience.
The servant goes to bed.
The patience rambles on
Musing on the library's lofty holes.

His pain is the servant's alive.
It pushes to the top stain of the wall
Its tree-top's head of excitement:
Baskets, birds, beetles, spools.
The light walls collapse next day.
Traffic is the reader's pictured face.
Dear, be the tree your sleep awaits;
Worms be your words, you not safe from ours.

Chaos

Don't ask me to go there again
The white is too painful
Better to forget it
the sleeping river spoke to the awake land

When they first drew the wires
across the field
slowly air settled
on the pools
The blue mirror came to light
Then someone feared the pools
To be armor enough might not someone
draw down the sky
Light emerged
The swimming motion

At last twilight that will not protect the leaves
Death that will not try to scream
Black beaches
That is why I sent you the black postcard that will never deafen
That is why land urges the well
The white is running in its grooves
The river slides under our dreams
but land flows more silently

The Orioles

What time the orioles came flying
Back to the homes, over the silvery dikes and seas,
The sad spring melted at a leap,
The shining clouds came over the hills to meet them.

The old house guards its memories, the birds
Stream over colored snow in summer
Or back into the magic rising sun in winter.
They cluster at the feeding station, and rags of song

Greet the neighbors. "Was that your voice?"
And in spring the mad caroling continues long after daylight
As each builds his hanging nest
Of pliant twigs and the softest moss and grasses.

But one morning you get up and the vermilion-colored
Messenger is there, bigger than life at the window.
"I take my leave of you; now I fly away
To the sunny reeds and marshes of my winter home."

And that night you gaze moodily
At the moonlit apple-blossoms, for of course
Horror and repulsion do exist! They do! And you wonder,
How long will the perfumed dung, the sunlit clouds cover my heart?

And then some morning when the snow is flying
Or it lines the black fir-trees, the light cries,
The excited songs start up in the yard!
The feeding station is glad to receive its guests,

But how long can the stopover last?
The cold begins when the last song retires,
And even when they fly against the trees in bright formation
You know the peace they brought was long overdue.

The Young Son

The screen of supreme good fortune curved his absolute smile into a celestial scream. These things (the most arbitrary that could exist) wakened denials, thoughts of putrid reversals as he traced the green paths to and fro. Here and there a bird sang, a rose silenced her expression of him, and all the gaga flowers wondered. But they puzzled the wanderer with their vague wearinesses. Is the conclusion, he asked, the road forced by concubines from exact meters of strategy? Surely the trees are hinged to no definite purpose or surface. Yet now a wonder would shoot up, all one color, and virtues would jostle each other to get a view of nothing—the crowded house, two faces glued fast to the mirror, corners and the bustling forest ever preparing, ever menacing its own shape with a shadow of the evil defenses gotten up and in fact already exhausted in some void of darkness, some kingdom he knew the earth could not even bother to avoid if the minutes arranged and divine lettermen with smiling cries were to come in the evening of administration and night which no cure, no bird ever more compulsory, no subject apparently intent on its heart's own demon would forestall even if the truths she told of were now being seriously lit, one by one, in the hushed and fast darkening room.

The Thinnest Shadow

He is sherrier
And sherriest.
A tall thermometer
Reflects him best.

Children in the street
Watch him go by.
"Is that the thinnest shadow?"
They to one another cry.

A face looks from the mirror
As if to say,
"Be supple, young man,
Since you can't be gay."

All his friends have gone
From the street corner cold.
His heart is full of lies
And his eyes are full of mold.

Canzone

Until the first chill
No door sat on the clay.
When Billy brought on the chill
He began to chill.
No hand can
Point to the chill
It brought. Where a chill
Was, the grass grows.
See how it grows.
Acts punish the chill
Showing summer in the grass.
The acts are grass.

Acts of our grass
Transporting chill
Over brazen grass
That retorts as grass
Leave the clay,
The grass,
And that which is grass.
The far formal forest can,
Used doubts can
Sit on the grass.
Hark! The sadness grows
In pain. The shadow grows.

All that grows
In deep shadow or grass
Is lifted to what grows.
Walking, a space grows.

Beyond, weeds chill
Toward night which grows.
Looking about, nothing grows.
Now a whiff of clay
Respecting clay
Or that which grows
Brings on what can.
And no one can.

The sprinkling can
Slumbered on the dock. Clay
Leaked from a can.
Normal heads can
Touch barbed-wire grass
If they can
Sing the old song of can
Waiting for a chill
In the chill
That without a can
Is painting less clay
Therapeutic colors of clay.

We got out into the clay
As a boy can.
Yet there's another kind of clay
Not arguing clay,
As time grows
Not getting larger, but mad clay
Looked for for clay,
And grass
Begun seeming, grass
Struggling up out of clay
Into the first chill
To be quiet and raucous in the chill.

The chill
Flows over burning grass.
Not time grows.
So odd lights can
Fall on sinking clay.

Errors

Jealousy. Whispered weather reports.
In the street we found boxes
Littered with snow, to burn at home.
What flower tolling on the waters
You stupefied me. We waxed,
Carnivores, late and alight
In the beaded winter. All was ominous, luminous.
Beyond the bed's veils the white walls danced
Some violent compunction. Promises,
We thought then of your dry portals,
Bright cornices of eavesdropping palaces,
You were painfully stitched to hours
The moon now tears up, scoffing at the unrinsed portions.
And loves adopted realm. Flees to water,
The coach dissolving in mists.
                              A wish
Refines the lines around the mouth
At these ten-year intervals. It fumed
Clear air of wars. It desired
Excess of core in all things. From all things sucked
A glossy denial. But look, pale day:
We fly hence. To return if sketched
In the prophet's silence. Who doubts it is true?

Illustration

A novice was sitting on a cornice
High over the city. Angels

Combined their prayers with those
Of the police, begging her to come off it.

One lady promised to be her friend.
"I do not want a friend," she said.

A mother offered her some nylons
Stripped from her very legs. Others brought

Little offerings of fruit and candy,
The blind man all his flowers. If any

Could be called successful, these were,
For that the scene should be a ceremony

Was what she wanted. "I desire
Monuments," she said. "I want to move

Figuratively, as waves caress
The thoughtless shore. You people I know

Will offer me every good thing
I do not want. But please remember

I died accepting them." With that, the wind
Unpinned her bulky robes, and naked

As a roc's egg, she drifted softly downward
Out of the angels' tenderness and the minds of men.

2.

Much that is beautiful must be discarded
So that we may resemble a taller

Impression of ourselves. Moths climb in the flame,
Alas, that wish only to be the flame:

They do not lessen our stature.
We twinkle under the weight

Of indiscretions. But how could we tell
That of the truth we know, she was

The somber vestment? For that night, rockets sighed
Elegantly over the city, and there was feasting:

There is so much in that moment!
So many attitudes toward that flame,

We might have soared from earth, watching her glide
Aloft, in her peplum of bright leaves.

But she, of course, was only an effigy
Of indifference, a miracle

Not meant for us, as the leaves are not
Winter's because it is the end.

Some Trees

These are amazing: each
Joining a neighbor, as though speech
Were a still performance.
Arranging by chance

To meet as far this morning
From the world as agreeing
With it, you and I
Are suddenly what the trees try

To tell us we are:
That their merely being there
Means something; that soon
We may touch, love, explain.

And glad not to have invented
Such comeliness, we are surrounded:
A silence already filled with noises,
A canvas on which emerges

A chorus of smiles, a winter morning.
Placed in a puzzling light, and moving,
Our days put on such reticence
These accents seem their own defense.

Hotel Dauphin

It was not something identical with my carnation-world
But its smallest possession—a hair or a sneeze—
I wanted. I remember
Dreaming on tan plush the wrong dreams

Of asking fortunes, now lost
In what snows? Is there anything
We dare credit? And we get along.
The soul resumes its teachings. Winter boats

Are visible in the harbor. A child writes
"La pluie." All noise is engendered
As we sit listening. I lose myself
In others' dreams.

Why no vacation from these fortunes, from the white hair
Of the old? These dreams of tennis?
Fortunately, the snow, cutting like a knife,
Protects too itself from us.

Not so with this rouge I send to you
At old Christmas. Here the mysteries
And the color of holly are embezzled—
Poor form, poor watchman for my holidays,

My days of name-calling and blood-letting.
Do not fear the exasperation of death
(Whichever way I go is solitary)
Or the candles blown out by your passing.

It breathes a proper farewell, the panic
Under sleep like grave under stone,
Warning of sad renewals of the spirit.
In cheap gardens, fortunes. Or we might never depart.

The Painter

Sitting between the sea and the buildings
He enjoyed painting the sea's portrait.
But just as children imagine a prayer
Is merely silence, he expected his subject
To rush up the sand, and, seizing a brush,
Plaster its own portrait on the canvas.

So there was never any paint on his canvas
Until the people who lived in the buildings
Put him to work: "Try using the brush
As a means to an end. Select, for a portrait,
Something less angry and large, and more subject
To a painter's moods, or, perhaps, to a prayer."

How could he explain to them his prayer
That nature, not art, might usurp the canvas?
He chose his wife for a new subject,
Making her vast, like ruined buildings,
As if, forgetting itself, the portrait
Had expressed itself without a brush.

Slightly encouraged, he dipped his brush
In the sea, murmuring a heartfelt prayer:
"My soul, when I paint this next portrait
Let it be you who wrecks the canvas."
The news spread like wildfire through the buildings:
He had gone back to the sea for his subject.

Imagine a painter crucified by his subject!
Too exhausted even to lift his brush,

He provoked some artists leaning from the buildings
To malicious mirth: "We haven't a prayer
Now, of putting ourselves on canvas,
Or getting the sea to sit for a portrait!"

Others declared it a self-portrait.
Finally all indications of a subject
Began to fade, leaving the canvas
Perfectly white. He put down the brush.
At once a howl, that was also a prayer,
Arose from the overcrowded buildings.

They tossed him, the portrait, from the tallest of the buildings;
And the sea devoured the canvas and the brush
As though his subject had decided to remain a prayer.

And You Know

The girls, protected by gold wire from the gaze
Of the onrushing students, live in an atmosphere of vacuum
In the old schoolhouse covered with nasturtiums.
At night, comets, shootings stars, twirling planets,
Suns, bits of illuminated pumice, and spooks hang over the old place;
The atmosphere is breathless. Some find the summer light
Nauseous and damp, but there are those
Who are charmed by it, going out into the morning.
We must rest here, for this is where the teacher comes.
On his desk stands a vase of tears.
A quiet feeling pervades the playroom. His voice clears
Through the interminable afternoon: "I was a child once
Under the spangled sun. Now I do what must be done.
I teach reading and writing and flaming arithmetic. Those
In my home come to me anxiously at night, asking how it goes.
My door is always open. I never lie, and the great heat warms me."

His door is always open, the fond schoolmaster!
We ought to imitate him in our lives,
For as a man lives, he dies. To pass away
In the afternoon, on the vast vapid bank
You think is coming to crown you with hollyhocks and lilacs, or in gold at
    the opera,
Requires that one shall have lived so much! And not merely
Asking questions and giving answers, but grandly sitting,
Like a great rock, through many years.
It is the erratic path of time we trace
On the globe, with moist fingertip, and surely, the globe stops;
We are pointing to England, to Africa, to Nigeria;
And we shall visit these places, you and I, and other places,

Including heavenly Naples, queen of the sea, where I shall be king and you
    will be queen,
And all the places around Naples.
So the good old teacher is right, to stop with his finger on Naples, gazing
    out into the mild December afternoon
As his star pupil enters the classroom in that elaborate black and yellow
    creation.
He is thinking of her flounces, and is caught in them as if they were made of
    iron, they will crush him to death!
Goodbye, old teacher, we must travel on, not to a better land, perhaps,
But to the England of the sonnets, Paris, Colombia, and Switzerland
And all the places with names, that we wish to visit—
Strasbourg, Albania,
The coast of Holland, Madrid, Singapore, Naples, Salonika, Liberia, and
    Turkey.
So we leave you behind with her of the black and yellow flounces.
You were always a good friend, but a special one.
Now as we brush through the clinging leaves we seem to hear you crying;
You want us to come back, but it is too late to come back, isn't it?
It is too late to go to the places with the names (what were they, anyway? just
    names).
It is too late to go anywhere but to the nearest star, that one, that hangs just
    over the hill, beckoning
Like a hand of which the arm is not visible. Goodbye, Father! Goodbye,
    pupils. Goodbye, my master and my dame.
We fly to the nearest star, whether it be red like a furnace, or yellow,
And we carry your lessons in our hearts (the lessons and our hearts are the
    same)
Out of the humid classroom, into the forever. Goodbye, Old Dog Tray.

And so they have left us feeling tired and old.
They never cared for school anyway.
And they have left us with the things pinned on the bulletin board,
And the night, the endless, muggy night that is invading our school.

He

He cuts down the lakes so they appear straight
He smiles at his feet in their tired mules.
He turns up the music much louder.
He takes down the vaseline from the pantry shelf.

He is the capricious smile behind the colored bottles.
He eats not lest the poor want some.
He breathes of attitudes the piney altitudes.
He indeed is the White Cliffs of Dover.

He knows that his neck is frozen.
He snorts in the vale of dim wolves.
He writes to say, "If ever you visit this island,
He'll grow you back to your childhood.

"He is the liar behind the hedge
He grew one morning out of candor.
He is his own consolation prize.
He has had his eye on you from the beginning."

He hears the weak cut down with a smile.
He waltzes tragically on the spitting housetops.
He is never near. What you need
He cancels with the air of one making a salad.

He is always the last to know.
He is strength you once said was your bonnet.
He has appeared in "Carmen."
He is after us. If you decide

He is important, it will get you nowhere.
He is the source of much bitter reflection.
He used to be pretty for a rat.
He is now over-proud of his Etruscan appearance.

He walks in his sleep into your life.
He is worth knowing only for the children
He has reared as savages in Utah.
He helps his mother take in the clothes-line.

He is unforgettable as a shooting star.
He is known as "Liverlips."
He will tell you he has had a bad time of it.
He will try to pretend his press agent is a temptress.

He looks terrible on the stairs.
He cuts himself on what he eats.
He was last seen flying to New York.
He was handing out cards which read:

"He wears a question in his left eye.
He dislikes the police but will associate with them.
He will demand something not on the menu.
He is invisible to the eyes of beauty and culture.

"He prevented the murder of Mistinguett in Mexico.
He has a knack for abortions. If you see
He is following you, forget him immediately:
He is dangerous even though asleep and unarmed."

Meditations of a Parrot

Oh the rocks and the thimble
The oasis and the bed
Oh the jacket and the roses.

All sweetly stood up the sea to me
Like blue cornflakes in a white bowl.
The girl said, "Watch this."

I come from Spain, I said.
I was purchased at a fair.
She said, "None of us know.

"There was a house once
Of dazzling canopies
And halls like a keyboard.

"These the waves tore in pieces."
(His old wound—
And all day: Robin Hood! Robin Hood!)

A Long Novel

What will his crimes become, now that her hands
Have gone to sleep? He gathers deeds

In the pure air, the agent
Of their factual excesses. He laughs as she inhales.

If it could have ended before
It began—the sorrow, the snow

Dropping, dropping its fine regrets.
The myrtle dries about his lavish brow.

He stands quieter than the day, a breath
In which all evils are one.

He is the purest air. But her patience,
The imperative. Become, trembles

Where hands have been before. In the foul air
Each snowflake seems a Piranesi

Dropping in the past; his words are heavy
With their final meaning. Milady! Mimosa! So the end

Was the same: the discharge of spittle
Into frozen air. Except that, in a new

Humorous landscape, without music,
Written by music, he knew he was a saint,

While she touched all goodness
As golden hair, knowing its goodness

Impossible, and waking and waking
As it grew in the eyes of the beloved.

The Way They Took

The green bars on you grew soberer
As I petted the lock, a crank
In my specially built shoes.
We hedged about leisure, feeling, walking
That day, that night. The day
Came up. The heads borne in peach vessels
Out of asking that afternoon droned.
You saw the look of some other people,
Huge husks of chattering boys
And girls unfathomable in lovely dresses
And remorseful and on the edge of darkness.
No firmness in that safe smile ebbing.
Tinkling sadness. The sun pissed on a rock.

That is how I came nearer
To what was on my shoulder. One day you were lunching
With a friend's mother; I thought how plebeian all this testimony,
That you might care to crave that, somehow
Before I would decide. Just think,
But I know now how romantic, how they whispered
Behind the lace of their aspiring
Opinions. And heaven will not care,
To raise our love
In scathing hymns. So beware and
Bye now. The jewels are for luck.

Sonnet

The barber at his chair
Clips me. He does as he goes.
He clips the hairs outside the nose.
Too many preparations, nose!
I see the raincoat this Saturday.
A building is against the sky—
The result is more sky.
Something gathers in painfully.

To be the razor—how would you like to be
The razor, blue with ire,
That presses me? This is the wrong way.
The canoe speeds toward a waterfall.
Something, prince, in our backward manners—
You guessed the reason for the storm.

The Pied Piper

Under the day's crust a half-eaten child
And further sores which eyesight shall reveal
And they live. But what of dark elders
Whose touch at nightfall must now be
To keep their promise? Misery
Starches the host's one bed, his hand
Falls like an axe on her curls:
"Come in, come in! Better that the winter
Blaze unseen, than we two sleep apart!"

Who in old age will often part
From single sleep at the murmur
Of acerb revels under the hill;
Whose children couple as the earth crumbles
In vanity forever going down
A sunlit road, for his love was strongest
Who never loved them at all, and his notes
Most civil, laughing not to return.

Answering a Question in the Mountains

I went into the mountains to interest myself
In the fabulous dinners of hosts distant and demure.

The foxes followed with endless lights.

Some day I am to build the wall
Of the box in which all angles are shown.
I shall bounce like a ball.
The towers of justice are waving
To describe the angles we describe.
Oh we have been so far
To instruct the birds in our cold ways.

Near me I heard a sound,
The line of a match struck in care.

It is late to be late.

2.

Let us ascend the hearts in our hearts.
Let us ascend trees in our heads,
The dull heads of trees.
It is pain in the hand of the ungodly
To witness all the sentries,
The perfumed toque of dawn,
The hysteric evening with empty hands.
The snow creeps by; many light years pass.

We see for the first time.
We shall see for the first time.
We have seen for the first time.

The snow creeps by; many light years pass.

3.

I cannot agree or seek
Since I departed in the laugh of diamonds
The hosts of my young days.

A Pastoral

Perhaps no vice endears me to the showboat,
Whose license permeates our deep south.
The shows are simple, not yet easy, with handsome
And toy horns trying tried and true melodies.
Silently, that vice might speak from the shade:
"Your capers have misdirected all your animals."

But, hating and laughing, risen with animals,
Who is denied admission to the showboat?
Nevertheless, because of tomorrow's shade
The lad intends to file with the green deep south.
His ankles seek the temple melodies.
His mischief stirs the rocks and keeps them handsome.

Tomorrow, finding them less handsome,
They might side with the foreseeing of animals.
From the corral the melodies
Would start, teaching the showboat
(Thick is the tambour, oversold the deep south)
Which flowers to press back into the shade.

My affairs wrapped in shade,
Myself shall mobilize that handsome
Energetic enemy of the deep south.
Lately worms have pestered the animals.
Alarmed at our actions, a glittering showboat
Fled from the glade of supposed melodies.

And no more in our society living melodies
Break forth under the little or no shade.

The days are guarded. A miserable showboat
Plies back and forth between the handsome
Rocks, unwatched by animals
Whose glistening breath wakens forgetfulness of the deep south.

Truly the lesson of the deep south
Is how to avoid lingering beyond melodies
That cleave to the heart before it learns the animals
Strangers are. Knowing shade
Is their apology, let us never excuse handsome
Terror, the crook'd finger of a disappearing showboat.

The psalmist thought the deep south a wonderful showboat
And to the animals he met in the shade
Said, "You are my melodies, and you are handsome."

Le livre est sur la table

All beauty, resonance, integrity,
Exist by deprivation or logic
Of strange position. This being so,

We can only imagine a world in which a woman
Walks and wears her hair and knows
All that she does not know. Yet we know

What her breasts are. And we give fullness
To the dream. The table supports the book,
The plume leaps in the hand. But what

Dismal scene is this? the old man pouting
At a black cloud, the woman gone
Into the house, from which the wailing starts?

2.

The young man places a bird-house
Against the blue sea. He walks away
And it remains. Now other

Men appear, but they live in boxes.
The sea protects them like a wall.
The gods worship a line-drawing

Of a woman, in the shadow of the sea
Which goes on writing. Are there
Collisions, communications on the shore

Or did all secrets vanish when
The woman left? Is the bird mentioned
In the waves' minutes, or did the land advance?

THE TENNIS COURT OATH

The Tennis Court Oath

What had you been thinking about
the face studiously bloodied
heaven blotted region
I go on loving you like water but
there is a terrible breath in the way all of this
You were not elected president, yet won the race
All the way through fog and drizzle .
When you read it was sincere the coasts
stammered with unintentional villages the
horse strains fatigued I guess . . . the calls . . .
I worry

the water beetle head
why of course reflecting all
then you redid you were breathing
I thought going down to mail this
of the kettle you jabbered as easily in the yard
you come through but
are incomparable the lovely tent
mystery you don't want surrounded the real
you dance
in the spring there was clouds .

The mulatress approached in the hall—the
lettering easily visible along the edge of the *Times*
in a moment the bell would ring but there was time
for the carnation laughed here are a couple of "other"

to one in yon house

The doctor and Philip had come over the road
Turning in toward the corner of the wall his hat on
reading it carelessly as if to tell you your fears were justified
the blood shifted you know those walls
wind off the earth had made him shrink
undeniably an oboe now the young
were there there was candy
to decide the sharp edge of the garment
like a particular cry not intervening called the dog "he's coming! he's
    coming" with an emotion felt it sink into peace
there was no turning back but the end was in sight
he chose this moment to ask her in detail about her family and the others
The person.   pleaded—"have more of these
not stripes on the tunic—or the porch chairs
will teach you about men—what it means"
to be one in a million pink stripe
and now could go away the three approached the doghouse
the reef.   Your daughter's
dream of my son understand prejudice
darkness in the hole
the patient finished
They could all go home now the hole was dark
lilacs blowing across his face glad he brought you

"They Dream Only of America"

They dream only of America
To be lost among the thirteen million pillars of grass:
"This honey is delicious
Though it burns the throat."

And hiding from darkness in barns
They can be grownups now
And the murderer's ash tray is more easily—
The lake a lilac cube.

He holds a key in his right hand.
"Please," he asked willingly.
He is thirty years old.
That was before

We could drive hundreds of miles
At night through dandelions.
When his headache grew worse we
Stopped at a wire filling station.

Now he cared only about signs.
Was the cigar a sign?
And what about the key?
He went slowly into the bedroom.

"I would not have broken my leg if I had not fallen
Against the living room table. What is it to be back
Beside the bed? There is nothing to do
For our liberation, except wait in the horror of it.

And I am lost without you."

Thoughts of a Young Girl

"It is such a beautiful day I had to write you a letter
From the tower, and to show I'm not mad:
I only slipped on the cake of soap of the air
And drowned in the bathtub of the world.
You were too good to cry much over me.
And now I let you go. Signed, The Dwarf."

I passed by late in the afternoon
And the smile still played about her lips
As it has for centuries. She always knows
How to be utterly delightful. Oh my daughter,
My sweetheart, daughter of my late employer, princess,
May you not be long on the way!

America

Piling upward
the fact the stars
In America the office hid
archives in his
stall . . .
Enormous stars on them
The cold anarchist standing
in his hat.
Arm along the rail
We were parked
Millions of us
The accident was terrible.
The way the door swept out
The stones piled up—
The ribbon—books.   miracle.   with moon and the stars

The pear tree
moving me
I am around   and in my sigh
The gift of a the stars.
The person
Horror—the morsels of his choice
Rebuked to me I
—in the apartment
the pebble we in the bed.
The roof—
rain—   pills—
Found among the moss
Hers wouldn't longer care—I don't know why.

Ribbons
over the Pacific
Sometimes we
The deep
additional
and more and more less deep
but hurting
under the fire
brilliant rain
to meet us.
Probably in
moulded fire
We make it
times of the year
the light falls from heaven
love
parting the separate lives
her fork   the
specs
notably fire.
We get unhappy, off
The love
All the house
Waste visits
Autumn brushes the hair
The girl has lived in this corner
In the sunlight all year.
getting up to speak
Your janitor tried
if it was ready
I was almost killed
now by reading
on trial
standing with the jar

in the door wrapper
of this year fire intangible
Spoon
glad the dirt around
the geraniums of last August's
dried in the yard
played for certain
person
of course the lathes around
the stars with privilege jerks
over the country last year we were disgusted meeting
misguided
their only answer pine tree
off of the land
to the wind
out of your medicine
health, light, death preoccupation, beauty.
So don't kill the
stone this is desert
to the arms
You girl
the sea in waves

3.

of the arsenal
shaded in public
a hand put up
lips—a house
A minute the music stops.
The day it began. Person
blocking the conductor
Is the janitor with the red cape
And the pot of flowers in one hand
His face hidden by the shelf
thought intangible.

So is this way
out into the paths
of the square
petals armed with a chain
arctic night
what with stars
rocks and that fascinating illumination
that buries my heart
itself a tribune for which dancers
come. Inch pageant
of history   shaping
More than the forms
can do quacks
the night over the baths
stirred in his sleep the janitor reaches for the wrench with which he'll kill the
    intruder
Terrain
Glistening
Doesn't resemble much the out of doors
We walked around   the hand
observe the smashing of the rain
into the door the night
can't keep   inside
perhaps feeling the sentry
the perfect disc
We walked toward the bush
the disc
something was the matter with the disc
bush had forgotten
apples on the crater
the northern
Messenger the snow
stone

Though I had never come here
This country, its laws of glass
And night majesty
Through the football
Lured far away
Wave helplessly
The country
lined with snow
only mush was served
piling up
the undesired stars
needed against the night
Forbidden categorically
but admitted
beyond the cape
the tree still grows
tears fall
And I am proud
of these stars in our flag we don't want
the flag of film
waving over the sky
toward us—citizens of some future state.
We despair in the room, but the stars
And night persist, knowing we don't want it
Some tassels first
then nothing—day
the odor.
In the hall. The stone.

Across the other sea, was
in progress
the halt sea
Tens of persons   blinded

Immediately the port, challenge
Argument
Pear tree
Only perforation
Chain to fall apart in his hand
Someday liberty
to be of the press
drank
perhaps the lotion
she added. Drank
the orders.
The fake
ones.
border
his misanthropy.   pear mist.
the act   imitation
his happy stance
position   peace
on earth
ignited fluid
before he falls
must come under this head
be liked, so may be
Tears, hopeless adoration, passions
the fruit of carpentered night
Visible late next day. Cars
blockade the streets   wish
the geraniums embracing
umbrella
falling his embrace he strangles
in his storage but in
this meant
one instance
A feather not snow blew against the window.
A signal from the great outside.

Two Sonnets

1. DIDO

The body's products become
Fatal to it. Our spit
Would kill us, but we
Die of our heat.
Though I say the things I wish to say
They are needless, their own flame conceives it.
So I am cheated of perfection.

The iodine bottle sat in the hall
And out over the park where crawled roadsters
The apricot and purple clouds were
And our blood flowed down the grating
Of the cream-colored embassy.
Inside it they had a record of "The St. Louis Blues."

2. THE IDIOT

O how this sullen, careless world
Ignorant of me is! Those rocks, those homes
Know not the touch of my flesh, nor is there one tree
Whose shade has known me for a friend.
I've wandered the wide world over.
No man I've known, no friendly beast
Has come and put its nose into my hands.
No maid has welcomed my face with a kiss.

Yet once, as I took passage
From Gibraltar to Cape Horn
I met some friendly mariners on the boat

And as we struggled to keep the ship from sinking
The very waves seemed friendly, and the sound
The spray made as it hit the front of the boat.

To Redouté

To true roses uplifted on the bilious tide of evening
And morning-glories dotting the crescent day
The oval shape responds:
My first is a haunting face
In the hanging-down hair.
My second is water:
I am a sieve.

My only new thing:
The penalty of light forever
Over the heads of those who were there
And back into the night, the cough of the finishing petal.

Once approved the magenta must continue
But the bark island sees
Into the light:
It grieves for what it gives:
Tears that streak the dusty firmament.

Night

The evening I offer you the easy aspirin of death
Boots on the golden age of landscape
You don't understand when I've
Smelled the smell of . . . I don't know
Now from opposite sides of the drawing
The nut of his birthday

Bringing night brings in also idea of death
Thought when she was sixteen . . . he'd take her out
But it did no good . . .   Fuss was
Over the comics like in board you seen
Growing in patch on them laurels. And after
Taken out behind the stairs and stood them
In the kitchen . . .   the flowers blowing in the window
Felt funny just the same . . .   on account of the stove
We moved to another place. Funny how eighteen years can make
All that difference . . .   the marble
We never wanted to go away
But the porch forced its way on
Acting kind of contented in the silvery wind
From who knows where . . .   the porcelain
Uh huh.

It was sometime after this
We were all sitting alone one night
One stops did you hear the colored flute
Brand of years tossed into ash can
The heap of detritus . . .   tickets to the bed
Detective women the entire scene
We'll make sides.

They stop for a moment.
His landlord turned him out
It a hot dog stand

. . . .

Was grown chilly
My brain concocted
It did the inspector
He had been wandering
Around the park in a delirium
After the fang had grown
Add dishes returned—flowers on them
Neutral daylight sitting things
Like it. It woofed. It liked it.

Ordeal a home and
My lake and sat down
We must the gin came faster in cups
Under the scissors mill just like you was sixteen
In the orange flowers a pale narcissus hung
You was saying the alligators the grove
And he plied a rod out of the gray
Fishing manure . . .   the gray roses the best
And the bed hung with violets
I was rampant to ask you she had been would circulate
The prisons . . .
Out of the storeroom never to
Back in the room they for the six weeks
Piercing the monocle . . .   because letters
The sad trash newspapers schedule complaint
To belong to me . . . .

It strikes me . . .   the robe loose
The overalls laying . . .
Gray and . . .   flimsy. You the cake
Hobbled over to get the and grand

Store out of peanuts dust his thin
Cane down near store and the powder
Under the runway where a little
Light falls just on the patch
Noise that thought came from his own leg
There are numerous
Distinct flavors
The peanut ship wells
Into the desert
The stand . . .   Velocipede
Pergolas next to the chance of numb hitting
In the rostrum he forgot the behind him
Murmur halls on half-wet beauty
Paper green big
Sense
Where the trout had originated from
Smuggled from youth and grown into a tree
Fallen halfway across house
To bring the pet
Over the flowered curtains around
Water capillaries magic
Lift on the dune . . .   screaming her part dumb

They vary, depending
Salmon left the sea, gradually to
Pale and watery
But he will never to the fly
It is dumb and night continually seeping up—like a reservoir
Of truth on the bandits
He asked the fish why she seemed to . . .
A jeweler's, smooth, and luggage
Next day beside the rail
Arranged for night the postman bent down
Delivered his stare into the grass
I guess the darkness stubbed its toe

We were growing away from that . . .   waiting
The pool of shade
Near the dress house . . . and she turned in
The fly beckon on the window
The kids came and we all went the briars.

"How Much Longer Will I Be Able
to Inhabit the Divine Sepulcher . . ."

How much longer will I be able to inhabit the divine sepulcher
Of life, my great love? Do dolphins plunge bottomward
To find the light? Or is it rock
That is searched? Unrelentingly? Huh. And if some day

Men with orange shovels come to break open the rock
Which encases me, what about the light that comes in then?
What about the smell of the light?
What about the moss?

In pilgrim times he wounded me
Since then I only lie
My bed of light is a furnace choking me
With hell (and sometimes I hear salt water dripping).

I mean it—because I'm one of the few
To have held my breath under the house. I'll trade
One red sucker for two blue ones. I'm
Named Tom. The

Light bounces off mossy rocks down to me
In this glen (the neat villa! which
When he'd had he would not had he of
And jests under the smarting of privet

Which on hot spring nights perfumes the empty rooms
With the smell of sperm flushed down toilets
On hot summer afternoons within sight of the sea.
If you knew why then professor) reads

To his friends: Drink to me only with
And the reader is carried away
By a great shadow under the sea.
Behind the steering wheel

The boy took out his own forehead.
His girlfriend's head was a green bag
Of narcissus stems. "OK you win
But meet me anyway at Cohen's Drug Store

In 22 minutes." What a marvel is ancient man!
Under the tulip roots he has figured out a way to be a religious animal
And would be a mathematician. But where in unsuitable heaven
Can he get the heat that will make him grow?

For he needs something or will forever remain a dwarf,
Though a perfect one, and possessing a normal-sized brain
But he has got to be released by giants from things.
And as the plant grows older it realizes it will never be a tree,

Will probably always be haunted by a bee
And cultivates stupid impressions
So as not to become part of the dirt. The dirt
Is mounting like a sea. And we say goodbye

Shaking hands in front of the crashing of the waves
That give our words lonesomeness, and make these flabby hands seem
    ours—
Hands that are always writing things
On mirrors for people to see later—

Do you want them to water
Plant, tear listlessly among the exchangeable ivy—
Carrying food to mouth, touching genitals—
But no doubt you have understood

It all now and I am a fool. It remains
For me to get better, and to understand you so
Like a chair-sized man. Boots
Were heard on the floor above. In the garden the sunlight was still purple

But what buzzed in it had changed slightly
But not forever . . .   but casting its shadow
On sticks, and looking around for an opening in the air, was quite as if it had
     never refused to exist differently. Guys
In the yard handled the belt he had made

Stars
Painted the garage roof crimson and black
He is not a man
Who can read these signs . . .   his bones were stays . . .
And even refused to live
In a world and refunded the hiss
Of all that exists terribly near us
Like you, my love, and light.

For what is obedience but the air around us
To the house? For which the federal men came
In a minute after the sidewalk
Had taken you home? ("Latin . . .   blossom . . . ")

After which you led me to water
And bade me drink, which I did, owing to your kindness.
You would not let me out for two days and three nights,
Bringing me books bound in wild thyme and scented wild grasses

As if reading had any interest for me, you . . .
Now you are laughing.
Darkness interrupts my story.
Turn on the light.

Meanwhile what am I going to do?
I am growing up again, in school, the crisis will be very soon.
And you twist the darkness in your fingers, you
Who are slightly older . . .

Who are you, anyway?
And it is the color of sand,
The darkness, as it sifts through your hand
Because what does anything mean,

The ivy and the sand? That boat
Pulled up on the shore? Am I wonder,
Strategically, and in the light
Of the long sepulcher that hid death and hides me?

Rain

I.

The spoon of your head
crossed by livid stems

The chestnuts' large clovers wiped

      You see only the white page its faint frame of red
      You hear the viola's death sound
      A woman sits in black and white tile

      Why, you are pale

Light sucks up what I did
In the room two months ago
Spray of darkness across the back,
Tree flowers . . .

Taxis took us far apart
And will . . .
      over the shuddering page of a sea
      The sofa

Hay
blown in the window
The boards dark as night sea
Pot of flowers fixed in the wind

      Last year . . .   the gray snow falling
      The building . . .   pictures
      His eye into the forest

And people alright
Those stiff lead rods
Silver in the afternoon light
Near where it stops
Where they drink tea from a glass smaller than a thimble
Head of shade

And many stiff little weeds that grew
beside the kidney-shaped lake
A wooden cage painted green
        sand
               And the green streets though parallel run
                  far from each other

Cupped under the small lead surface of that cloud you see you are
going to die
Burnt by the powder of that view
              The day of the week will not save you

Mixture of air and wind
Sand then mud
A flower, lost in someone's back yard.

2.

The first coffee of the morning
Soon the stars.

       and broken feldspar   black
     squares against the light
   message—a handwriting
      Dip pen in solution

They would be playing now
    The sky
Flowers sucked in—stone ranunculus

amaryllis—red
Freesia and existence

The letter arrives—seeing the stamp
The van
New York under the umbrella

A photograph of what

Fumes
Features in the lake
The light
The shadow of a hand
soft on the lock
staring wax
scraped with a pin, reflection of the face
The time
principal thing
Train
Hand holding watch
silver vase
against the plaid

Comfort me
The hedge coming up to meet me that way in the dried red sun
The meadows down I mean
At night
Curious—I'd seen this tall girl

I urge the deep prune of the mirror
That stick she carries
The book—a trap

The facts have hinged on my reply

calm

Hat against the sky
Eyes of forest

memory of cars
You buried in the hot avenue: and to all of them, you cannot be and are,
naming me.

3.

The missing letter—the crumb of confidence
His love boiling up to me
Forever will I be the only
In sofa I know
The darkness on his back
Fleeing to darkness of my side

It is the time
We do not live in but on
And this young man
like a soldier
Into the dust
Words drip from the wound
Spring mounts in me
of dandelion—lots of it
And the little one
the hooded lost one
near the pillow

A fine young man

4.

The storm coming—
Not to have ever been exactly on this street with cats
Because the houses were vanishing behind a cloud
The plants on the rugs look nice
Yet I have never been here before

Glass

regime

Which is in the tepee of the great city
I build to you every moment
Ice lily of the sewers
In a thousand thoughts
Mindful in a thousand dresser drawers you pull out
Mufti of the gray crocus silent on the wood diamond floor
Or if I asked you for a game with rods and balls
You stood up with me to play

But fatal laxity undoes
The stiff, dark and busy streets
Through which any help must roll.
The third of runners who are upon are past you
The opal snows the moppet
You behind me in the van
The flat sea rushing away

A White Paper

And if he thought that
All was foreign—
As, gas and petrol, en-
gine full of seeds, barking to hear the night
The political contaminations

Of what he spoke,
Spotted azaleas brought to meet him
Sitting next day
The judge, emotions,
The crushed paper heaps.

Leaving the Atocha Station

The arctic honey blabbed over the report causing darkness
And pulling us out of there experiencing it
he meanwhile . . .   And the fried bats they sell there
dropping from sticks, so that the menace of your prayer folds . . .
Other people . . .   flash
the garden are you boning
and defunct covering . . .   Blind dog expressed royalties . . .
comfort of your perfect tar grams nuclear world bank tulip
Favorable to   near the night pin
loading formaldehyde.   the table torn from you
Suddenly   and we are close
Mouthing the root   when you think
generator   homes enjoy leered

The worn stool blazing   pigeons from the roof
             driving tractor to squash
Leaving the Atocha Station   steel
infected bumps the screws
   everywhere   wells
abolished top ill-lit
scarecrow falls   Time, progress and good sense
strike of shopkeepers dark blood
no forest you can name drunk scrolls
the completely new Italian hair . . .
Baby . . .   ice falling off the port
The centennial   Before we can

              old   eat
members with their chins
            so high up   rats

      relaxing the cruel discussion
  suds   the painted corners
white   most aerial
     garment crow
            and when the region took us back
the person left us like birds
  it was fuzz on the passing light
over disgusted heads, far into amnesiac
permanent house depot   amounts he can
     decrepit mayor . . .   exalting flea
for that we turn around
experiencing it is not to go into
the epileptic prank forcing bar
to borrow out onto tide-exposed fells
over her morsel, she chasing you
and the revenge he'd get
establishing the vultural over
rural area cough protection
murdering quintet. Air pollution terminal
the clean fart genital enthusiastic toe prick album serious evening flames
the lake over your hold   personality
     lightened . . .   roar
You are freed
      including barrels
head of the swan   forestry
the night and stars fork
That is, he said
   and rushing under the hoops of
equations probable
     absolute mush   the right
entity   chain store   sewer opened their books
     The flood dragged you
     I coughed to the window
last month: juice, earlier
like the slacks   to be declining

the peaches   more
   fist
sprung expecting the cattle
false loam   imports
         next time around

White Roses

The worst side of it all—
The white sunlight on the polished floor—
Pressed into service,
And then the window closed
And the night ends and begins again.
Her face goes green, her eyes are green;
In the dark corner playing "The Stars and Stripes Forever." I try to describe
    for you,
But you will not listen, you are like the swan.

No stars are there,
No stripes,
But a blind man's cane poking, however clumsily, into the inmost corners of
    the house.
Nothing can be harmed! Night and day are beginning again!
So put away the book,
The flowers you were keeping to give someone:
Only the white, tremendous foam of the street has any importance,
The new white flowers that are beginning to shoot up about now.

The Suspended Life

She is under heavy sedation
Seeing the world. The drink
Controls the tooth
Weather information clinic
Tomorrow morning. She started
On her round-the-world cruise
Aboard the *Zephyr.* The boy sport
A dress. The girl,
Slacks. Each carried a magazine—
A package of sea the observatory
Introduced me to canned you.
Only a few cases of plague
Announced in Oporto, the schools
Reopen in the fresh September breeze.
Teeth are munching salads
Tragedy and forest fires return
To the pitted, happy town.
A jungle of matter
Floats over the piles.
A major insulted the naval
Doom. The buttons' pill
Descended the trunk with a shout.
Servitude leapt from old age. Sky
Imagined us happy. The black
Trees impinged on the balloon. It follows
We were mean subsequently
To those who were near us,
The nude sleeping mechanically,
The foundation boy under the plant.
You tittered that in the milady of rocks

The sea was expanding neutral.
The stair carpet plunged into blankness.

"The igloo sun, while I was away,
Chastened the wolverine towels.
Isn't Idaho the wolverine state
Anyway Ohio is the flower state
New York is the key state.
Bandana is the population state.
In the hay states of Pennsylvania and Arkansas
I lay down and slept.
The cross delirium tremens state of Mississippi
Led me to further discoveries:
Timbuctoo, for instance. And Ashtabula,
The towel city. The wolverines
Had almost faded off the towels, the frigid pallor
Of the arctic sun was responsible."

"Isn't Montpelier the capital of the ditch state?
I remember as a child reading about some bombs
That had been placed on a tram.
They were green and in a cone-shaped pile
To look like a fir tree.
Many people were fooled.
Others in faraway places
Like Aberdeen or the Shetland Islands
Were unhappy about the affair.
What can you do with people far away?
Only those near me, like Bob,
Mean to me what Uncle Ben means to me
When he comes in, wiping a block of ice
On a chipmunk dishtowel, his face glittering
With the pleasure of being already absent.
Or when someone places a cabbage on a stump
I think I am with them, I think of their name:

Julian. Do you see
The difference between weak handshakes
And freezing to death in a tub of ice and snow
Called a home by some, but it lacks runners,
Do you? When through the night
Pure sobs denote the presence
Of supernatural yearning you think
Of all those who have been near you
Who might have formed a wall
Of demarcation around your sorrow,
Of those who offered you a coffee."

The chariot moved apart
And those who had been whispering
Pulled away, as though offended
By a sudden noise. Night grew clear
Over Mount Hymettus
And sudden day unbuttoned her blouse.
The travellers drew near a lake
Whose palm trees and chalets
Seemed indifferent, transparent
And so the trip stays
Close to hope and death. Dun lamps
Reveal a stone signpost.
We have lived here a long time.
The lips suggest a tragedy
No heart can make clear.
The glass blobs form an exclamation point.
The green shall not pierce your tippling sanctity,
The weather continues, the children are on their way to school.

A Life Drama

Yellow curtains
Are in fashion,
Murk plectrum,
Fatigue and smoke of nights
And recording of piano in factory.
Of the hedge
The woods
Stained by water running over
Factory is near
Workers near the warmth of their nights
And plectrum. Factory
Of cigar. The helium burned
All but the man. And the
Child. The heart. Moron.
Headed slum
Woods coming back
The sand
Lips   hips   The sand poured away over
The slum and the fountain
Man and child
Cigar and palace
Sand and hips
The factory and the palace. Like we
Vote. The man and the rose.
The man is coming back—take the rose.

And scoot over car door
Back into pulp. The race reads print—
Trees—The man races to the print.
The child and the rose and the cigar are there at the edge of the fountain

"The bath of the mountains" in a way.
The factory to be screwed onto palace
The workers—happy
Lost memory lost mess happy
Opium rose
You cheat you are our face
Lost danger
Going close to the bowl you said a word
Me. You forgot the piano. It is
The one thing that can destroy us.
The partridges and the wild fowl and the other game hens
Have gone to their nests near water undisturbed
The sunset stains the water of the lake,
Plectrum. There are birches in the trees,
White with fine black markings, like stalks.
Tears invade the privacy of private lives
In the house overlooking the park
The piano is seldom mute
The plectrum on the lawn vanishes
Tears invade the jealousy of the regent's bosom
Walking at twilight by the path that leads to the factory
The floor a pool. When the cigar
Explodes
The tears a fifth time of the workers pulling down the board through the
    trees
Plectrum
Darkness invades the tears exploding in the bosom
Walking the little boy the enormous dog and red ball
In the house by the marshes
Where they gave up
Soldiers in blue
The merchant returns. The map
Shut up. Across the sea
Now in another way of life carrying the food
To the edge of the mouth

Pausing at the end of the lane the hips
Waiting cigar long ago
Plectrum two three
Before killing after coming so far
Day declines jealously in the house by the park
Under the mill
The child falls asleep on the chalk breast.

Our Youth

Of bricks . . .   Who built it? Like some crazy balloon
When love leans on us
Its nights . . .   The velvety pavement sticks to our feet.
The dead puppies turn us back on love.

Where we are. Sometimes
The brick arches led to a room like a bubble, that broke when you entered it
And sometimes to a fallen leaf.
We got crazy with emotion, showing how much we knew.

The Arabs took us. We knew
The dead horses. We were discovering coffee,
How it is to be drunk hot, with bare feet
In Canada. And the immortal music of Chopin

Which we had been discovering for several months
Since we were fourteen years old. And coffee grounds,
And the wonder of hands, and the wonder of the day
When the child discovers her first dead hand.

Do you know it? Hasn't she
Observed you too? Haven't you been observed to her?
My, haven't the flowers been? Is the evil
In't? What window? What did you say there?

Heh? Eh? Our youth is dead.
From the minute we discover it with eyes closed
Advancing into mountain light.
Ouch . . .   You will never have that young boy,

That boy with the monocle
Could have been your father
He is passing by. No, that other one,
Upstairs. He is the one who wanted to see you.

He is dead. Green and yellow handkerchiefs cover him.
Perhaps he will never rot, I see
That my clothes are dry. I will go.
The naked girl crosses the street.

Blue hampers . . .   Explosions,
Ice . . .   The ridiculous
Vases of porphyry. All that our youth
Can't use, that it was created for.

It's true we have not avoided our destiny
By weeding out the old people.
Our faces have filled with smoke. We escape
Down the cloud ladder, but the problem has not been solved.

The Ticket

The experience of writing you these love letters . . .
Fences not concluding, nothing, no even, water in your eye, seeming
    anything
The garden in mist, perhaps, but egocentricity makes up for that, the winter
    locusts, whitened
Her hand not leading anywhere. Her head into the yard, maples, a stump
    seen through a gauze of bottles, ruptures—
You had no permission, to carry anything out, working to carry out the
    insane orders given you to raze
The box, red, funny going underground
And, being no reason suspicious, mud of the day, the plaid—I was near you
    where you want to be
Down in the little house writing you.

Though afterwards tears seem skunks
And the difficult position we in to light the world
Of awe, mush raging, the stump again
And as always before
The scientific gaze, perfume, millions, tall laugh
That was ladder though not of uncertain, innocuous truths, the felt
    branch—
To a ditch of wine and tubs, spraying the poster with blood, telegraph, all the
    time
Automatically taking the things in, that had not been spoiled, sordid.

An Additional Poem

Where then shall hope and fear their objects find?
The harbor cold to the mating ships,
And you have lost as you stand by the balcony
With the forest of the sea calm and gray beneath.
A strong impression torn from the descending light
But night is guilty. You knew the shadow
In the trunk was raving
But as you keep growing hungry you forget.
The distant box is open. A sound of grain
Poured over the floor in some eagerness—we
Rise with the night let out of the box of wind.

Measles

There was no longer any need for the world to be divided
Into bunny, when he had chased the hare.
He had to be
Pressure, so disappeared from the air.
I understand . . . to accept the ball.
To inspire the painted wall
She limited the hall.

A mouse with crew-
Cut rang the bell, the wall
Fell into the sewer garden. Perhaps some football'll
Square you off, save you a minute
That he fell.

Was it only ten months ago
The general installed? Pine
Offered foreign . . . warmonger
Piloting a contraption
Above the dotted fields, seizes
The contrast. The branches
Urge his pain. He sees.
The trees is to be considered to him
Like we in the way you say saga.
Perfect, the emery wheel.
There was no reason to play. Pennies, these I can give you. I have nothing
    else, and the air . . . I ought to, but I cannot, feeling the air and you there.
    I cannot set you free, whispering only to be there.

I write, trying to economize
These lines, tingling. The very earth's

A pension. My life story
I am toying with the idea.
I'm perfectly capable (signature)
The kerosene white branches the stadium

There is no reason to be cold
Underneath, it is calm today.
For the moment, clement day
Observes our transactions with kindly eye.
There is no reason to suppose
Anything of the kind will occur.
I oppose with all the forces of my will
Your declaration. You are right
To do so. The street catches auburn
Reflections, the start is here.
You may have been well.
You limit me to what I say.
The sense of the words is
With a backward motion, pinning me
To the daylight mode of my declaration.

But ah, night may not tell
The source! I feel well
Under the dinner table. He is playing a game
With me, about credits.
I have to check in the hall
About something.
The invitation arrived
On the appointed day.
By nightfall he and I were between.
The street rages with toil.
Can you let yourself, a moment, put down your work?

Faust

If only the phantom would stop reappearing!
Business, if you wanted to know, was punk at the opera.
The heroine no longer appeared in *Faust*.
The crowds strolled sadly away. The phantom
Watched them from the roof, not guessing the hungers
That must be stirred before disappointment can begin.

One day as morning was about to begin
A man in brown with a white shirt reappearing
At the bottom of his yellow vest, was talking hungers
With the silver-haired director of the opera.
On the green-carpeted floor no phantom
Appeared, except yellow squares of sunlight, like those in *Faust*.

That night as the musicians for *Faust*
Were about to go on strike, lest darkness begin
In the corridors, and through them the phantom
Glide unobstructed, the vision reappearing
Of blonde Marguerite practicing a new opera
At her window awoke terrible new hungers

In the already starving tenor. But hungers
Are just another topic, like the new Faust
Drifting through the tunnels of the opera
(In search of lost old age? For they begin
To notice a twinkle in his eye. It is cold daylight reappearing
At the window behind him, itself a phantom

Window, painted by the phantom
Scene painters, sick of not getting paid, of hungers

For a scene below of tiny, reappearing
Dancers, with a sandbag falling like a note in *Faust*
Through purple air. And the spectators begin
To understand the bleeding tenor star of the opera.)

That night the opera
Was crowded to the rafters. The phantom
Took twenty-nine curtain calls. "Begin!
Begin!" In the wings the tenor hungers
For the heroine's convulsive kiss, and Faust
Moves forward, no longer young, reappearing

And reappearing for the last time. The opera
Faust would no longer need its phantom.
On the bare, sunlit stage the hungers could begin.

The Lozenges

The Division was unsuitable
He thought. He was tempted not to fulfilling order written down
To him. The award on the wall
Believing it belonged to him.
Working and dreaming, getting the sun always right
In the end, he had supplanted the technician
With the bandage. Invented a new cradle.
The factory yard resounded
Filling up with air. Spring, outside
The window jammed almost shut, wafted its enormous bubble amidships.
Tell me, asparagus fern
Are you troubled by the cold night air?
The plane had passed him,
Bound for Copenhagen with smiling officers.
Lighter than air, I guess. I jest
Was playing the piano of your halitosis
A bridge into amber. Seven bargains popped into the sloop.
Venemously she aimed the pot of flowers
At his head—a moth-eaten curtain hid the fire extinguisher.

We all have graves to travel from, vigorously exerting
The strongest possible influence on those about us.
The children sleep—mountains—absorbing us into the greater part of us;
We had seen the sun dance.
Ribbons cover it—the carnival brought
The thermometer down to absolute zero.
People unknown in the depot
A lot of valuable medicine being stolen
Climate in your eyes. I have to tell
The doctor entered, a wet Limburger cheese sandwich in his hand.

He was crying. His little daughter, next to him
Was about fourteen years old. Her crying fit
Was not yet over. You could go out of the house
The saffron paving stones were aware of this
Pond leading down to the sea.
As though too much dew obscured the newspaper
A band of polyps decorating it
For the optician's lenses never told you
Until today, that is, how many crawfish
I detest you. We slowly stoked the rusted platinum engine.
Only about three more kilometers now
Tabby had been notified. The ball of sperm
And then we . . . It too faded into light
An oriental thing, curved that lissome day might fit
There was rain and dew
You hanging on the clothes horse
Thought it funny the mushrooms
Water moccasins and Dutch elm disease.
If only pockets contained the auditorium,
He, the young girl in business,
The girl Samson told you about when they came to get him out
Unpacked the old Chevrolet—upholstery and such
The horse rocketing us into a nightmare world of champagne
You surprised more kinks. After all, a rabbit
Screaming paeans of praise—from mortar.

Frigid disappointment skins the wall of a bald world.
Release shadow upon men—in their heaviness
Siding with hours in their flight
Turning over the subconscious—and all fly
With him—the radio, astronomy lessons,
The broken pageant, the girls'
Dormitory.

The Ascetic Sensualists

All . . . All these numbers easily . . . Why . . .
Unwashed feet and then . . . typhoid fever . . .
The leading drains multiplied, then over ocean head
Is a dangerous feed broken easily.
The reeds came up to her, lying without life
Standing halfway to the shore. Then they came over and . . .

Calm clouds borne over. The reeds, not strife.
These were thoughts of happiness
In the dark pasture
Remembering from the other time.
The old man ignored.

These times, by water, the members
Balloting, proud stain adrift
Over the glass air.
See, you must acknowledge.
For big charity ball. The autumn leaves
Among lead crescents, and wig—

Never-to-be-forgotten conjectures
Concerning the originality
Caves and dynamic arches and the used green
Encrusted the tube.
The mirror, the child's scream
Is perplexed, managing to end the sentence.

The scissors, this season, old newspaper.
The brown suit. Hunted unsuccessfully,
To be torn down later

The horse said.
You called midway between the jaws,
Mediterranean bus strike
At the four corners of the world
She stood, stinking. The cart unleashed
Ashes over every part of the century;
Some of us were working—the cat.
You pill . . . on the porch
Workers bravo. Before the universe.

Only a small edge of dime protected the issued utter blank darkness from the
silver regal porch factory inscribed pearl-handled revolver raped gun to the ul-
timate tease next to the door fifth gum. Your Balzac open the foot scrounge
lamp tube traffic gun. Gun is over, war banished, tottering lamp gun. Hic the
perfect screw slow giggles to be sky raffia. The person or persons molested.
These led directly to:

FIRST FUNERAL

The sky hopes the vanilla bastard
Axle busted over fifth dimwit slump.
The reason ejected. Impossibility of their purple paper trails.
Hold collar, basted.

SECOND FUNERAL

Candy rigors upset the train
From Boston to Newport.
I was reading *Vogue* in the car—suddenly
Cream or lace—to be manufactured this year like in loom.
The room in which the loom
Dispelled thunder, cracked tennis under the eaves. Gone to work.

THIRD FUNERAL

Hardly was believed New England eyes
At fast report, tacked up in factory
Before the holidays.

After the holidays
The jar filled rapidly . . .

FOURTH FUNERAL

So we sabotaged the car
The rangers loved. Not to protect
Is to give all, we found
Under the topical night.
The weeds, miserable, and yet, topmast,
The performance is worth knives.

We shall not call you
On that. Panorama. Over the glue garage
The sky was blue fudge.
The sky was white as flour—the sky
Like some baker's apron. Or the margarine
Of an April day. Pig. The sea. Ancient smoke.

FIFTH FUNERAL

After the New Year
The tide changed.
Green thorns flushed in from the New England coasts and swamps,
All kinds of things
To make you think. Oh heart
You need these things, leaves and nubile weeds,
I guess, ever present.
They changed the time
And we were supposed to be back an hour earlier.

SIXTH FUNERAL

The colored balls were like distant lights on the plaque horizon.
There was room for but one ball.

SEVENTH FUNERAL

The thrush of those who await the month

Of decapitated return, and thankless sight.
Through steering wheel
Brown woods or weeds
And brown-ribbed dress, violent
In the sun. The birds
And all your deeds. They bids.

EIGHTH FUNERAL

A glass of water in home
To where we had come out of the hole
Crying, the running water
Announced our engagement.
The dog ran over us
The ball with all his might.
We might escape, in the daylight
The barn of his personal loss.

NINTH FUNERAL

There was a slow rejoining of his
Original position, the maelstrom.
Lights were brought. The beds, sentenced.
The tulips grew redder. He smiled over
The desk. The persons abolished
Grew to stand in the tank his sin made.
—the vice-twins.

TENTH FUNERAL

A passion of daisies real
The embossed white of the silver head.
Among the stars it is time
Going slowly down to where
You were asked not to participate, where
Hard mud trails reiterate
Brougham capital.

Stones. Loggia

The least astonished were the wetter veterans who had come to pray and prac-
tice, unaware as yet that the basilica's southern tip was submerged—you to
whom I write, can you believe them this instant far from ideal palms? That the
farewell was taking place? That's why the funeral décors—black gingerbread
for the trip, I suppose will want something other than nauseating clear sea
framed in window—to eat, I mean, just as our mind takes up the vases, deposit
hard baked clay on hard mud or stone—the loggia in the picture. You see well,
the perverted things you wanted gone in a group of colored lights all lucky for
you. Besides, sometime the question will return—count on asking—the bald
leader smile up at your dark window in the nothing sunlight—just because you
correctly ask that one day and now nothing more, politeness and the broad
seas.

Landscape

The pest asked us to re-examine the screws he held.
Just then the barman squirted juice over the lumps.
It decided to vote for ink (the village).
There was surprise at the frozen ink
That was brought in and possibly rotten.
Several new lumps were revealed
Near Penalty Avenue. The bathers' tree
Explained ashes. The pilot knew.
All over the country the rapid extension meter
Was thrown out of court . . .   the tomatoes . . .

The charcoal mines were doing well
At 9½ per cent. A downy hill
Announced critical boredom for the bottler
Of labor tonic. It seemed there was no more
Steering-wheel oil or something—you had better
Call them about it—I don't know,
I predisposed the pests toward blue rock.
The barometer slides slowly down the wall
It has finished registering data.
The glass sanctuary repeated the panic
Of Morgan's Hill.

You knew those square doctrines had—
Come apart . . .   the paper lining had gotten
Unpinned, or unstuck, and blue balloons
Poured out over the foul street, creasing
The original paper outside. The ladder failed.

A Last World

These wonderful things
Were planted on the surface of a round mind that was to become our present
time.
The mark of things belongs to someone
But if that somebody was wise
Then the whole of things might be different
From what it was thought to be in the beginning, before an angel bandaged
the field glasses.
Then one could say nothing hear nothing
Of what the great time spoke to its divisors.
All borders between men were closed.
Now all is different without having changed
As though one were to pass through the same street at different times
And nothing that is old can prefer the new.
An enormous merit has been placed on the head of all things
Which, bowing down, arrive near the region of their feet
So that the earth-stone has stared at them in memory at the approach of an
error.
Still it is not too late for these things to die
Provided that an anemone will grab them and rush them to the wildest
heaven.
But having plucked oneself, who could live in the sunlight?
And the truth is cold, as a giant's knee
Will seem cold.

Yet having once played with tawny truth
Having once looked at a cold mullet on a plate on a table supported by the
weight of the inconstant universe
He wished to go far away from himself.

There were no baskets in those jovial pine-tree forests, and the waves pushed
    without whitecaps
In that foam where he wished to be.

Man is never without woman, the neuter sex
Casting up her equations, looks to her lord for loving kindness
For man smiles never at woman.
In the forests a night landslide could disclose that she smiled.
Guns were fired to discourage dogs into the interior
But woman—never. She is completely out of this world.
She climbs a tree to see if he is coming
Sunlight breaks at the edges of the wet lakes
And she is happy, if free
For the power he forces down at her like a storm of lightning.

Once a happy old man
One can never change the core of things, and light burns you the harder for
    it.
Glad of the changes already and if there are more it will never be you that
    minds
Since it will not be you to be changed, but in the evening in the severe lamp-
    light doubts come
From many scattered distances, and do not come too near.
As it falls along the house, your treasure
Cries to the other men; the darkness will have none of you, and you are
    folded into it like mint into the sound of haying.
It was ninety-five years ago that you strolled in the serene little port; under
    an enormous cornice six boys in black slowly stood.
Six frock coats today, six black fungi tomorrow,
And the day after tomorrow—but the day after tomorrow itself is blackening
    dust.
You court obsidian pools
And from a tremendous height twilight falls like a stone and hits you.

You who were always in the way
Flower
Are you afraid of trembling like breath
But there is no breath in seriousness; the lake howls for it.
Swiftly sky covers earth, the wrong breast for a child to suck, and that,
What have you got there in your hand?
It is a stone

So the passions are divided into tiniest units
And of these many are lost, and those that remain are given at nightfall to
    the uneasy old man
The old man who goes skipping along the roadbed.
In a dumb harvest
Passions are locked away, and states of creation are used instead, that is to say
    synonyms are used.

Honey
On the lips of elders is not contenting, so
A firebrand is made. Woman carries it,
She who thought herself good only for bearing children is decked out in the
    lace of fire
And this is exactly the way she wanted it, the trees coming to place
    themselves in her
In a rite of torpor, dust.
A bug carries the elixir
Naked men pray the ground and chew it with their hands
The fire lives
Men are nabbed
She her bonnet half off is sobbing there while the massacre yet continues
    with a terrific thin energy
A silver blaze calms the darkness.

Rest undisturbed on the dry of the beach
Flower

And night stand suddenly sideways to observe your bones
Vixen

Do men later go home
Because we wanted to travel
Under the kettle of trees
We thought the sky would melt to see us
But to tell the truth the air turned to smoke,
We were forced back onto a foul pillow that was another place.
Or were lost by our comrades
Somewhere between heaven and no place, and were growing smaller.
In another place a mysterious mist shot up like a wall, down which trickled
    the tears of our loved ones.
Bananas rotten with their ripeness hung from the leaves, and cakes and
    jewels covered the sand.
But these were not the best men
But there were moments of the others
Seen through indifference, only bare methods
But we can remember them and so we are saved.

A last world moves on the figures;
They are smaller than when we last saw them caring about them.
The sky is a giant rocking horse
And of the other things death is a new office building filled with modern
    furniture,
A wise thing, but which has no purpose for us.

Everything is being blown away;
A little horse trots up with a letter in its mouth, which is read with eagerness
As we gallop into the flame.

The New Realism

I have lost the beautiful dreams
That enlisted on waking,
Cold and waiting. That world is a war now
The portable laugh eclipsing another place
The warrior's bonnet holds sand.
The blond headdress is soggy
The ray carried your picture away
If space could imagine a pilot
The clouds were rags, wheat the sun
A small dancer decorated the coverlet with gore
A perforated fountain assumed
That the center cravat was the right one
The one with peach halves and violets
And buzzing soda water
Out of the serene
Blackening with space, its blankness
Cast waterward, the grim engine
Chugging, denial at first
You see you cannot do this to me
Why, we were differing
The eyes and clitoris a million miles from
The small persistent tug.
The tree streamed with droppings
Mountain air the subject of our three conversations
The child skipped happily over
The western pages—even better than it is
Stones of day
Police formed a boundary to the works
Where we played
A torn page with a passionate oasis

Shall we ask them to
The kitty, the outgrown stone keeps up
The grass and solid ovaries
A pineapple near
And the lumber over the rear plant
You especially not because you're known
That tree of noon—pretext of your roots
Are among several dopes
On the loony stock exchange
Near your dumb bank.
You often asked me after hours
The glass pinnacle, its upkeep and collapse
Knowing that if we were in a barn
Straw panels would . . .   Confound it
The arboretum is bursting with jasmine and lilac
And all I can smell here is newsprint
The tea went down
All went down easily
He keeps coming back, the curse
Of pliant dawns
Braiding afternoons—a whistle be the result
On some nights in their climate president
His term packed with ice
The sideboard burst under millions of candles
And hope . . . a gray Niagara.

Under the crushed water on the rock
Dove affects man . . . in his burden
Compounded of cannibalism and hush
Mice roar and an Ethiop
Sprinkles lead beads over the clay babe
Once the oxygen is removed the
Arms can move freely again.
The soldiers sigh comfortably
In their garrison, you do not trust me any more.

A rainy day brought us the truth
The suffragette had proclaimed
And the wax had shuffled
Only beauty offered sin
Out of the round and the oval
Something to match the edges of dawn
The house where it took place
Pardon on the face of the tall wall
That land burned season on it scum
The fence removed and all the tile gone.
Again, going up in a balloon
Reading from the pages of the telephone directory
The scooter and the Ethiop had gotten away
The building was to be torn down
A pleasant wink . . . you said the sun was setting
And there were only more rollers,
More Nile . . .   In these moments I often think of the man
Who . . . payments acceded to the night
Of his claim a perfect universe
Onyx, imperturbable, moderate . . . you see the session was letting out
One came up to me
They veil the sky
Cast down in new purity, the cargo
A sky, the lever anyway
The plantation crew of three
Were never awarded.   Mixed
With undistinguishable day, and night, the new moon
Turning with ash under the way
Crowds into the night stopped at fall
Lights stream undeniably away
The purgation is cheap. Blocked by a heavy truck
Shift your ballast, radiant
In gingham
The sheriff
Culled, all superior, and the grain

Disappeared forever, the haven
Which the ranch
Torn flower topping curious day.
A mast of all not eliminated
Fixing the way you smile
The sunbeams carried to me
The trail . . . stopped only where you overstepped
And libation. The answer had ended,
Clouds mounted swiftly, the furniture
Ages away by the torn page of the book
Forgotten in the sun
The pink moth close to its border
A millionth change
If we must go on
And the oasis in flames
The desert muted, the Nubians plunged in dreams
Scared by owls. You have to exact the forfeit
We change this concave block, the difference between us three
The peak guards mist his door
A table for three
The light goes out—it exudes
Your idea—perched on some utterly crass sign
Not the hardest either, but adoption is no way
There was calm rapture in the way she spoke
Perhaps I would get over the way the joke
Always turned against me, in the end.
The bars had been removed from all the windows
There was something quiet in the way the light entered
Her trousseau. Wine fished out of the sea—they hadn't known
We were coming relaxed forever
We stood off the land because if you get too far
From a perfume you can squeeze the life out of it
One seal came into view and then the others
Yellow in the vast sun.
A watchdog performed and they triumphed

The day was bleak—ice had replaced air
The sigh of the children to former music
Supplanting the mutt's yelps.
This was as far as she would go—
A tavern with plants.
Dynamite out over the horizon
And a sequel, and a racket. Dolphins repelling
The sand. Swarms of bulldozers
Wrecked the site, and she died laughing
Because only once does prosperity let you get away
On your doorstep she used to explain
How if the returning merchants in the morning hitched the rim of the van
In the evening one must be very quick to give them the slip.
The judge knocked. The zinnias
Had never looked better—red, yellow, and blue
They were, and the forget-me-nots and dahlias
At least sixty different varieties
As the shade went up
And the ambulance came crashing through the dust
Of the new day, the moon and the sun and the stars,
And the iceberg slowly sank
In the volcano and the sea ran far away
Yellow over the hot sand, green as the green trees.

The Unknown Travelers

Lugged to the gray arbor,
I have climbed this snow-stone on my face,
My stick, but what, snapped the avalanche
The air filled with slowly falling rocks

Breathed in deeply—arrived,
The white room, a table covered
With a towel, mug of ice—fear
Among the legs of a chair, the ashman,
Purple and gray she starts upright in her chair.

Europe

1.

To employ her
construction ball
Morning fed on the
light blue wood
of the mouth
        cannot understand
feels deeply)

2.

A wave of nausea—
numerals

3.

a few berries

4.

the unseen claw
Babe asked today
The background of poles roped over
into star jolted them

5.

filthy or into backward drenched flung heaviness
lemons asleep pattern crying

6.

The month of elephant—
embroidery over where
ill page sees.

7.

What might have
       children singing
the horses
       the seven
breaths under tree, fog
clasped—absolute, unthinking
menace to our way of life.
uh unearth more cloth
This could have been done—
This could not be done

8.

In the falling twilight of the wintry afternoon all looked dull and cheerless.
The car stood outside with Ronald Pryor and Collins attending to some slight
engine trouble—the fast, open car which Ronnie sometimes used to such ad-
vantage. It was covered with mud, after the long run from Suffolk, for they had
started from Harbury long before daylight, and, until an hour ago, had been
moving swiftly up the Great North Road, by way of Stanford, Grantham and
Doncaster to York. There they had turned away to Ripon, where, for an hour,
they had eaten and rested. In a basket the waiter had placed some cold food
with some bread and a bottle of wine, and this had been duly transferred to the
car.

All was now ready for the continuance of the journey.

9.

The decision in his life
soul elsewhere
the gray hills
out there on the road darkness
covering lieutenant

       there is a cure

10.

He had mistaken his book for garbage

11.

The editor realized
    its gradual abandonment
    a kind of block where other men come down
    spoiling the view
    wept blood
    on the first page and following snow
    gosh flowers upset ritual
      a mass of black doves
over the scooter, snow outlining the tub
    flower until dawn

12.

that surgeon must operate

I had come across
to the railway from the Great North
Road, which I had followed up to London.

13.

the human waste cannibals designed the master and his life

robot you underground sorrow to the end
can unlack horsemen. Storm seems berries—
until the truth can be explained
Nothing can exist. Rain
blossomed in the highlands—a
secret to annul grass sticks—razor today engraved sobs.
The lion's skin—ears, to travel.

14.

Before the waste
went up
Before she had worked
The sunlight in the square—
apples, oranges, the compass
tears of joy—over rotten stone flesh
His dyspepsia uncorked—that's
    leaf of the story
  mitigated

15.

Absolve me from the hatred I never
she—all are wounded against
Zeppelin—wounded carrying dying
three colors over land
thistles again closed around voice.
She is dying—
automatically—
wanting to see you again, but the stone
must be rebuilt. Time stepped

16.

before I started
I was forced to   flying
she said.

higher and higher on
next tree, am as wire
when canvas the must spread
           to new junk

17.

I moved up

glove
the field

18.

I must say I
suddenly
she left the room, oval tear tonelessly fell.

19.

Life pursued down these cliffs.
the omened birds
intrusion; skated, at night
clear waves of weather
fur you bring genius
over hell's curiosity
the librarian shabbily books on
You cannot illusion; the dust.
abstract vermin the garden worn smiles

20.

That something desperate was to be attempted was,
however, quite plain.

21.

Night hunger
of berry . . .   stick

22.

"Beautiful morning for a flip miss," remarked the mechanic in brown overalls.
"Are you going up alone."

23.

"Then I'll take the bombs out," he said, and at once removed the six powerful bombs from the rack, the projectiles intended for the destruction of Zeppelins.

24.

The tables gleamed—soft lighting
    covered the place

There was a certain pleasure in all this for him.
The twelve girls wept. She willed him
loveliest diamond of the tree; the old lawyer kept his mule there.
They had gone. The weather was very pure that night like
leaves of paper placed on the black—the opal
crescent still dangled on the little chain—
a pleasant memory of a kiss, completely
given to recollection. Only
faded water remained. The last memory left.

25.

She was dying but had time for him—
brick. Men were carrying the very heavy things—dark purple, like
    flowers.
Bowl lighted up the score just right

26.

water
                    thinking
                        a

27.

A notice:

wishing you were a
　　the bottle really　　　before the washed
　　　　handed over to her:
　　　　　hundreds
light over her
　　hanging her
you can remember

29

Have you encouraged judge
　　inked commentary
approaching obvious battle
summer night less ecstatic
　　　　train over scream . . .　　mountain
　　　into woods

sweetheart . . .　　　　　　　　　the stamp
　　ballooning you
vision I thought you
forget, encouraging your vital organs.
Telegraph. The rifle—a page folded over.

More upset, wholly meaningless, the willing sheath
glide into fall . . .　　mercury　to passing
the war you said won—milling around the picket fence, and noise of
　　　the engine from the sky
and flowers—here is a bunch
the war won out of cameos.
And somehow the perfect warrior is fallen.

31

They wore red
the three children dragged into next year

sad . . .   gold under the feet.
sadly more music is divine to them.

32.

The snow stopped falling
on the head of the stranger.
In a moment the house would be dark

33.

mirrors—insane

34.

dying for they do not
the hole no crow can
and finally the day of thirst
in the air.
whistles carbon dioxide. Cold
pavement grew. The powerful machine
The tractor, around edge
the listless children. Good night
staining the naughty air
with marvelous rings. You are going there.
Weeps. The wreath not decorating.
The kids pile over the ample funeral hill.
had arrived from London
                    o'clock
baited tragically
This time the others grew.
The others waited
by the darkening pool—"a world of silence"
you can't understand their terror
means more to these people   waste
the runt crying in the pile of colored
snapshots offal in the wind
that's the way we do it terror

the hand of the large person falls
to the desk. The people all leave.
the industries begin
moments   puts on the silencer
You crab into the night

35·

The sheiks protest use of
aims. In the past
coal has protected their
O long, watchful hour.
the engines had been humming
stones of March in the gray woods
still, the rods, could not they take long
More anthems until dust
flocks disguised machine. The stone
the valentine couldn't save . . .   Hooks

36.

he ran the machine swiftly across the frosty grass.
Soon he rose, and skimming the trees, soon
soared away into the darkness.

37·

From where Beryl sat she saw the glow
of the little electric bulb set over the instruments shining into
her lover's strong clean-shaven face, and, by the compass, gathered
        that
they had described a half-circle, and, though
still rising rapidly, were now heading eastward in
the direction of the sea.

38.

The roar of the engine, of course,
rendered speech impossible,

while the mist was very chilly, causing her to draw her brown woollen
    comforter around her legs.
There was no sign of light anywhere below
—all was a bright black void.

39.

The few children
Seeds under the glare
The formal tragedy of it all
Mystery for man—engines humming
Parachutes opening.
The newspaper being read
Beside the great gas turbine
The judge calls his assistant over
And together they try to piece together the secret message contained
    in today's paper.

40.

The police
Had been forgotten
Scarlet, blue, and canary
Heads tossing on the page
    grunting to the coatroom
there was another ocean, ballads and legends, the children returning
    to the past—head

41.

She was saying into the distance
    It was a sad day
the riders drinking in the car
haze of trees behind
               dummy woods
  plans and sketches
  soda, glasses, ice

bumped off
"with these strange symbols."

42.

the club had bought aperture

43.

Their hidden storage (to you, murder)
but what testimony buried under colored sorrow
—the nerve

children called upon
assassination this racket.

44.

He ran the ferret
backing him hard nest
        The chil—
One day the children particularly surrounded
he had read about him.

45.

Like a long room
Monsignor
        pushed away it
studio artificially small
        pine rounds

46.

The last time she crossed close to Berck,
        beyond Paris-Plage, she passed over Folke-
stone, and then over to Cape Gris-Nez
        alone into the night

Or he hides bodies
stone night,
pleasant city, gray
      hides
perfect dictionary for you
valentine not wanted storm under the
snow backed rubbers
The city hides, desolate
rocks snow tile hides
over the door marked "The literature
beginning veins hide the mind
robot—"—capped by all.   release.

Then she studied her map, took her bearings
and, drawing on her ample gauntlet gloves
            (for it had become chilly)
she followed a straight line of railway leading through Suffolk
    and Norfolk

I'm on my way to Hull

   grinned the girl

It was in German. The aviator and his
observer climbed out of the seats and stood
with Mr. Aylesworth, chatting and laughing.

They were written upon English paper, and English penny
    stamps are upon them . . .

they can be put into any post-box . . .   They
mostly contain instructions to our good friends in Great
     Britain.

52.

The rose

          dirt

   dirt you
pay
The buildings
is tree

Undecided

protest

        This planet

53.

The vegetable wagon had not been placed yet
Scotchmen with their plaids—all the colorful
Photography, horror of all
That has died
The hundred year old stones—deceived
by the mind of these things—the stairs
climbing up out of dark hollyhocks
old, dirt, smell of the most terrifying thing in the world.

54.

"He is probably one of the gang."

55.

   mood seems the sort
   to brag
   end

56.

songs like
You came back to me
you were wrong about the gravestone
that nettles hide quietly
The son is not ours.

57.

Precise mechanisms
Love us.

He came over the hill
He held me in his arms—it was marvelous.

But the map of Europe
shrinks around naked couples

Even as you lick the stamp
A brown dog lies down beside you and dies

In the city an eleven year old girl with pig tails
Tied with a yellow ribbon takes the trolley

All of this ends somewhere—the book is replaced on the shelf
By an unseen hand

We are not more loved than now
The newspaper is ruining your eyes.

58.

The professor—a large "S"
One kitten escaped
Take plane

                    or death by hanging
And naturally it is all over again, beginning to get tired you realize

                              59.
                    The real thing the matter
                         with him you see studio end
                      of day masked
                    you didn't see him—he went
                    escape is over on the lighted steps
                    "My blood went into this."
                    Misunderstandings arise cathedral
                    twenty years later.   catching sight of him
                    his baggy trousers the porch daylight
                    playing tennis before we realize the final dream is razed
                    Today, of course.

                              60.

Wing

            Bostonian

        and his comments
    thirty-three years old the day
        of his third birthday the legs
    Lenin de Gaulle three days later
        also comparing simple

                              61.

reflecting trout

                              62.

All of us fear the secret
guarded too carefully
        An assortment

63.

she ran along the grass for a short distance
couple of beers
eats   being corpse tables

64.

ice   dirt
five minutes
get your money back
        the hole screamed
two persons
            two cut flowers

65.

nothing is better than
glowing coals
The perfect animal
during the summer, sleep of brine and ice

66.

She followed a straight line leading
due north through Suffolk and Norfolk.

67.

over the last few years

there is one terrifying
    wild
        the error of sleep
            love

68.

The straight line out of sight
of beads
decades cheapest
the more   post card
"genius"

69.

because it is
That is to say

70.

Her last dollar

71.

They must hold against
The fire rain
or when sometime it seems
upward, hands down
against
pilloried
sell quickly took her bearings
did not appear entirely
upper hand of her
a height of five thousand feet

72.

The village (using the new headache system) were cut
With the stops running
A French or Swiss
had hit bottom and gotten back up
wild margins are possible
The gold a "call"
options his life . . . flea

73.

A least
four days
A surprise
mothers
suppose
Is not a "images"
to "arrange"
He is a descendant, for example
The Swiss bank—a village

74.

Man come for one in humanity
the lowest pickpocket helps

75.

Like the public,
reactions
from Crystal Palace

76.

A roar
"sweetness and light"
pickpocket—stem
and more scandalous . . . well, forgotten
The snow is around storm
He laughed lightly at cliff
and used that term

77.

"Perhaps you've heard of her. She's a great flying woman."

"Oh yes," replied the stranger. "I've seen things about
her in the papers. Does she fly much?"

78.

applauding itself—wiser
    more gun   I come from the district
four times carrying a small,
        oval
the movie was also
        in the entire crystal

79.

to stroll down Main Street
the dignified and paternal image
telegraph—magnificent

            dump
porch
        flowers   store
weed local relatives
            whine

80.

multitude headquarters about there
Because there are no
because the majority is toxic
An exquisite sense—like pretzels . . .
He was sent to the state senate
wage conceal his disapproval
The arguments situation lawyers worthlessness sullen cafeterias

81.

    barcarolle

82.

The silencer. "Is he not . . . "

83.

Soon after noon, carrying a narrow,

84.

about her

85.

    ghost of stone—massive
        hangs halfway
polishing
      whose winding
Strong, sad, half-city
    gardens
           from the bridge of
    stair
      broom
    recent   past   symbolized
hair   banana
does not evoke a concrete image
the splendid

86.

nourished on the
railings of bare stone—

87.

Your side
is majestic—the dry wind
timeless tones.   a deep sigh
dragged up with a piercing scream
the clean, crisp air
aging on the villas

little openings for her bath
facades of the—all alike, the hard rain
"the dignity of this fortress."

88.

the invaders
         so bad just now
      go up and see the shabby traveller
            ordered a pint
At half-past two, the visitor, taking
      his bag, set out on a tour of the
      village.   An endeavor
               remained

rolls on them

      at night

89.

This car has some private
      more than one cottage the chintzes were bright its
      brass candlestick forgotten
      twenty-five cents.
      could offer was a feeble

90.

I have a perfect memory and

the sky seems to pass
      a couple of them like a huge bowl

and encircle the earth

91.

flanked by his lieutenants—lemon—
his chief outside
"If I am wrong
    a fine sieve
telephones   I do not
strong nature who wrote of him while starving himself

92.

to be dying, he gets them into magazines
and some of them mangy and rabid
hardly seemed necessary.

I was horrified. I felt sorry for him.
No branch without . . .
down to the lakes the ornamental
bronze—isn't it fear that

Hand in hand like fire
and in your souls

93.

A searchlight sweeping
picked up "The Hornet"
Hardly had he undressed when he
heard again that low swish of
"The Hornet" on her return from scouting circuit of the
    Thames estuary
solidifying disguises

who died in an automobile accident
had developed a
then, imperceptibly

94.

The snow has begun to fall on Paris
It is barely noon

95.

Between the legs of her
Cobwebs the lip reads chewing
and taste seem uncertain;
powerless creating images
shut up and leave me . . . Hush! This
two men who have
        most profoundly
            the islanders

96.

Mr. Bean remained indoors
at the small boats
of our defences, our intentions

97.

out upon the lawn after a few months in the village

    big
"Like some of my friends
Otherwise we'll chop off his head

98.

This was the third thing
another giant

99.

dark wool, summer
and winter

100.

gun metal—her right foot in both hands
                things

101.

the doctor, comb
                Sinn Fein

102.

                dress

103.

streaming sweeping the surface
long-handled twig-brooms
                starving
wall   great   trees

104.

blaze			aviators	
	out		dastardly	

105.

We must be a little more wary in
                future, dear

106.

she was trying to make sense of
what was quick laugh
hotel—cheap for them
caverns the bed
        box of cereal

Ere long a flare was lit
I don't understand wreckage

107.

blue smoke?   The steel bolts
It was as though   having been replaced
She had   by a painting of
the river   one of wood!
above the water   Ronnie, thoughtfully

of the silencer

plot to kill both of us, dear.

pet

oh

it that she was there

108.

the bridge crosses
dragon   ships
canal lock
was effect
There are but two seasons
the map of Paris
through the center of the sheet
character
sewers empty into under the
literally choked the river with
bodies
"on the coast, I think . . . "

passing over

109.

Magnificent trees—the old
chateau—he said he was

going home for their needs
only the other—
exchanged another meaning
here lately
the inn-keeper's

110.

Dry, the bush
settling   Everybody

knows him
close to the Thwaite
passing close to where
The bookshop
were crouched in conceal-
up a steep, narrow path
to the summit of Black Hill
recognized him
lavatory—dogging
his footsteps

out to sea

111.

Half an hour later
Ronald recognized him.
They suddenly saw a beam of intense, white light,
A miniature searchlight of great brilliance,
—pierce the darkness, skyward.

They now recognized to be a acetylene,
a cylinder mounted
upon a light tripod of aluminum
with a bright reflector behind the gas jet,

that the light began to "wink,"
    three times in quick succession
the Morse letter "S."

Slowly the beam turned from north to south,
making the Morse "S." upon the clouds,
time after time.

Suddenly the light was shut off—for five minutes by
    Ronald's watch no flicker was shown
Then suddenly, once again, the series of S's was repeated
in a semicircle from north to south
and back again.

Another five minutes passed in darkness

Once more the light opened out and commenced
to signal the Morse flashes and flares,
"N.F.", "N.F."
followed by a long beam of
light skyward, slowly sweeping in a circle

                        the breath

To the Same Degree

From the frozen yelps squirted lust
Unavoidably but without waste, though certain rusks
Were being distributed. Water mains, you imitate
Our positive statement, when through the disgusting air
With mantle of leaves, possibly forgetting old
Seizure, in some fishing village, the barbed leaves
Close to the ground, in some automobile on the grounds
Things contained in the universal consciousness:
Wool, brooks, books, the Carpathians, a caterpillar, rivalries
Today we could see all the way to the ditch.
The possibility of fastening a ball
To anything, weary unexplored
The river continued to pour out its volume of water
Like an enraged smell. The horse disappeared
With the cart. We were near a larger body
Of water in the north
To some factory of climate

Earnestly so-and-so
The fresh lumps pointed
To Valhalla, the oboes
Torturing the hobo's visor
The "Poet's Wife" ran aground
The laxative had been
Administered . . . on the grounds
Of legality. Full ugly night
With blistering blasts
Fist of aloes, aground
With only a certain amount of hair
Cloves, you tax our
Thorax weary from apes
Ball
Unexpected
The tall stork approached
This time the expenses were enormous

A fault deep in the earth
Of manners unquenchable
Or sold to be eaten out of hand
The enormous cans
You contaminated our layers.
The wretch vanished. There is no more sirup, nothing to
   dominate
As frogs will flock together, when the scudding
Hares out of the west churned by the stain
Of erratic paradise, so fish will in schools
Close to the pond, rage, action
Contriving to will heartburn—in case of glare
Parenthesis uncle
A package of drought next door
Customers absorbed, mist getting redder
Two entries that day. Poured into one hole
And you remember to mark the exhausted shepherd
The marble of his Swedish copper forehead, and all that?

And chirping bogs
The anxious gardens' stare
Agreement was possible. In the apartment fallen
The tree began to take root. The promise of fire
The sky and the storks began, the job
Pleasure, earliest of the guests, prick
With hand of flour execrating
The keys. The pursar. With the time
Pushing to the great bear
The boar—which do you prefer?
Some juice was served in glasses
And you could moisten your rusk.
This is perhaps the best time to point out
That I was alone—a large wheel.

Soon after they began to leave
In little groups first, then by tens.

The Passive Preacher

the year books
authored the heart bees—
Beers over beads somewhat
broken off from the rest
Quit the tenement
the person slides affect in excrement
on the sides
the janitor and cap, the flat
over the trees
years of patient
on the patient, enamel
sink
washbasin
Please, the pride of the
the three
threaded over, the fluke
the midwinter flood
we were how we liked to
carry it
the blood—full of
and when the mediocrity
cashed in
the mediocrity
fallen for the doom landing swivel
to the next
not to be free of
and the comparison pointed to
the exit light
By frivolous sails
you, that other, and the third one you were become by

and the recent
nuisance
miscreant eating
the last time you on land to
all the old ones eaten
or carried away in marvel
as though the pagoda
and really carried away all
the way shouted at
crimson the day after
you removed the shin
having only forgotten the grave
but permanent as the night's infection
on the needle end
on that needle land

The Shower

The water began to fall quite quietly
As pipes decorate laminations of
City unit buses pass through.
A laborer dragging luggage examined
The wet place near a bug.
It sifted slowly down the sides of buildings flat
The permanent way to make a race.
So simple was the ally. Trying the lips
The spaced demons never breaking.
They imagine something different from what it is.

Just a fat man with sunglasses
Moving through shine—the uncle in the mirror—
As it is beginning again these are the proportions—
He lauds her with a smile.

Miles away in the country the performance included glue.
The abandoned airfield will have to have the imagination now
To be august, gray, against oneself

These things that are the property of only the few.

Idaho

During the past few months, Biff had become quite a frequent visitor to Carol's apartment.

He never failed to marvel at the cool, corrected elegance of the place as contrasted with its warm, rippling, honey-blonde occupant. The apothecary jars,

Chippendale furniture,

and wall-to-wall carpeting were strangely out of keeping with Carol's habitual "Hiya good lookin'" as she came forward to greet him, wrapped in one of those big fuzzy bathrobes and drying her hair on a Turkish towel. Or were his calculations somehow awry? Was there, deep within this warm, vital-seeming presence a steel vein so thin as to be almost invisible? Or was this, too, a mistake?

Their whole conduct had been, up to now, not impersonal exactly, but utterly devoid of any recognition of sex-consciousness. In conversation they had "swapped backgrounds," as Biff called it. Carol, her eyes wet with tears at the picture of his isolation in the crowded rectory, had uttered a deep sigh at her own recital of being left for the first eight years of her life to the sole care of Patches.

With the unconscious dramatic heightening that always goes with a sympathetic audience, each of them, intensely serious and really moved, had lifted corners of the veil for the other to peep through. They had been very close to each other in attention, in sympathy, in response, but with none of the subtle emphasis which marks the recognized intrusion of sex. Carol was aware today, however, that Biff had suddenly become obsessed with a sense of her; that he had caught fire. She was aware of

vast excitement,

apprehension,

a mental

"Can I give you a hand?"

She gave a little cry that was silenced by mouth on
         uttermost tingling nerve
"Carol!" he said. Can this be the one time
      ??

                             She had known how from
Biff: The last Rhode Island reds are
          "diet of hamburgers and orange juice"
   Exactly what kind of perfection??
I see into fields of timothy
          one
the others   time
          change
,,,,,,,and they walked back,
       small hand-assemblies

       "What does it mean?????????????"

      Carol laughed. Among other things,
        till I've finished it. It's the reason of
      dropped into Brentano's.
           get some of the
    a pile of these. I just grabbed one . . .
        —Oh, by the way, there's a tele-
"See?" She pointed to the table.
Cornelia unfolded the piece of crude blue paper that is a French telegra.
    # # # # # # # # # # # # #
          The mouth of weeds

      marriage." She shivered. "It's—it's a death!"

         2.

      The door of the studio slammed.
      "Hullo, honey!" Cornelia said.
  was the last practical   from now on, whispers
    leading into the night

flowers, moral turpitude,
She had had more than enough. Why, in Stone Age
vessels
But that doesn't explain. Her mind opened it-
Every tendril of thought,,,,,,,,,,
It sees through a magnifying glass
genius
a special aureole
Niagara of affliction.   had learned this
heard it
into the
window   the long   platform at Oxford, and Carol lowered the
When the train stopped the army
You had nothing about it. That's no Bob!!!!!!!!!!!!!!!!

A whistle blew shrilly
the slow evening
silver note
the main road automobiles
majestic stag-beetles, with a high, sweet hum
that moment for long
thoughts and low red voices
the mood was shattered
"twenty-seven"   Just as that act changes
nerve-centers
birthdays—
She rose from the table abruptly. "You must smoke your
cigar alone tonight. I—I'm going out in the car. She went
upstairs and changed into a different pair of shoes
and a sweater.
Jim was pouring himself another glass of port as she came down.
,,,,,,,,,,,,,,,,,,,,,, "I won't be very long,",,,,,,,,,,,,,,,,,,,,, she said.   # # # # # # # #

nodded. "Take care of yourself." She closed the door behind her and went
down through

the garden. A carnation struck her hand as she passed. She picked it,

sniffed deeply, and put the stalk in her mouth. "Twenty-seven! Twenty-seven!" She went into the garage, a little house of wood, tucked into the bank at the edge of the road. It was Jim's car, a present from Carol. She had earned it in the year

following the exhibition, had learned to drive it at an automobile school in London, and had a special low bunk designed for Jim alongside the driver's seat. The carnation made a crimson

splash against her cheek as she drove out

and headed down the hill towards the main road. Up in the cottage Patches "Good 'eavens! Is that

> For who dies
> The crocus ideally
> On life's playing field
> The "never mind" rubbish
> All, all fixed
> running water
> And the proper names,
> blood out of courage
> to fix
> to feel
> the stem of air

great, senseless knob

brownies ahead and the clutch. "Twenty-seven!   Twenty-seven!"

sniffed loudly
the car window
listening car had ceased.

A whistle blew shrilly.

RIVERS AND MOUNTAINS

These Lacustrine Cities

These lacustrine cities grew out of loathing
Into something forgetful, although angry with history.
They are the product of an idea: that man is horrible, for instance,
Though this is only one example.

They emerged until a tower
Controlled the sky, and with artifice dipped back
Into the past for swans and tapering branches,
Burning, until all that hate was transformed into useless love.

Then you are left with an idea of yourself
And the feeling of ascending emptiness of the afternoon
Which must be charged to the embarrassment of others
Who fly by you like beacons.

The night is a sentinel.
Much of your time has been occupied by creative games
Until now, but we have all-inclusive plans for you.
We had thought, for instance, of sending you to the middle of the desert,

To a violent sea, or of having the closeness of the others be air
To you, pressing you back into a startled dream
As sea-breezes greet a child's face.
But the past is already here, and you are nursing some private project.

The worst is not over, yet I know
You will be happy here. Because of the logic
Of your situation, which is something no climate can outsmart.
Tender and insouciant by turns, you see

You have built a mountain of something,
Thoughtfully pouring all your energy into this single monument,
Whose wind is desire starching a petal,
Whose disappointment broke into a rainbow of tears.

Rivers and Mountains

On the secret map the assassins
Cloistered, the Moon River was marked
Near the eighteen peaks and the city
Of humiliation and defeat—wan ending
Of the trail among dry, papery leaves
Gray-brown quills like thoughts
In the melodious but vast mass of today's
Writing through fields and swamps
Marked, on the map, with little bunches of weeds.
Certainly squirrels lived in the woods
But devastation and dull sleep still
Hung over the land, quelled
The rioters turned out of sleep in the peace of prisons
Singing on marble factory walls
Deaf consolation of minor tunes that pack
The air with heavy invisible rods
Pent in some sand valley from
Which only quiet walking ever instructs.
The bird flew over and
Sat—there was nothing else to do.
Do not mistake its silence for pride or strength
Or the waterfall for a harbor
Full of light boats that is there
Performing for thousands of people
In clothes some with places to go
Or games. Sometimes over the pillar
Of square stones its impact
Makes a light print.

So going around cities
To get to other places you found
It all on paper but the land
Was made of paper processed
To look like ferns, mud or other
Whose sea unrolled its magic
Distances and then rolled them up
Its secret was only a pocket
After all but some corners are darker
Than these moonless nights spent as on a raft
In the seclusion of a melody heard
As though through trees
And you can never ignite their touch
Long but there were homes
Flung far out near the asperities
Of a sharp, rocky pinnacle
And other collective places
Shadows of vineyards whose wine
Tasted of the forest floor
Fisheries and oyster beds
Tides under the pole
Seminaries of instruction, public
Places for electric light
And the major tax assessment area
Wrinkled on the plan
Of election to public office
Sixty-two years old bath and breakfast
The formal traffic, shadows
To make it not worth joining
After the ox had pulled away the cart.

Your plan was to separate the enemy into two groups
With the razor-edged mountains between.
It worked well on paper
But their camp had grown

To be the mountains and the map
Carefully peeled away and not torn
Was the light, a tender but tough bark
On everything. Fortunately the war was solved
In another way by isolating the two sections
Of the enemy's navy so that the mainland
Warded away the big floating ships.
Light bounced off the ends
Of the small gray waves to tell
Them in the observatory
About the great drama that was being won
To turn off the machinery
And quietly move among the rustic landscape
Scooping snow off the mountains rinsing
The coarser ones that love had
Slowly risen in the night to overflow
Wetting pillow and petal
Determined to place the letter
On the unassassinated president's desk
So that a stamp could reproduce all this
In detail, down to the last autumn leaf
And the affliction of June ride
Slowly out into the sun-blackened landscape.

Last Month

No changes of support—only
Patches of gray, here where sunlight fell.
The house seems heavier
Now that they have gone away.
In fact it emptied in record time.
When the flat table used to result
A match recedes, slowly, into the night.
The academy of the future is
Opening its doors and willing
The fruitless sunlight streams into domes,
The chairs piled high with books and papers.

The sedate one is this month's skittish one
Confirming the property that,
A timeless value, has changed hands.
And you could have a new automobile
Ping pong set and garage, but the thief
Stole everything like a miracle.
In his book there was a picture of treason only
And in the garden, cries and colors.

Civilization and Its Discontents

A people chained to aurora
I alone disarming you

Millions of facts of distributed light

Helping myself with some big boxes
Up the steps, then turning to no neighborhood;
The child's psalm, slightly sung
In the hall rushing into the small room.
Such fire! leading away from destruction.
Somewhere in outer ether I glimpsed you
Coming at me, the solo barrier did it this time,
Guessing us staying, true to be at the blue mark
Of the threshold. Tired of planning it again and again,
The cool boy distant, and the soaked-up
Afterthought, like so much rain, or roof.

The miracle took you in beside him.
Leaves rushed the window, there was clear water and the sound of a lock.
Now I never see you much any more.
The summers are much colder than they used to be
In that other time, when you and I were young.
I miss the human truth of your smile,
The halfhearted gaze of your palms,
And all things together, but there is no comic reign
Only the facts you put to me. You must not, then,
Be very surprised if I am alone: it is all for you,
The night, and the stars, and the way we used to be.

There is no longer any use in harping on
The incredible principle of daylong silence, the dark sunlight
As only the grass is beginning to know it,
The wreath of the north pole,
Festoons for the late return, the shy pensioners
Agasp on the lamplit air. What is agreeable
Is to hold your hand. The gravel
Underfoot. The time is for coming close. Useless
Verbs shooting the other words far away.
I had already swallowed the poison
And could only gaze into the distance at my life
Like a saint's with each day distinct.
No heaviness in the upland pastures. Nothing
In the forest. Only life under the huge trees
Like a coat that has grown too big, moving far away,
Cutting swamps for men like lapdogs, holding its own,
Performing once again, for you and for me.

If the Birds Knew

It is better this year.
And the clothes they wear
In the gray unweeded sky of our earth
There is no possibility of change
Because all of the true fragments are here.
So I was glad of the fog's
Taking me to you
Undetermined summer thing eaten
Of grief and passage—where you stay.
The wheel is ready to turn again.
When you have gone it will light up.
The shadow of the spokes to drown
Your departure where the summer knells
Speak to grown dawn.
There is after all a kind of promise
To the affair of the waiting weather.
We have learned not to be tired
Among the lanterns of this year of sleep
But someone pays—no transparency
Has ever hardened us before
To long piers of silence, and hedges
Of understanding, difficult passing
From one lesson to the next and the coldness
Of the consistency of our lives'
Devotion to immaculate danger.
A leaf would have settled the disturbance
Of the atmosphere, but at that high
Valley's point disbanded

Clouds that rocks smote newly
The person or persons involved
Parading slowly through the sunlit fields
Not only as though the danger did not exist
But as though the birds were in on the secret.

Into the Dusk-Charged Air

Far from the Rappahannock, the silent
Danube moves along toward the sea.
The brown and green Nile rolls slowly
Like the Niagara's welling descent.
Tractors stood on the green banks of the Loire
Near where it joined the Cher.
The St. Lawrence prods among black stones
And mud. But the Arno is all stones.
Wind ruffles the Hudson's
Surface. The Irawaddy is overflowing.
But the yellowish, gray Tiber
Is contained within steep banks. The Isar
Flows too fast to swim in, the Jordan's water
Courses over the flat land. The Allegheny and its boats
Were dark blue. The Moskowa is
Gray boats. The Amstel flows slowly.
Leaves fall into the Connecticut as it passes
Underneath. The Liffey is full of sewage,
Like the Seine, but unlike
The brownish-yellow Dordogne.
Mountains hem in the Colorado
And the Oder is very deep, almost
As deep as the Congo is wide.
The plain banks of the Neva are
Gray. The dark Saône flows silently.
And the Volga is long and wide
As it flows across the brownish land. The Ebro
Is blue, and slow. The Shannon flows
Swiftly between its banks. The Mississippi
Is one of the world's longest rivers, like the Amazon.

It has the Missouri for a tributary.
The Harlem flows amid factories
And buildings. The Nelson is in Canada,
Flowing. Through hard banks the Dubawnt
Forces its way. People walk near the Trent.
The landscape around the Mohawk stretches away;
The Rubicon is merely a brook.
In winter the Main
Surges; the Rhine sings its eternal song.
The Rhône slogs along through whitish banks
And the Rio Grande spins tales of the past.
The Loir bursts its frozen shackles
But the Moldau's wet mud ensnares it.
The East catches the light.
Near the Escaut the noise of factories echoes
And the sinuous Humboldt gurgles wildly.
The Po too flows, and the many-colored
Thames. Into the Atlantic Ocean
Pours the Garonne. Few ships navigate
On the Housatonic, but quite a few can be seen
On the Elbe. For centuries
The Afton has flowed.
                          If the Rio Negro
Could abandon its song, and the Magdalena
The jungle flowers, the Tagus
Would still flow serenely, and the Ohio
Abrade its slate banks. The tan Euphrates would
Sidle silently across the world. The Yukon
Was choked with ice, but the Susquehanna still pushed
Bravely along. The Dee caught the day's last flares
Like the Pilcomayo's carrion rose.
The Peace offered eternal fragrance
Perhaps, but the Mackenzie churned livid mud
Like tan chalk-marks. Near where
The Brahmaputra slapped swollen dikes

Was an opening through which the Limmat
Could have trickled. A young man strode the Churchill's
Banks, thinking of night. The Vistula seized
The shadows. The Theiss, stark mad, bubbled
In the windy evening. And the Ob shuffled
Crazily along. Fat billows encrusted the Dniester's
Pallid flood, and the Fraser's porous surface.
Fish gasped amid the Spree's reeds. A boat
Descended the bobbing Orinoco. When the
Marne flowed by the plants nodded
And above the glistering Gila
A sunset as beautiful as the Athabaska
Stammered. The Zambezi chimed. The Oxus
Flowed somewhere. The Parnahyba
Is flowing, like the wind-washed Cumberland.
The Araguía flows in the rain.
And, through overlying rocks the Isère
Cascades gently. The Guadalquiver sputtered.
Someday time will confound the Indre,
Making a rill of the Hwang. And
The Potomac rumbles softly. Crested birds
Watch the Ucayali go
Through dreaming night. You cannot stop
The Yenisei. And afterwards
The White flows strongly to its . . .
Goal. If the Tyne's shores
Hold you, and the Albany
Arrest your development, can you resist the Red's
Musk, the Meuse's situation?
A particle of mud in the Neckar
Does not turn it black. You cannot
Like the Saskatchewan, nor refuse
The meandering Yangtze, unleash
The Genesee. Does the Scamander
Still irrigate crimson plains? And the Durance

And the Pechora? The São Francisco
Skulks amid gray, rubbery nettles. The Liard's
Reflexes are slow, and the Arkansas erodes
Anthracite hummocks. The Paraná stinks.
The Ottawa is light emerald green
Among grays. Better that the Indus fade
In steaming sands! Let the Brazos
Freeze solid! And the Wabash turn to a leaden
Cinder of ice! The Marañón is too tepid, we must
Find a way to freeze it hard. The Ural
Is freezing slowly in the blasts. The black Yonne
Congeals nicely. And the Petit-Morin
Curls up on the solid earth. The Inn
Does not remember better times, and the Merrimack's
Galvanized. The Ganges is liquid snow by now;
The Vyatka's ice-gray. The once-molten Tennessee's
Curdled. The Japurá is a pack of ice. Gelid
The Columbia's gray loam banks. The Don's merely
A giant icicle. The Niger freezes, slowly.
The interminable Lena plods on
But the Purus' mercurial waters are icy, grim
With cold. The Loing is choked with fragments of ice.
The Weser is frozen, like liquid air.
And so is the Kama. And the beige, thickly flowing
Tocantins. The rivers bask in the cold.
The stern Uruguay chafes its banks,
A mass of ice. The Hooghly is solid
Ice. The Adour is silent, motionless.
The lovely Tigris is nothing but scratchy ice
Like the Yellowstone, with its osier-clustered banks.
The Mekong is beginning to thaw out a little
And the Donets gurgles beneath the
Huge blocks of ice. The Manzanares gushes free.
The Illinois darts through the sunny air again.
But the Dnieper is still ice-bound. Somewhere

The Salado propels its floes, but the Roosevelt's
Frozen. The Oka is frozen solider
Than the Somme. The Minho slumbers
In winter, nor does the Snake
Remember August. Hilarious, the Canadian
Is solid ice. The Madeira slavers
Across the thawing fields, and the Plata laughs.
The Dvina soaks up the snow. The Sava's
Temperature is above freezing. The Avon
Carols noiselessly. The Drôme presses
Grass banks; the Adige's frozen
Surface is like gray pebbles.

Birds circle the Ticino. In winter
The Var was dark blue, unfrozen. The
Thwaite, cold, is choked with sandy ice;
The Ardèche glistens feebly through the freezing rain.

The Ecclesiast

"Worse than the sunflower," she had said.
But the new dimension of truth had only recently
Burst in on us. Now it was to be condemned.
And in vagrant shadow her mothball truth is eaten.
In cool, like-it-or-not shadow the humdrum is consumed.
Tired housewives begat it some decades ago,
A small piece of truth that if it was honey to the lips
Was also millions of miles from filling the place reserved for it.
You see how honey crumbles your universe
Which seems like an institution—how many walls?

Then everything, in her belief, was to be submerged
And soon. There was no life you could live out to its end
And no attitude which, in the end, would save you.
The monkish and the frivolous alike were to be trapped in death's capacious
    claw
But listen while I tell you about the wallpaper—
There was a key to everything in that oak forest
But a sad one. Ever since childhood there
Has been this special meaning to everything.
You smile at your friend's joke, but only later, through tears.

For the shoe pinches, even though it fits perfectly.
Apples were made to be gathered, also the whole host of the world's ailments
    and troubles.
There is no time like the present for giving in to this temptation.
Tomorrow you'll weep—what of it? There is time enough
Once the harvest is in and the animals put away for the winter
To stand at the uncomprehending window cultivating the desert
With salt tears which will never do anyone any good.

My dearest I am as a galleon on salt billows.
Perfume my head with forgetting all about me.

For some day these projects will return.
The funereal voyage over ice-strewn seas is ended.
You wake up forgetting. Already
Daylight shakes you in the yard.
The hands remain empty. They are constructing an osier basket
Just now, and across the sunlight darkness is taking root anew
In intense activity. You shall never have seen it just this way
And that is to be your one reward.

Fine vapors escape from whatever is doing the living.
The night is cold and delicate and full of angels
Pounding down the living. The factories are all lit up,
The chime goes unheard.
We are together at last, though far apart.

The Recent Past

Perhaps we ought to feel with more imagination.
As today the sky 70 degrees above zero with lines falling
The way September moves a lace curtain to be near a pear,
The oddest device can't be usual. And that is where
The pejorative sense of fear moves axles. In the stars
There is no longer any peace, emptied like a cup of coffee
Between the blinding rain that interviews.

You were my quintuplets when I decided to leave you
Opening a picture book the pictures were all of grass
Slowly the book was on fire, you the reader
Sitting with specs full of smoke exclaimed
How it was a rhyme for "brick" or "redder."
The next chapter told all about a brook.
You were beginning to see the relation when a tidal wave
Arrived with sinking ships that spelled out "Aladdin."
I thought about the Arab boy in his cave
But the thoughts came faster than advice.
If you knew that snow was a still toboggan in space
The print could rhyme with "fallen star."

The Thousand Islands

Keeping warm now, while it lasts
In the life we must suppose, continuance
Quickens the scrap which falls to us.

Painless rigors, like thistledown,
Strapped to us like a heavy pack
The massed air hanging above.

The tether of you to this bank
To understand the flesh left splinters.
Depths of understanding preside
Shelving steeply into a kind of flow
Stumble happily as through a miracle
Opening around you
Pinned to the moment.
Your eyes reflect a hunting scene.

A promise of so much that is to come,
Extracted, accepted gladly
But within its narrow limits
No knowledge yet, nothing which can be used.

You are grateful for the imaginary pause.

No one had imagined that the storm would be like this
To discover its heart. The blind enemy
Exalting the possibility of defeat
Behind glass first unthinkable then not so much
It would be better if one smile
The one successful day drew darkness from the folds around it.

Meadows then might melt into something
For play, the necessity gone. But your
Idea is not continuing—a swift imperfect
Condensation of the indifference you feel
To be the worn fiber and bone which must surround you
For the permanence of what's already happened in you.

Blackness plays no part; the eye
Is black but there is no depth.
It is the surface black which attacks the shape,
Bending it to present uses.
The face on the door a hundred million years old
Slightly smaller than real life
To accept the cold air and bread
And cause, in the distance, an old satisfaction.

Their simplest construction rising slowly toward
Your neutral ceiling in which are capsized
Forever afternoon smells and rich zero disturbance
As you unharness the horse moves slowly back
Changing too the position escapes you mild and drawn

And prisons think restlessly shifting
There are ever new arrivals
New standard of living and expunging
With a shout something you'd rather have

These equators fixed you'd esteemed
The discovery
Only lacking to fail eagerly
The approach of the cool marble subject
An aphrodisiac in its tall gray flowering
Into separate lengths later lost
Brought down with it hesitancy

The bend clouds' arrow and rutted woods.
At Pine Creek imitation the circle
Had swallowed the useless mystery again
As clouds reappear after rains.

A Blessing in Disguise

Yes, they are alive and can have those colors,
But I, in my soul, am alive too.
I feel I must sing and dance, to tell
Of this in a way, that knowing you may be drawn to me.

And I sing amid despair and isolation
Of the chance to know you, to sing of me
Which are you. You see,
You hold me up to the light in a way

I should never have expected, or suspected, perhaps
Because you always tell me I am you,
And right. The great spruces loom.
I am yours to die with, to desire.

I cannot ever think of me, I desire you
For a room in which the chairs ever
Have their backs turned to the light
Inflicted on the stone and paths, the real trees

That seem to shine at me through a lattice toward you.
If the wild light of this January day is true
I pledge me to be truthful unto you
Whom I cannot ever stop remembering.

Remembering to forgive. Remember to pass beyond you into the day
On the wings of the secret you will never know.
Taking me from myself, in the path
Which the pastel girth of the day has assigned to me.

I prefer "you" in the plural, I want "you,"
You must come to me, all golden and pale
Like the dew and the air.
And then I start getting this feeling of exaltation.

Clepsydra

Hasn't the sky? Returned from moving the other
Authority recently dropped, wrested as much of
That severe sunshine as you need now on the way
You go. The reason why it happened only since
You woke up is letting the steam disappear
From those clouds when the landscape all around
Is hilly sites that will have to be reckoned
Into the total for there to be more air: that is,
More fitness read into the undeduced result, than land.
This means never getting any closer to the basic
Principle operating behind it than to the distracted
Entity of a mirage. The half-meant, half-perceived
Motions of fronds out of idle depths that are
Summer. And expansion into little draughts.
The reply wakens easily, darting from
Untruth to willed moment, scarcely called into being
Before it swells, the way a waterfall
Drums at different levels. Each moment
Of utterance is the true one; likewise none are true,
Only is the bounding from air to air, a serpentine
Gesture which hides the truth behind a congruent
Message, the way air hides the sky, is, in fact,
Tearing it limb from limb this very moment: but
The sky has pleaded already and this is about
As graceful a kind of non-absence as either
Has a right to expect: whether it's the form of
Some creator who has momentarily turned away,
Marrying detachment with respect, so that the pieces
Are seen as parts of a spectrum, independent
Yet symbolic of their spaced-out times of arrival;

Whether on the other hand all of it is to be
Seen as no luck. A recurring whiteness like
The face of stone pleasure, urging forward as
Nostrils what only meant dust. But the argument,
That is its way, has already left these behind: it
Is, it would have you believe, the white din up ahead
That matters: unformed yells, rocketings,
Affected turns, and tones of voice called
By upper shadows toward some cloud of belief
Or its unstated circumference. But the light
Has already gone from there too and it may be that
It is lines contracting into a plane. We hear so much
Of its further action that at last it seems that
It is we, our taking it into account rather, that are
The reply that prompted the question, and
That the latter, like a person waking on a pillow
Has the sensation of having dreamt the whole thing,
Of returning to participate in that dream, until
The last word is exhausted; certainly this is
Peace of a sort, like nets drying in the sun,
That we must progress toward the whole thing
About an hour ago. As long as it is there
You will desire it as its tag of wall sinks
Deeper as though hollowed by sunlight that
Just fits over it; it is both mirage and the little
That was present, the miserable totality
Mustered at any given moment, like your eyes
And all they speak of, such as your hands, in lost
Accents beyond any dream of ever wanting them again.
To have this to be constantly coming back from—
Nothing more, really, than surprise at your absence
And preparing to continue the dialogue into
Those mysterious and near regions that are
Precisely the time of its being furthered.
Seeing it, as it was, dividing that time,

Casting colored paddles against the welter
Of a future of disunion just to abolish confusion
And permit level walks into the gaze of its standing
Around admiringly, it was then, that it was these
Moments that were the truth, although each tapered
Into the distant surrounding night. But
Wasn't it their blindness, instead, and wasn't this
The fact of being so turned in on each other that
Neither would ever see his way clear again? It
Did not stagger the imagination so long as it stayed
This way, comparable to exclusion from the light of the stars
That drenched every instant of that being, in an egoistic way,
As though their round time were only the reverse
Of some more concealable, vengeful purpose to become known
Once its result had more or less established
The look of the horizon. But the condition
Of those moments of timeless elasticity and blindness
Was being joined secretly so
That their paths would cross again and be separated
Only to join again in a final assumption rising like a shout
And be endless in the discovery of the declamatory
Nature of the distance traveled. All this is
Not without small variations and surprises, yet
An invisible fountain continually destroys and refreshes the previsions.
Then is their permanence merely a function of
The assurance with which it's understood, assurance
Which, you might say, goes a long way toward conditioning
Whatever result? But there was no statement
At the beginning. There was only a breathless waste,
A dumb cry shaping everything in projected
After-effects orphaned by playing the part intended for them,
Though one must not forget that the nature of this
Emptiness, these previsions,
Was that it could only happen here, on this page held
Too close to be legible, sprouting erasures, except that they

Ended everything in the transparent sphere of what was
Intended only a moment ago, spiraling further out, its
Gesture finally dissolving in the weather.
It was the long way back out of sadness
Of that first meeting: a half-triumph, an imaginary feeling
Which still protected its events and pauses, the way
A telescope protects its view of distant mountains
And all they include, the coming and going,
Moving correctly up to other levels, preparing to spend the night
There where the tiny figures halt as darkness comes on,
Beside some loud torrent in an empty yet personal
Landscape, which has the further advantage of being
What surrounds without insisting, the very breath so
Honorably offered, and accepted in the same spirit.
There was in fact pleasure in those high walls.
Each moment seemed to bore back into the centuries
For profit and manners, and an old way of looking that
Continually shaped those lips into a smile. Or it was
Like standing at the edge of a harbor early on a summer morning
With the discreet shadows cast by the water all around
And a feeling, again, of emptiness, but of richness in the way
The whole thing is organized, on what a miraculous scale,
Really what is meant by a human level, with the figures of giants
Not too much bigger than the men who have come to petition them:
A moment that gave not only itself, but
Also the means of keeping it, of not turning to dust
Or gestures somewhere up ahead
But of becoming complicated like the torrent
In new dark passages, tears and laughter which
Are a sign of life, of distant life in this case.
And yet, as always happens, there would come a moment when
Acts no longer sufficed and the calm
Of this true progression hardened into shreds
Of another kind of calm, returning to the conclusion, its premises
Undertaken before any formal agreement had been reached, hence

A writ that was the shadow of the colossal reason behind all this
Like a second, rigid body behind the one you know is yours.
And it was in vain that tears blotted the contract now, because
It had been freely drawn up and consented to as insurance
Against the very condition it was now so efficiently
Seeking to establish. It had reduced that other world,
The round one of the telescope, to a kind of very fine powder or dust
So small that space could not remember it.
Thereafter any signs of feeling were cut short by
The comfort and security, a certain elegance even,
Like the fittings of a ship, that are after all
The most normal things in the world. Yes, perhaps, but the words
"After all" are important for understanding the almost
Exaggerated strictness of the condition, and why, in spite of this,
It seemed the validity of the former continuing was
Not likely to be reinstated for a long time.
"After all," that too might be possible, as indeed
All kinds of things are possible in the widening angle of
The day, as it comes to blush with pleasure and increase,
So that light sinks into itself, becomes dark and heavy
Like a surface stained with ink: there was something
Not quite good or correct about the way
Things were looking recently: hadn't the point
Of all this new construction been to provide
A protected medium for the exchanges each felt of such vital
Concern, and wasn't it now giving itself the airs of a palace?
And yet her hair had never been so long.
It was a feeling of well-being, if you will, as though a smallest
Distant impulse had rendered the whole surface ultra-sensitive
But its fierceness was still acquiescence
To the nature of this goodness already past
And it was a kind of sweet acknowledgment of how
The past is yours, to keep invisible if you wish
But also to make absurd elaborations with
And in this way prolong your dance of non-discovery

In brittle, useless architecture that is nevertheless
The map of your desires, irreproachable, beyond
Madness and the toe of approaching night, if only
You desire to arrange it this way. Your acts
Are sentinels against this quiet
Invasion. Long may you prosper, and may your years
Be the throes of what is even now exhausting itself
In one last effort to outwit us; it could only be a map
Of the world: in their defeat such peninsulas as become
Prolongations of our reluctance to approach, but also
Fine days on whose memorable successions of events
We shall be ever afterwards tempted to dwell. I am
Not speaking of a partially successful attempt to be
Opposite; anybody at all can read that page, it has only
To be thrust in front of him. I mean now something much broader,
The sum total of all the private aspects that can ever
Become legible in what is outside, as much in the rocks
And foliage as in the invisible look of the distant
Ether and in the iron fist that suddenly closes over your own.
I see myself in this totality, and meanwhile
I am only a transparent diagram, of manners and
Private words with the certainty of being about to fall.
And even this crumb of life I also owe to you
For being so close as to seal out knowledge of that other
Voluntary life, and so keep its root in darkness until your
Maturity when your hair will actually be the branches
Of a tree with the light pouring through them.
It intensifies echoes in such a way as to
Form a channel to absorb every correct motion.
In this way any direction taken was the right one,
Leading first to you, and through you to
Myself that is beyond you and which is the same thing as space,
That is the stammering vehicles that remain unknown,
Eating the sky in all sincerity because the difference
Can never be made up: therefore, why not examine the distance?

It seemed he had been repeating the same stupid phrase
Over and over throughout his life; meanwhile
Infant destinies had suavely matured; there was
To be a meeting or collection of them that very evening.
He was out of it of course for having lain happily awake
On the tepid fringes of that field or whatever
Whose center was beginning to churn darkly, but even more for having
The progression of minutes by accepting them, as one accepts drops of rain
As they form a shower, and without worrying about the fine weather that
    will come after.
Why shouldn't all climate and all music be equal
Without growing? There should be an invariable balance of
Contentment to hold everything in place, ministering
To stunted memories, helping them stand alone
And return into the world, without ever looking back at
What they might have become, even though in doing so they
Might just once have been the truth that, invisible,
Still surrounds us like the air and is the dividing force
Between our slightest steps and the notes taken on them.
It is because everything is relative
That we shall never see in that sphere of pure wisdom and
Entertainment much more than groping shadows of an incomplete
Former existence so close it burns like the mouth that
Closes down over all your effort like the moment
Of death, but stays, raging and burning the design of
Its intentions into the house of your brain, until
You wake up alone, the certainty that it
Wasn't a dream your only clue to why the walls
Are turning on you and why the windows no longer speak
Of time but are themselves, transparent guardians you
Invented for what there was to hide. Which was now
Grown up, or moved away, as a jewel
Exists when there is no one to look at it, and this
Existence saps your own. Perhaps you are being kept here
Only so that somewhere else the peculiar light of someone's

Purpose can blaze unexpectedly in the acute
Angles of the rooms. It is not a question, then,
Of having not lived in vain. What is meant is that this distant
Image of you, the way you really are, is the test
Of how you see yourself, and regardless of whether or not
You hesitate, it may be assumed that you have won, that this
Wooden and external representation
Returns the full echo of what you meant
With nothing left over, from that circumference now alight
With ex-possibilities become present fact, and you
Must wear them like clothing, moving in the shadow of
Your single and twin existence, waking in intact
Appreciation of it; while morning is still and before the body
Is changed by the faces of evening.

The Skaters

These decibels
Are a kind of flagellation, an entity of sound
Into which being enters, and is apart.
Their colors on a warm February day
Make for masses of inertia, and hips
Prod out of the violet-seeming into a new kind
Of demand that stumps the absolute because not new
In the sense of the next one in an infinite series
But, as it were, pre-existing or pre-seeming in
Such a way as to contrast funnily with the unexpectedness
And somehow push us all into perdition.

Here a scarf flies, there an excited call is heard.

The answer is that it is novelty
That guides these swift blades o'er the ice,
Projects into a finer expression (but at the expense
Of energy) the profile I cannot remember.
Colors slip away from and chide us. The human mind
Cannot retain anything except perhaps the dismal two-note theme
Of some sodden "dump" or lament.

But the water surface ripples, the whole light changes.

We children are ashamed of our bodies
But we laugh and, demanded, talk of sex again
And all is well. The waves of morning harshness
Float away like coal-gas into the sky.
But how much survives? How much of any one of us survives?

The articles we'd collect—stamps of the colonies
With greasy cancellation marks, mauve, magenta and chocolate,
Or funny-looking dogs we'd see in the street, or bright remarks.
One collects bullets. An Indianapolis, Indiana man collects slingshots of all
     epochs, and so on.

Subtracted from our collections, though, these go on a little while, collecting
     aimlessly. We still support them.
But so little energy they have! And up the swollen sands
Staggers the darkness fiend, with the storm fiend close behind him!
True, melodious tolling does go on in that awful pandemonium,
Certain resonances are not utterly displeasing to the terrified eardrum.
Some paroxysms are dinning of tambourine, others suggest piano room or
     organ loft
For the most dissonant night charms us, even after death. This, after all, may
     be happiness: tuba notes awash on the great flood, ruptures of xylophone,
     violins, limpets, grace-notes, the musical instrument called serpent, viola
     da gambas, aeolian harps, clavicles, pinball machines, electric drills, *que
     sais-je encore!*
The performance has rapidly reached your ear; silent and tear-stained, in the
     post-mortem shock, you stand listening, awash
With memories of hair in particular, part of the welling that is you,
The gurgling of harp, cymbal, glockenspiel, triangle, temple block, English
     horn and metronome! And still no presentiment, no feeling of pain before
     or after.
The passage sustains, does not give. And you have come far indeed.

Yet to go from "not interesting" to "old and uninteresting,"
To be surrounded by friends, though late in life,
To hear the wings of the spirit, though far. . . .
Why do I hurriedly undrown myself to cut you down?
"I am yesterday," and my fault is eternal.
I do not expect constant attendance, knowing myself insufficient for your
     present demands
And I have a dim intuition that I am that other "I" with which we began.

My cheeks as blank walls to your tears and eagerness
Fondling that other, as though you had let him get away forever.

The evidence of the visual henceforth replaced
By the great shadow of trees falling over life.

A child's devotion
To this normal, shapeless entity. . . .

Forgotten as the words fly briskly across, each time
Bringing down meaning as snow from a low sky, or rabbits flushed from a
    wood.
How strange that the narrow perspective lines
Always seem to meet, although parallel, and that an insane ghost could do
    this,
Could make the house seem so much farther in the distance, as
It seemed to the horse, dragging the sledge of a perspective line.
Dim banners in the distance, to die. . . . And nothing put to rights. The pigs
    in their cages

And so much snow, but it is to be littered with waste and ashes
So that cathedrals may grow. Out of this spring builds a tolerable
Affair of brushwood, the sea is felt behind oak wands, noiselessly pouring.
Spring with its promise of winter, and the black ivy once again
On the porch, its yellow perspective bands in place
And the horse nears them and weeps.

So much has passed through my mind this morning
That I can give you but a dim account of it:
It is already after lunch, the men are returning to their positions around the
    cement mixer
And I try to sort out what has happened to me. The bundle of Gerard's
    letters,
And that awful bit of news buried on the back page of yesterday's paper.
Then the news of you this morning, in the snow. Sometimes the interval

Of bad news is so brisk that . . . And the human brain, with its tray of
images
Seems a sorcerer's magic lantern, projecting black and orange cellophane
shadows
On the distance of my hand . . . The very reaction's puny,
And when we seek to move around, wondering what our position is now,
what the arm of that chair.

A great wind lifted these cardboard panels
Horizontal in the air. At once the perspective with the horse
Disappeared in a *bigarrure* of squiggly lines. The image with the crocodile in
it became no longer apparent.
Thus a great wind cleanses, as a new ruler
Edits new laws, sweeping the very breath of the streets
Into posterior trash. The films have changed—
The great titles on the scalloped awning have turned dry and blight-colored.
No wind that does not penetrate a man's house, into the very bowels of the
furnace,
Scratching in dust a name on the mirror—say, and what about letters,
The dried grasses, fruits of the winter—gosh! Everything is trash!
The wind points to the advantages of decay
At the same time as removing them far from the sight of men.
The regent of the winds, Aeolus, is a symbol for all earthly potentates
Since holding this sickening, festering process by which we are cleansed
Of afterthought.
               A girl slowly descended the line of steps.

The wind and treason are partners, turning secrets over to the military
police.

Lengthening arches. The intensity of minor acts. As skaters elaborate their
distances,
Taking a separate line to its end. Returning to the mass, they join each other
Blotted in an incredible mess of dark colors, and again reappearing to take
the theme

Some little distance, like fishing boats developing from the land different
    parabolas,
Taking the exquisite theme far, into farness, to Land's End, to the ends of
    the earth!

But the livery of the year, the changing air
Bring each to fulfillment. Leaving phrases unfinished,
Gestures half-sketched against woodsmoke. The abundant sap
Oozes in girls' throats, the sticky words, half-uttered, unwished for,
A blanket disbelief, quickly supplanted by idle questions that fade in turn.
Slowly the mood turns to look at itself as some urchin
Forgotten by the roadside. New schemes are got up, new taxes,
Earthworks. And the hours becomes light again.
Girls wake up in it.

It is best to remain indoors. Because there is error
In so much precision. As flames are fanned, wishful thinking arises
Bearing its own prophets, its pointed ignoring. And just as a desire
Settles down at the end of a long spring day, over heather and watered shoot
    and dried rush field,
So error is plaited into desires not yet born.

Therefore the post must be resumed (is being falsified
To be forever involved, tragically, with one's own image?).
The studio light suddenly invaded the long casement—values were what
She knows now. But the floor is being slowly pulled apart
Like straw under those limpid feet.
And Helga, in the minuscule apartment in Jersey City
Is reacting violet to the same kind of dress, is drawing death
Again in blossoms against the reactionary fire . . . pulsing
And knowing nothing to superb lambent distances that intercalate
This city. Is the death of the cube repeated. Or in the musical album.

It is time now for a general understanding of

The meaning of all this. The meaning of Helga, importance of the setting,
   etc.
A description of the blues. Labels on bottles
And all kinds of discarded objects that ought to be described.
But can one ever be sure of which ones?
Isn't this a death-trap, wanting to put too much in
So the floor sags, as under the weight of a piano, or a piano-legged girl
And the whole house of cards comes dinning down around one's ears!
But this is an important aspect of the question
Which I am not ready to discuss, am not at all ready to,
This leaving-out business. On it hinges the very importance of what's novel
Or autocratic, or dense or silly. It is as well to call attention
To it by exaggeration, perhaps. But calling attention
Isn't the same thing as explaining, and as I said I am not ready
To line phrases with the costly stuff of explanation, and shall not,
Will not do so for the moment. Except to say that the carnivorous
Way of these lines is to devour their own nature, leaving
Nothing but a bitter impression of absence, which as we know involves
   presence, but still.
Nevertheless these are fundamental absences, struggling to get up and be off
   themselves.

This, thus, is a portion of the subject of this poem
Which is in the form of falling snow:
That is, the individual flakes are not essential to the importance of the
   whole's becoming so much of a truism
That their importance is again called in question, to be denied further out,
   and again and again like this.
Hence, neither the importance of the individual flake,
Nor the importance of the whole impression of the storm, if it has any, is
   what it is,
But the rhythm of the series of repeated jumps, from abstract into positive
   and back to a slightly less diluted abstract.

Mild effects are the result.

I cannot think any more of going out into all that, will stay here
With my quiet *schmerzen*. Besides the storm is almost over
Having frozen the face of the bust into a strange style with the lips
And the teeth the most distinct part of the whole business.

It is this madness to explain. . . .

What is the matter with plain old-fashioned cause-and-effect?
Leaving one alone with romantic impressions of the trees, the sky?
Who, actually, is going to be fooled one instant by these phony explanations,
Think them important? So back we go to the old, imprecise feelings, the
Common knowledge, the importance of duly suffering and the occasional
    glimpses
Of some balmy felicity. The world of Schubert's lieder. I am fascinated
Though by the urge to get out of it all, by going
Further in and correcting the whole mismanaged mess. But am afraid I'll
Be of no help to you. Good-bye.

As balloons are to the poet, so to the ground
Its varied assortment of trees. The more assorted they are, the
Vaster his experience. Sometimes
You catch sight of them on a level with the top story of a house,
Strung up there for publicity purposes. Or like those bubbles
Children make with a kind of ring, not a pipe, and probably using some
    detergent
Rather than plain everyday soap and water. Where was I? The balloons
Drift thoughtfully over the land, not exactly commenting on it;
These are the range of the poet's experience. He can hide in trees
Like a hamadryad, but wisely prefers not to, letting the balloons
Idle him out of existence, as a car idles. Traveling faster
And more furiously across unknown horizons, belted into the night
Wishing more and more to be unlike someone, getting the whole thing
(So he believes) out of his system. Inventing systems.
We are a part of some system, thinks he, just as the sun is part of
The solar system. Trees brake his approach. And he seems to be wearing but

Half a coat, viewed from one side. A "half-man" look inspiring the disgust of
　　honest folk
Returning from chores, the milk frozen, the pump heaped high with a
　　chapeau of snow,
The "No Skating" sign as well. But it is here that he is best,
Face to face with the unsmiling alternatives of his nerve-wracking existence.
Placed squarely in front of his dilemma, on all fours before the lamentable
　　spectacle of the unknown.
Yet knowing where men are coming from. It is this, to hold the candle up to
　　the album.

2.

Under the window marked "General Delivery" . . .

This should be a letter
Throwing you a minute to one side,
Of how this tossing looks harmonious from a distance,
Like sea or the tops of trees, and how
Only when one gets closer is its sadness small and appreciable.
It can be held in the hand.

All this must go into a letter.
Also the feeling of being lived, looking for people,
And gradual peace and relaxation.

But there's no personal involvement:
These sudden bursts of hot and cold
Are wreathed in shadowless intensity
Whose moment saps them of all characteristics.
Thus beginning to rest you at once know.

Once there was a point in these islands,
Coming to see where the rock had rotted away,
And turning into a tiny speck in the distance.

But war's savagery. . . . Even the most patient scholar, now
Could hardly reconstruct the old fort exactly as it was.
That trees continue to wave over it. That there is also a small museum
      somewhere inside.
That the history of costume is no less fascinating than the history of great
      migrations.
I'd like to bugger you all up,
Deliberately falsify all your old suck-ass notions
Of how chivalry is being lived. What goes on in beehives.
But the whole filthy mess, misunderstandings included,
Problems about the tunic button etc. How much of any one person is there.

Still, after bananas and spoonbread in the shadow of the old walls
It is cooling to return under the eaves in the shower
That probably fell while we were inside, examining bowknots,
Old light-bulb sockets, places where the whitewash had begun to flake
With here and there an old map or illustration. Here's one for instance—
Looks like a weather map . . . or a coiled bit of wallpaper with a design
Of faded hollyhocks, or abstract fruit and gumdrops in chains.

But how is it that you are always indoors, peering at too heavily canceled
      stamps through a greasy magnifying glass?
And slowly the incoherencies of day melt in
A general wishful thinking of night
To peruse certain stars over the bay.
Cataracts of peace pour from the poised heavens
And only fear of snakes prevents us from passing the night in the open air.
The day is definitely at an end.

Old heavens, you used to tweak above us,
Standing like rain whenever a salvo . . . Old heavens,
You lying there above the old, but not ruined, fort,
Can you hear, there, what I am saying?

For it is you I am parodying,

Your invisible denials. And the almost correct impressions
Corroborated by newsprint, which is so fine.
I call to you there, but I do not think that you will answer me.

For I am condemned to drum my fingers
On the closed lid of this piano, this tedious planet, earth
As it winks to you through the aspiring, growing distances,
A last spark before the night.

There was much to be said in favor of storms
But you seem to have abandoned them in favor of endless light.
I cannot say that I think the change much of an improvement.
There is something fearful in these summer nights that go on forever. . . .

We are nearing the Moorish coast, I think, in a **bateau**.
I wonder if I will have any friends there
Whether the future will be kinder to me than the past, for example,
And am all set to be put out, finding it to be not.

Still, I am prepared for this voyage, and for anything else you may care to
   mention.
Not that I am not afraid, but there is very little time left.
You have probably made travel arrangements, and know the feeling.
Suddenly, one morning, the little train arrives in the station, but oh, so big

It is! Much bigger and faster than anyone told you.
A bewhiskered student in an old baggy overcoat is waiting to take it.
"Why do you want to go there," they all say. "It is better in the other
   direction."
And so it is. There people are free, at any rate. But where you are going no
   one is.

Still there are parks and libraries to be visited, "la Bibliothèque Municipale,"
Hotel reservations and all that rot. Old American films dubbed into the
   foreign language,

Coffee and whiskey and cigar stubs. Nobody minds. And rain on the bristly
    wool of your topcoat.
I realize that I never knew why I wanted to come.

Yet I shall never return to the past, that attic,
Its sailboats are perhaps more beautiful than these, these I am leaning
    against,
Spangled with diamonds and orange and purple stains,
Bearing me once again in quest of the unknown. These sails are life itself to
    me.

I heard a girl say this once, and cried, and brought her fresh fruit and fishes,
Olives and golden baked loaves. She dried her tears and thanked me.
Now we are both setting sail into the purplish evening.
I love it! This cruise can never last long enough for me.

But once more, office desks, radiators—No! That is behind me.
No more dullness, only movies and love and laughter, sex and fun.
The ticket seller is blowing his little horn—hurry before the window slams
    down.
The train we are getting onto is a boat train, and the boats are really boats
    this time.

But I heard the heavens say—Is it right? This continual changing back and
    forth?
Laughter and tears and so on? Mightn't just plain sadness be sufficient for
    him?
No! I'll not accept that any more, you bewhiskered old caverns of blue!
This is just right for me. I am cozily ensconced in the balcony of my face

Looking out over the whole darn countryside, a beacon of satisfaction
I am. I'll not trade places with a king. Here I am then, continuing but ever
    beginning
My perennial voyage, into new memories, new hope and flowers
The way the coasts glide past you. I shall never forget this moment

Because it consists of purest ecstasy. I am happier now than I ever dared
  believe
Anyone could be. And we finger down the dog-eared coasts. . . .
It is all passing! It is past! No, I am here,
Bellow the coasts, and even the heavens roar their assent

As we pick up a lemon-colored light horizontally
Projected into the night, the night that heaven
Was kind enough to send, and I launch into the happiest dreams,
Happier once again, because tomorrow is already here.

Yet certain kernels remain. Clouds that drift past sheds—
Read it in the official bulletin. We shan't be putting out today.
The old stove smoked worse than ever because rain was coming down its
  chimney.
Only the bleary eye of fog accosted one through the mended pane.

Outside, the swamp water lapped the broken wood step.
A rowboat was moored in the alligator-infested swamp.
Somewhere, from deep in the interior of the jungle, a groan was heard.
Could it be . . . ? Anyway, a rainy day—wet weather.

The whole voyage will have to be canceled.
It would be impossible to make different connections.
Anyway the hotels are all full at this season. The junks packed with refugees
Returning from the islands. Sea-bream and flounder abound in the muddied
  waters. . . .

They in fact represent the backbone of the island economy.
That, and cigar rolling. Please leave your papers at the desk as you pass out,
You know. "The Wedding March." Ah yes, that's the way. The couple descend
The steps of the little old church. Ribbons are flung, ribbons of cloud

And the sun seems to be coming out. But there have been so many false
  alarms. . . .

No, it's happened! The storm is over. Again the weather is fine and clear.
And the voyage? It's on! Listen everybody, the ship is starting,
I can hear its whistle's roar! We have just time enough to make it to the
    dock!

And away they pour, in the sulfurous sunlight,
To the aqua and silver waters where stands the glistening white ship
And into the great vessel they flood, a motley and happy crowd
Chanting and pouring down hymns on the surface of the ocean. . . .

Pulling, tugging us along with them, by means of streamers,
Golden and silver confetti. Smiling, we laugh and sing with the revelers
But are not quite certain that we want to go—the dock is so sunny and
    warm.
That majestic ship will pull up anchor who knows where?

And full of laughter and tears, we sidle once again with the other passengers.
The ground is heaving under foot. Is it the ship? It could be the dock. . . .
And with a great whoosh all the sails go up. . . . Hideous black smoke
    belches forth from the funnels
Smudging the gold carnival costumes with the gaiety of its jet-black soot

And, as into a tunnel the voyage starts
Only, as I said, to be continued. The eyes of those left standing on the dock
    are wet
But ours are dry. Into the secretive, vaporous night with all of us!
Into the unknown, the unknown that loves us, the great unknown!

So man nightly
Sparingly descends
The birches and the hay   all of him
Pruned, erect for vital contact. As the separate mists of day slip
Uncomplainingly into the atmosphere. Loving you? The question sinks into
That mazy business

About writing or to have read it in some book
To silently move away. At Gannosfonadiga the pumps
Working, argent in the thickening sunset, like boys' shoulders

And you return to the question as to a calendar of November
Again and again consulting the surface of that enormous affair
I think not to have loved you   but the music
Petting the enameled   slow-imagined stars

A concert of dissatisfaction whereby   gutter and dust seep
To engross the mirrored image and its landscape:

As when
                through darkness and mist
                                    the pole-bringer
                                        demandingly watches
I am convinced these things are of some importance.

Firstly, it is a preparing to go outward
Of no planet limiting the enjoyment
Of motion—hips free of embarrassment etc.

The figure 8 is a perfect symbol
Of the freedom to be gained in this kind of activity.
The perspective lines of the barn are another and different kind of example
(Viz. "Rigg's Farm, near Aysgarth, Wensleydale," or the "Sketch at Norton")
In which we escape ourselves—putrefying mass of prevarications etc.—
In remaining close to the limitations imposed.

Another example is this separate dying
Still keeping in mind the coachmen, servant girls, duchesses, etc. (cf. Jeremy
    Taylor)
Falling away, rhythm of too-wet snow, but parallel
With the kind of rhythm substituting for "meaning."

Looked at from this angle the problem of death and survival
Ages slightly. For the solutions are millionfold, like waves of wild geese
    returning in spring.
Scarcely we know where to turn to avoid suffering, I mean
There are so many places.

So, coachman-servile, or scullion-slatternly, but each place is taken.

The lines that draw nearer together are said to "vanish."
The point where they meet is their vanishing point.

Spaces, as they recede, become smaller.

But another, more urgent question imposes itself—that of poverty.
How to excuse it to oneself? The wetness and coldness? Dirt and grime?
Uncomfortable, unsuitable lodgings, with a depressing view?
The peeled geranium flowering in a rusted tomato can,
Framed in a sickly ray of sunlight, a tragic chromo?

A broken mirror nailed up over a chipped enamel basin, whose turbid waters
Reflect the fly-specked calendar—with ecstatic Dutch girl clasping tulips—
On the far wall. Hanging from one nail, an old velvet hat with a tattered bit
    of veiling—last remnant of former finery.
The bed well made. The whole place scrupulously clean, but cold and damp.

All this, wedged into a pyramidal ray of light, is my own invention.

But to return to our tomato can—those spared by the goats
Can be made into a practical telephone, the two halves being connected by a
    length of wire.
You can talk to your friend in the next room, or around corners.
An American inventor made a fortune with just such a contraption.
The branches tear at the sky—

Things too tiny to be remembered in recorded history—the backfiring of a bus

In a Paris street in 1932, and all the clumsy seductions and amateur paintings done,
Clamber to join in the awakening
To take a further role in my determination. These clown-shapes
Filling up the available space for miles, like acres of red and mustard pom-poms
Dusted with a pollen we call "an air of truth." Massed mounds
Of Hades it is true. I propose a general housecleaning
Of these true and valueless shapes which pester us with their raisons d'être
Whom no one (that is their weakness) can ever get to like.

There are moving parts to be got out of order,
However, in the flame fountain. Add gradually one ounce, by measure, of sulphuric acid
To five or six ounces of water in an earthenware basin. Add to it, also gradually, about three-quarters of an ounce of granulated zinc.
A rapid production of hydrogen gas will instantly take place. Then add,
From time to time, a few pieces of phosphorus the size of a pea.
A multitude of gas bubbles will be produced, which will fire on the surface of the effervescing liquid.
The whole surface of the liquid will become luminous, and fire balls, with jets of fire,
Will dart from the bottom, through the fluid with great rapidity and a hissing noise.

Sure, but a simple shelter from this or other phenomena is easily contrived.

But how luminous the fountain! Its sparks seem to aspire to reach the sky!
And so much energy in those bubbles. A wise man could contemplate his face in them
With impunity, but fools would surely do better not to approach too close
Because any intense physical activity like that implies danger for the unwary and the uneducated. Great balls of fire!
In my day we used to make "fire designs," using a saturated solution of nitrate of potash.

Then we used to take a smooth stick, and using the solution as ink, draw
    with it on sheets of white tissue paper.
Once it was thoroughly dry, the writing would be invisible.
By means of a spark from a smoldering match ignite the potassium nitrate at
    any part of the drawing,
First laying the paper on a plate or tray in a darkened room.
The fire will smolder along the line of the invisible drawing until the design
    is complete.

Meanwhile the fire fountain is still smoldering and welling,
Casting off a hellish stink and wild fumes of pitch
Acrid as jealousy. And it might be
That flame writing might be visible right there, in the gaps in the smoke
Without going through the bother of the solution-writing.
A word here and there—"promise" or "beware"—you have to go the long
    way round
Before you find the entrance to that side is closed.
The phosphorescent liquid is still heaving and boiling, however.
And what if this insane activity were itself a kind of drawing
Of April sidewalks, and young trees bursting into timid leaf
And dogs sniffing hydrants, the fury of spring beginning to back up along
    their veins?
Yonder stand a young boy and girl leaning against a bicycle.
The iron lamppost next to them disappears into the feathery, unborn leaves
    that suffocate its top.

A postman is coming up the walk, a letter held in his outstretched hand.
This is his first day on the new job, and he looks warily around
Alas not seeing the hideous bulldog bearing down on him like sixty, its
    hellish eyes fixed on the seat of his pants, jowls a-slaver.
Nearby a young woman is fixing her stocking. Watching her, a chap with a
    hat
Is about to walk into the path of a speeding hackney cabriolet. The line of
    lampposts
Marches up the street in strict array, but the lamp-parts

Are lost in feathery bloom, in which hidden faces can be spotted, for this is a
  puzzle scene.
The sky is white, yet full of outlined stars—it must be night,
Or an early springtime evening, with just a hint of dampness and chill in the
  air—
Memory of winter, hint of the autumn to come—
Yet the lovers congregate anyway, the lights twinkle slowly on.
Cars move steadily along the street.
It is a scene worthy of the poet's pen, yet it is the fire demon
Who has created it, throwing it up on the dubious surface of a
  phosphorescent fountain
For all the world like a poet. But love can appreciate it,
Use or misuse it for its own ends. Love is stronger than fire.

The proof of this is that already the heaving, sucking fountain is paling away
Yet the fire-lines of the lovers remain fixed, as if permanently, on the air of
  the lab.
Not for long though. And now they too collapse,
Giving, as they pass away, the impression of a bluff,
Its craggy headlands outlined in sparks, its top crowned with a zigzag
Of grass and shrubs, pebbled beach at the bottom, with flat sea
Holding a few horizontal lines. Then this vision, too, fades slowly away.

3.

Now you must shield with your body if necessary (you
Remind me of some lummox I used to know) the secret your body is.
Yes, you are a secret and you must NEVER tell it—the vapor
Of the stars would quickly freeze you to death, like a tear-stiffened
  handkerchief
Held in liquid air. No, but this secret is in some way the fuel of
Your living apart. A hearth fire picked up in the glow of polished
Wooden furniture and picture frames, something to turn away from and
  move back to—
Understand? This is all a part of you and the only part of you.

Here comes the answer: is it because apples grow
On the tree, or because it is green? One average day you may
    never know
How much is pushed back into the night, nor what may return
To sulk contentedly, half asleep and half awake
By the arm of a chair pointed into
The painting of the hearth fire, or reach, in a coma,
Out of the garden for foreign students.
Be sure the giant would know falling asleep, but the frozen
    droplets reveal
A mixed situation in which the penis
Scored the offer by fixed marches into what is.
One black spot remained.

If I should . . . If I said you were there
The . . . towering peace around us might
Hold up the way it breaks—the monsoon
Move a pebble, to the plumbing contract, cataract.
There has got to be only—there is going to be
An accent on the portable bunch of grapes
The time the mildewed sea cast the
Hygrometer too far away. You read into it
The meaning of tears, survey of our civilization.

Only one thing exists: the fear of death. As widows are a prey to
    loan sharks
And Cape Hatteras to hurricanes, so man to the fear of dying, to
    the
Certainty of falling. And just so it permits him to escape from
    time to time
Amid fields of boarded-up posters: "Objects, as they recede,
    appear to become smaller
And all horizontal receding lines have their vanishing point upon
    the line of sight,"

Which is some comfort after all, for our volition to see must
    needs condition these phenomena to a certain degree.
But it would be rash to derive too much confidence from a
    situation which, in the last analysis, scarcely warrants it.
What I said first goes: sleep, death and hollyhocks
And a new twilight stained, perhaps, a slightly unearthlier
    periwinkle blue,
But no dramatic arguments for survival, and please no magic
    justification of results.

Uh . . . stupid song . . . that weather bonnet
Is all gone now. But the apothecary biscuits dwindled.
Where a little spectral
Cliffs, teeming over into irony's
Gotten silently inflicted on the passages
Morning undermines, the daughter is.

    Its oval armor
    Protects it then, and the poisonous filaments hanging down
    Are armor as well, or are they the creature itself, screaming
    To protect itself? An aggressive weapon, as well as a plan of
        defense?
    Nature is still liable to pull a few fast ones, which is why I can't
        emphasize enough
    The importance of adhering to my original program. Remember,
    No hope is to be authorized except in exceptional cases
    To be decided on by me. In the meantime, back to dreaming,
    Your most important activity.

The most difficult of all is an arrangement of hawthorn leaves.
But the sawing motion of desire, throwing you a moment to one side . . .
And then the other, will, I think, permit you to forget your dreams for a little
    while.
In reality you place too much importance on them. *"Frei aber Einsam"* (Free
    but Alone)

Ought to be your motto. If you dream at all, place a cloth over your face:
Its expression of satisfied desire might be too much for some spectators.

> The west wind grazes my cheek, the droplets come pattering
> down;
> What matter now whether I wake or sleep?
> The west wind grazes my cheek, the droplets come pattering
> down;
> A vast design shows in the meadow's parched and trampled
> grasses.
> Actually a game of "fox and geese" has been played there, but the
> real reality,
> Beyond truer imaginings, is that it is a mystical design full of a
> certain significance,
> Burning, sealing its way into my consciousness.
> Smooth out the sad flowers, pick up where you left off
> But leave me immersed in dreams of sexual imagery:
> Now that the homecoming geese unfurl in waves on the west
> wind
> And cock covers hen, the farmhouse dog slavers over his bitch,
> and horse and mare go screwing through the meadow!
> A pure scream of things arises from these various sights and smells
> As steam from a wet shingle, and I am happy once again
> Walking among these phenomena that seem familiar to me from
> my earliest childhood.

The gray wastes of water surround
My puny little shoal. Sometimes storms roll
Tremendous billows far up on the gray sand beach, and the morning
After, odd tusked monsters lie stinking in the sun.
They are inedible. For food there is only
Breadfruit, and berries garnered in the jungle's inner reaches,
Wrested from scorpion and poisonous snake. Fresh water is a problem.
After a rain you may find some nestling in the hollow trunk of a tree, or in
hollow stones.

One's only form of distraction is really
To climb to the top of the one tall cliff to scan the distances.
Not for a ship, of course—this island is far from all the trade routes—
But in hopes of an unusual sight, such as a school of dolphins at play,
A whale spouting, or a cormorant bearing down on its prey.
So high this cliff is that the pebble beach far below seems made of gravel.
Halfway down, the crows and choughs look like bees.
Near by are the nests of vultures. They cluck sympathetically in my direction,
Which will not prevent them from rending me limb from limb once I have
    keeled over definitively.
Further down, and way over to one side, are eagles;
Always fussing, fouling their big nests, they always seem to manage to turn
    their backs to you.
The glass is low; no doubt we are in for a storm.

Sure enough: in the pale gray and orange distances to the left, a
Waterspout is becoming distinctly visible.
Beautiful, but terrifying;
Delicate, transparent, like a watercolor by that nineteenth-century
    Englishman whose name I forget.
(I am beginning to forget everything on this island. If only I had been
    allowed to bring my ten favorite books with me—
But a weathered child's alphabet is my only reading material. Luckily,
Some of the birds and animals on the island are pictured in it—the albatross,
    for instance—that's a name I never would have remembered.)

It looks as though the storm-fiend were planning to kick up quite a ruckus
For this evening. I had better be getting back to the tent
To make sure everything is shipshape, weight down the canvas with extra
    stones,
Bank the fire, and prepare myself a little hardtack and tea
For the evening's repast. Still, it is rather beautiful up here,
Watching the oncoming storm. Now the big cloud that was in front of the
    waterspout

Seems to be lurching forward, so that the waterspout, behind it, looks more
    like a three-dimensional photograph.
Above me, the sky is a luminous silver-gray. Yet rain, like silver porcupine
    quills, has begun to be thrown down.
All the lightning is still contained in the big black cloud however. Now
    thunder claps belch forth from it,
Causing the startled vultures to fly forth from their nests.
I really had better be getting back down, I suppose.

Still it is rather fun to linger on in the wet,
Letting your clothes get soaked. What difference does it make? No one will
    scold me for it,
Or look askance. Supposing I catch cold? It hardly matters, there are no
    nurses or infirmaries here
To make an ass of one. A really serious case of pneumonia would suit me fine.
Ker-choo! There, now I'm being punished for saying so. Aw, what's the use.
I really am starting down now. Good-bye, Storm-fiend. Good-bye, vultures.

In reality of course the middle-class apartment I live in is nothing like a
    desert island.
Cozy and warm it is, with a good library and record collection.
Yet I feel cut off from the life in the streets.
Automobiles and trucks plow by, spattering me with filthy slush.
The man in the street turns his face away. Another island-dweller, no doubt.
In a store or crowded café, you get a momentary impression of warmth:
Steam pours out of the espresso machine, fogging the panes with their
    modern lettering
Of a kind that has only been available for about a year. The headlines offer
    you
News that is so new you can't realize it yet. A revolution in Argentina! Think
    of it! Bullets flying through the air, men on the move;
Great passions inciting to massive expenditures of energy, changing the lives
    of many individuals.
Yet it is all offered as "today's news," as if we somehow had a right to it, as
    though it were a part of our lives

That we'd be silly to refuse. Here, have another—crime or revolution? Take
    your pick.

None of this makes any difference to professional exiles like me, and that
    includes everybody in the place.
We go on sipping our coffee, thinking dark or transparent thoughts . . .
Excuse me, may I have the sugar. Why certainly—pardon me for not having
    passed it to you.
A lot of bunk, none of them really care whether you get any sugar or not.
Just try asking for something more complicated and see how far it gets you.
Not that I care anyway, being an exile. Nope, the motley spectacle offers no
    charms whatsoever for me—
And yet—and yet I feel myself caught up in its coils—
Its defectuous movement is that of my reasoning powers—
The main point has already changed, but the masses continue to tread the
    water
Of backward opinion, living out their mandate as though nothing had
    happened.
We step out into the street, not realizing that the street is different,
And so it shall be all our lives; only, from this moment on, nothing will ever
    be the same again. Fortunately our small pleasures and the monotony of
    daily existence
Are safe. You will wear the same clothes, and your friends will still want to
    see you for the same reasons—you fill a definite place in their lives, and
    they would be sorry to see you go.

There has, however, been this change, so complete as to be invisible:
You might call it . . . "passion" might be a good word.
I think we will call it that for easy reference. This room, now, for instance, is
    all black and white instead of blue.
A few snowflakes are floating in the airshaft. Across the way
The sun was sinking, casting gray
Shadows on the front of the buildings.

Lower your left shoulder.
Stand still and do not seesaw with your body.

Any more golfing hints, Charlie?

Plant your feet squarely. Grasp your club lightly but firmly in the hollow of
　　your fingers.
Slowly swing well back and complete your stroke well through, pushing to
　　the very end.

"All up and down de whole creation," like magic-lantern slides projected on
　　the wall of a cavern: castles, enchanted gardens, etc.

The usual anagrams of moonlight—a story
That subsides quietly into plain historical fact.
You have chosen the customary images of youth, old age and death
To keep harping on this traditional imagery. The reader

Will not have been taken in.
He will have managed to find out all about it, the way people do.
The moonlight congress backs out then. And with a cry
He throws the whole business into the flames: books, notes, pencil diagrams,
　　everything.

No, the only thing that interests him is day
And its problems. *Freiheit! Freiheit!* To be out of these dusty cells once and
　　for all
Has been the dream of mankind since the beginning of the universe.

His day is breaking over the eastern mountains, at least that's the way he tells
　　it.
Only the crater of becoming—a sealed consciousness—resists the profaning
　　mass of the sun.
You who automatically sneer at everything that comes along, except your
　　own work, of course,

Now feel the curious force of the invasion; its soldiers, all and some,
A part of you the minute they appear. It is as though workmen in blue
    overalls
Were constantly bringing on new props and taking others away: that is how
    you feel the drama going past you, powerless to act in it.
To have it all be over! To wake suddenly on a hillside
With a valley far below—the clouds—

That is the penance you have already done:
January, March, February. You are living toward a definition
Of the peaceful appetite, then you see
Them standing around limp and hungry like adjacent clouds.

Soon there is to be exchange of ideas and
Far more beautiful handshake, under the coat of
Weather is undecided right now.
Postpone the explanation.
The election is to be held tomorrow, under the trees.

You felt the months keep coming up
And it is December again,
The snow outside. Or is it June full of sun
And the prudent benefits of sun, but still the postman comes.
The true meaning of some of his letters is slight—

Another time I thought I could see myself.
This too proved illusion, but I could deal with the way
I keep returning on myself like a plank
Like a small boat blown away from the wind.

It all ends in a smile somewhere,
Notes to be taken on all this,
And you can see in the dark, of which the night
Is the continuation of your ecstasy and apprehension.

4.

The wind thrashes the maple seed-pods,
The whole brilliant mass comes spattering down.

This is my fourteenth year as governor of C province.
I was little more than a lad when I first came here.
Now I am old but scarcely any wiser.
So little are white hair and a wrinkled forehead a sign of wisdom!

To slowly raise oneself
Hand over hand, lifting one's entire weight;
To forget there was a possibility
Of some more politic movement. That freedom, courage
And pleasant company could exist.
That has always been behind you.

An earlier litigation: wind hard in the tops
Of the baggy eucalyptus branches.

Today I wrote, "The spring is late this year.
In the early mornings there is hoarfrost on the water meadows.
And on the highway the frozen ruts are papered over with ice."

The day was gloves.

How far from the usual statement
About time, ice—the weather itself had gone.

I mean this. Through the years
You have approached an inventory
And it is now that tomorrow
Is going to be the climax of your casual
Statement about yourself, begun
So long ago in humility and false quietude.

The sands are frantic
In the hourglass. But there is time
To change, to utterly destroy
That too-familiar image
Lurking in the glass
Each morning, at the edge of the mirror.

The train is still sitting in the station.
You only dreamed it was in motion.

There are a few travelers on Z high road.
Behind a shutter, two black eyes are watching them.
They belong to the wife of P, the high-school principal.

The screen door bangs in the wind, one of the hinges is loose.
And together we look back at the house.
It could use a coat of paint
Except that I am too poor to hire a workman.
I have all I can do to keep body and soul together
And soon, even that relatively simple task may prove to be beyond my
   powers.

That was a good joke you played on the other guests.
A joke of silence.

One seizes these moments as they come along, afraid
To believe too much in the happiness that might result
Or confide too much of one's love and fear, even in
Oneself.

The spring, though mild, is incredibly wet.
I have spent the afternoon blowing soap bubbles
And it is with a feeling of delight I realize I am
All alone in the skittish darkness.

The birch-pods come clattering down on the weed-grown marble pavement.
And a curl of smoke stands above the triangular wooden roof.

Seventeen years in the capital of Foo-Yung province!
Surely woman was born for something
Besides continual fornication, retarded only by menstrual cramps.

I had thought of announcing my engagement to you
On the day of the first full moon of X month.

The wind has stopped, but the magnolia blossoms still
Fall with a plop onto the dry, spongy earth.
The evening air is pestiferous with midges.

There is only one way of completing the puzzle:
By finding a hog-shaped piece that is light green shading to buff at one side.

It is the beginning of March, a few
Russet and yellow wallflowers are blooming in the border
Protected by moss-grown, fragmentary masonry.

One morning you appear at breakfast
Dressed, as for a journey, in your worst suit of clothes.
And over a pot of coffee, or, more accurately, rusted water
Announce your intention of leaving me alone in this cistern-like house.
In your own best interests I shall decide not to believe you.

I think there is a funny sand bar
Beyond the old boardwalk
Your intrigue makes you understand.

"At thirty-two I came up to take my examination at the university.
The U wax factory, it seemed, wanted a new general manager.
I was the sole applicant for the job, but it was refused me.

So I have preferred to finish my life
In the quietude of this floral retreat."

The tiresome old man is telling us his life story.

Trout are circling under water—

Masters of eloquence
Glisten on the pages of your book
Like mountains veiled by water or the sky.

The "second position"
Comes in the seventeenth year
Watching the meaningless gyrations of flies above a sill.

Heads in hands, waterfall of simplicity.
The delta of living into everything.

The pump is busted. I shall have to get it fixed.

Your knotted hair
Around your shoulders
A shawl the color of the spectrum

Like that marvelous thing you haven't learned yet.

To refuse the square hive,
                                        postpone the highest . . .

The apples are all getting tinted
In the cool light of autumn.

The constellations are rising
In perfect order: Taurus, Leo, Gemini.

THE DOUBLE DREAM OF SPRING

The Task

They are preparing to begin again:
Problems, new pennant up the flagpole
In a predicated romance.

About the time the sun begins to cut laterally across
The western hemisphere with its shadows, its carnival echoes,
The fugitive lands crowd under separate names.
It is the blankness that succeeds gaiety, and Everyman must depart
Out there into stranded night, for his destiny
Is to return unfruitful out of the lightness
That passing time evokes. It was only
Cloud-castles, adept to seize the past
And possess it, through hurting. And the way is clear
Now for linear acting into that time
In whose corrosive mass he first discovered how to breathe.

Just look at the filth you've made,
See what you've done.
Yet if these are regrets they stir only lightly
The children playing after supper,
Promise of the pillow and so much in the night to come.
I plan to stay here a little while
For these are moments only, moments of insight,
And there are reaches to be attained,
A last level of anxiety that melts
In becoming, like miles under the pilgrim's feet.

Spring Day

The immense hope, and forbearance
Trailing out of night, to sidewalks of the day
Like air breathed into a paper city, exhaled
As night returns bringing doubts

That swarm around the sleeper's head
But are fended off with clubs and knives, so that morning
Installs again in cold hope
The air that was yesterday, is what you are,

In so many phases the head slips from the hand.
The tears ride freely, laughs or sobs:
What do they matter? There is free giving and taking;
The giant body relaxed as though beside a stream

Wakens to the force of it and has to recognize
The secret sweetness before it turns into life—
Sucked out of many exchanges, torn from the womb,
Disinterred before completely dead—and heaves

Its mountain-broad chest. "They were long in coming,
Those others, and mattered so little that it slowed them
To almost nothing. They were presumed dead,
Their names honorably grafted on the landscape

To be a memory to men. Until today
We have been living in their shell.
Now we break forth like a river breaking through a dam,
Pausing over the puzzled, frightened plain,

And our further progress shall be terrible,
Turning fresh knives in the wounds
In that gulf of recreation, that bare canvas
As matter-of-fact as the traffic and the day's noise."

The mountain stopped shaking; its body
Arched into its own contradiction, its enjoyment,
As far from us lights were put out, memories of boys and girls
Who walked here before the great change,

Before the air mirrored us,
Taking the opposite shape of our effort,
Its inseparable comment and corollary
But casting us further and further out.

Wha—what happened? You are with
The orange tree, so that its summer produce
Can go back to where we got it wrong, then drip gently
Into history, if it wants to. A page turned; we were

Just now floundering in the wind of its colossal death.
And whether it is Thursday, or the day is stormy,
With thunder and rain, or the birds attack each other,
We have rolled into another dream.

No use charging the barriers of that other:
It no longer exists. But you,
Gracious and growing thing, with those leaves like stars,
We shall soon give all our attention to you.

Plainness in Diversity

Silly girls your heads full of boys
There is a last sample of talk on the outer side
Your stand at last lifts to dumb evening:
It is reflected in the steep blue sides of the crater,
So much water shall wash over these our breaths
Yet shall remain unwashed at the end. The fine
Branches of the fir tree catch at it, ebbing.
Not on our planet is the destiny
That can make you one.

To be placed on the side of some mountain
Is the truer story, with the breath only
Coming in patches at first, and then the little spurt
The way a steam engine starts up eventually.
The sagas purposely ignore how better off it was next day,
The feeling in between the chapters, like fins.
There is so much they must say, and it is important
About all the swimming motions, and the way the hands
Came up out of the ocean with original fronds,
The famous arrow, the girls who came at dawn
To pay a visit to the young child, and how, when he grew up to be a man
The same restive ceremony replaced the limited years between,
Only now he was old, and forced to begin the journey to the sun.

Soonest Mended

Barely tolerated, living on the margin
In our technological society, we were always having to be rescued
On the brink of destruction, like heroines in *Orlando Furioso*
Before it was time to start all over again.
There would be thunder in the bushes, a rustling of coils,
And Angelica, in the Ingres painting, was considering
The colorful but small monster near her toe, as though wondering whether
    forgetting
The whole thing might not, in the end, be the only solution.
And then there always came a time when
Happy Hooligan in his rusted green automobile
Came plowing down the course, just to make sure everything was O.K.,
Only by that time we were in another chapter and confused
About how to receive this latest piece of information.
Was it information? Weren't we rather acting this out
For someone else's benefit, thoughts in a mind
With room enough and to spare for our little problems (so they began to
    seem),
Our daily quandary about food and the rent and bills to be paid?
To reduce all this to a small variant,
To step free at last, minuscule on the gigantic plateau—
This was our ambition: to be small and clear and free.
Alas, the summer's energy wanes quickly,
A moment and it is gone. And no longer
May we make the necessary arrangements, simple as they are.
Our star was brighter perhaps when it had water in it.
Now there is no question even of that, but only
Of holding on to the hard earth so as not to get thrown off,
With an occasional dream, a vision: a robin flies across
The upper corner of the window, you brush your hair away

And cannot quite see, or a wound will flash
Against the sweet faces of the others, something like:
This is what you wanted to hear, so why
Did you think of listening to something else? We are all talkers
It is true, but underneath the talk lies
The moving and not wanting to be moved, the loose
Meaning, untidy and simple like a threshing floor.

These then were some hazards of the course,
Yet though we knew the course *was* hazards and nothing else
It was still a shock when, almost a quarter of a century later,
The clarity of the rules dawned on you for the first time.
They were the players, and we who had struggled at the game
Were merely spectators, though subject to its vicissitudes
And moving with it out of the tearful stadium, borne on shoulders, at last.
Night after night this message returns, repeated
In the flickering bulbs of the sky, raised past us, taken away from us,
Yet ours over and over until the end that is past truth,
The being of our sentences, in the climate that fostered them,
Not ours to own, like a book, but to be with, and sometimes
To be without, alone and desperate.
But the fantasy makes it ours, a kind of fence-sitting
Raised to the level of an esthetic ideal. These were moments, years,
Solid with reality, faces, namable events, kisses, heroic acts,
But like the friendly beginning of a geometrical progression
Not too reassuring, as though meaning could be cast aside some day
When it had been outgrown. Better, you said, to stay cowering
Like this in the early lessons, since the promise of learning
Is a delusion, and I agreed, adding that
Tomorrow would alter the sense of what had already been learned,
That the learning process is extended in this way, so that from this
    standpoint
None of us ever graduates from college,
For time is an emulsion, and probably thinking not to grow up
Is the brightest kind of maturity for us, right now at any rate.

And you see, both of us were right, though nothing
Has somehow come to nothing; the avatars
Of our conforming to the rules and living
Around the home have made—well, in a sense, "good citizens" of us,
Brushing the teeth and all that, and learning to accept
The charity of the hard moments as they are doled out,
For this is action, this not being sure, this careless
Preparing, sowing the seeds crooked in the furrow,
Making ready to forget, and always coming back
To the mooring of starting out, that day so long ago.

Summer

There is that sound like the wind
Forgetting in the branches that means something
Nobody can translate. And there is the sobering "later on,"
When you consider what a thing meant, and put it down.

For the time being the shadow is ample
And hardly seen, divided among the twigs of a tree,
The trees of a forest, just as life is divided up
Between you and me, and among all the others out there.

And the thinning-out phase follows
The period of reflection. And suddenly, to be dying
Is not a little or mean or cheap thing,
Only wearying, the heat unbearable,

And also the little mindless constructions put upon
Our fantasies of what we did: summer, the ball of pine needles,
The loose fates serving our acts, with token smiles,
Carrying out their instructions too accurately—

Too late to cancel them now—and winter, the twitter
Of cold stars at the pane, that describes with broad gestures
This state of being that is not so big after all.
Summer involves going down as a steep flight of steps

To a narrow ledge over the water. Is this it, then,
This iron comfort, these reasonable taboos,
Or did you mean it when you stopped? And the face
Resembles yours, the one reflected in the water.

It Was Raining in the Capital

It was raining in the capital
And for many days and nights
The one they called the Aquarian
Had stayed alone with her delight.

What with the winter and its business
It had fallen to one side
And she had only recently picked it up
Where the other had died.

Between the pages of the newspaper
It smiled like a face.
Next to the drugstore on the corner
It looked to another place.

Or it would just hang around
Like sullen clouds over the sun.
But—this was the point—it was real
To her and to·everyone.

For spring had entered the capital
Walking on gigantic feet.
The smell of witch hazel indoors
Changed to narcissus in the street.

She thought she had seen all this before:
Bundles of new, fresh flowers,
All changing, pressing upward
To the distant office towers.

Until now nothing had been easy,
Hemmed in by all that shit—
Horseshit, dogshit, birdshit, manshit—
Yes, she remembered having said it,

Having spoken in that way, thinking
There could be no road ahead,
Sobbing into the intractable presence of it
As one weeps alone in bed.

Its chamber was narrower than a seed
Yet when the doorbell rang
It reduced all that living to air
As *"kyrie eleison"* it sang.

Hearing that music he had once known
But now forgotten, the man,
The one who had waited casually in the dark
Turned to smile at the door's span.

He smiled and shrugged—a lesson
In the newspaper no longer
But fed by the ink and paper
Into a sign of something stronger

Who reads the news and takes the bus
Going to work each day
But who was never born of woman
Nor formed of the earth's clay.

Then what unholy bridegroom
Did the Aquarian foretell?
Or was such lively intelligence
Only the breath of hell?

It scarcely mattered at the moment
And it shall never matter at all
Since the moment will not be replaced
But stand, poised for its fall,

Forever. "This is what my learning
Teaches," the Aquarian said,
"To absorb life through the pores
For the life around you is dead."

The sun came out in the capital
Just before it set.
The lovely death's head shone in the sky
As though these two had never met.

Variations, Calypso and Fugue
on a Theme of Ella Wheeler Wilcox

"For the pleasures of the many
May be ofttimes traced to one
As the hand that plants an acorn
Shelters armies from the sun."
And in places where the annual rainfall is .0071 inches
What a pleasure to lie under the tree, to sit, stand, and get up under the tree!
Im wunderschönen Monat Mai
The feeling is of never wanting to leave the tree,
Of predominantly peace and relaxation.
Do you step out from under the shade a moment,
It is only to return with renewed expectation, of expectation fulfilled.
Insecurity be damned! There is something to all this, that will not elude us:
Growing up under the shade of friendly trees, with our brothers all around.
And truly, young adulthood was never like this:
Such delight, such consideration, such affirmation in the way the day goes
     'round together.
Yes, the world goes 'round a good deal faster
When there are highlights on the lips, unspoken and true words in the heart,
And the hand keeps brushing away a strand of chestnut hair, only to have it
     fall back into place again.
But all good things must come to an end, and so one must move forward
Into the space left by one's conclusions. Is this growing old?
Well, it is a good experience, to divest oneself of some tested ideals, some old
     standbys,
And even finding nothing to put in their place is a good experience,
Preparing one, as it does, for the consternation that is to come.
But—and this is the gist of it—what if I dreamed it all,
The branches, the late afternoon sun,
The trusting camaraderie, the love that watered all,
Disappearing promptly down into the roots as it should?

For later in the vast gloom of cities, only there you learn
How the ideas were good only because they had to die,
Leaving you alone and skinless, a drawing by Vesalius.
This is what was meant, and toward which everything directs:
That the tree should shrivel in 120-degree heat, the acorns
Lie around on the worn earth like eyeballs, and the lead soldiers shrug and
    slink off.

So my youth was spent, underneath the trees
I always moved around with perfect ease

I voyaged to Paris at the age of ten
And met many prominent literary men

Gazing at the Alps was quite a sight
I felt the tears flow forth with all their might

A climb to the Acropolis meant a lot to me
I had read the Greek philosophers you see

In the Colosseum I thought my heart would burst
Thinking of all the victims who had been there first

On Mount Ararat's side I began to grow
Remembering the Flood there, so long ago

On the banks of the Ganges I stood in mud
And watched the water light up like blood

The Great Wall of China is really a thrill
It cleaves through the air like a silver pill

It was built by the hand of man for good or ill
Showing what he can do when he decides not to kill

But of all the sights that were seen by me
In the East or West, on land or sea,
The best was the place that is spelled H-O-M-E.

Now that once again I have achieved home
I shall forbear all further urge to roam

There is a hole of truth in the green earth's rug
Once you find it you are as snug as a bug

Maybe some do not like it quite as much as you
That isn't all you're going to do.

You must remember that it is yours
Which is why nobody is sending you flowers

This age-old truth I to thee impart
Act according to the dictates of your art

Because if you don't no one else is going to
And that person isn't likely to be you.

It is the wind that comes from afar
It is the truth of the farthest star

In all likelihood you will not need these
So take it easy and learn your ABC's

And trust in the dream that will never come true
'Cause that is the scheme that is best for you
And the gleam that is the most suitable too.

"MAKE MY DREAM COME TRUE." This message, set in 84-point Hobo type, startled in the morning editions of the paper: the old, half-won security troubles the new pause. And with the approach of the holidays, the present is clearly here to stay: the big brass band of its particular moment's consciousness invades the plazas and the narrow alleys. Three-fourths of the houses in this city are on narrow stilts, finer than a girl's wrists: it is largely a question of keeping one's feet dry, and of privacy. In the morning you forget what the punishment was. Probably it was something like eating a pretzel or going into the back yard. Still, you can't tell. These things could be a lot clearer without hurting anybody. But it does not follow that such issues will produce the most dynamic capital gains for you.

Friday. We are really missing you.

"The most suitable," however, was not the one specially asked for nor the one hanging around the lobby. It was just the one asked after, day after day—what spilled over, claimed by the spillway. The distinction of a dog, of how a dog walks. The thought of a dog walking. No one ever referred to the incident again. The case was officially closed. Maybe there were choruses of silent gratitude, welling up in the spring night like a column of cloud, reaching to the very rafters of the sky—but this was their own business. The point is no ear ever heard them. Thus, the incident, to call it by one of its names—choice, conduct, absent-minded frown might be others—came to be not only as though it had never happened, but as though it never *could* have happened. Sealed into the wall of all that season's coming on. And thus, for a mere handful of people—roustabouts and degenerates, most of them—it became the only true version. Nothing else mattered. It was bread by morning and night, the dates falling listlessly from the trees—man, woman, child, festering glistering in a single orb. The reply to "hello."

Pink purple and blue
The way you used to do

The next two days passed oddly for Peter and Christine, and were among the most absorbing they had ever known. On the one hand, a vast open basin—or sea; on the other a narrow spit of land, terminating in a copse, with a few broken-down outbuildings lying here and there. It made no difference that the bey—b-e-y this time, oriental potentate—had ordained their release, there was this funny feeling that they should always be there, sustained by looks out over the ether, missing Mother and Alan and the others but really quiet, in a kind of activity that offers its own way of life, sunflower chained to the sun. Can it ever be resolved? Or are the forms of a person's thoughts controlled by inexorable laws, as in Dürer's Adam and Eve? So mutually exclusive, and so steep—Himalayas jammed side by side like New York apartment buildings. Oh the blame of it, the de-crescendo. My vice is worry. Forget it. The continual splitting up, the ear-shattering volumes of a polar ice-cap breaking up are just what you wanted. You've got it, so shut up.

The crystal haze
For days and days

Lots of sleep is an important factor, and rubbing the eyes. Getting off the subway he suddenly felt hungry. He went into one place, a place he knew, and ordered a hamburger and a cup of coffee. He hadn't been in this neighborhood in a long time—not since he was a kid. He used to play stickball in the vacant lot across the street. Sometimes his bunch would get into a fight with some of the older boys, and he'd go home tired and bleeding. Most days were the same though. He'd say "Hi" to the other kids and they'd say "Hi" to him. Nice bunch of guys. Finally he decided to take a turn past the old grade school he'd attended as a kid. It was a rambling structure of yellow brick, now gone in seediness and shabbiness which the late-afternoon shadows mercifully softened. The gravel playground in front was choked with weeds. Large trees and shrubbery would do no harm flanking the main entrance. Time farted.

The first shock rattles the cruets in their stand,
The second rips the door from its hinges.

"My dear friend," he said gently, "you said you were Professor Hertz. You must pardon me if I say that the information startles and mystifies me. When you are stronger I have some questions to ask you, if you will be kind enough to answer them."

No one was prepared for the man's answer to that apparently harmless statement.

Weak as he was, Gustavus Hertz raised himself on his elbow. He stared wildly about him, peering fearfully into the shadowy corners of the room.

"I will tell you nothing! Nothing, do you hear?" he shrieked. "Go away! Go away!"

The song tells us of our old way of living,
Of life in former times. Fragrance of florals,
How things merely ended when they ended,
Of beginning again into a sigh. Later

Some movement is reversed and the urgent masks
Speed toward a totally unexpected end
Like clocks out of control. Is this the gesture
That was meant, long ago, the curving in

Of frustrated denials, like jungle foliage
And the simplicity of the ending all to be let go
In quick, suffocating sweetness? The day
Puts toward a nothingness of sky

Its face of rusticated brick. Sooner or later,
The cars lament, the whole business will be hurled down.
Meanwhile we sit, scarcely daring to speak,
To breathe, as though this closeness cost us life.

The pretensions of a past will some day
Make it over into progress, a growing up,
As beautiful as a new history book
With uncut pages, unseen illustrations,

And the purpose of the many stops and starts will be made clear:
Backing into the old affair of not wanting to grow
Into the night, which becomes a house, a parting of the ways
Taking us far into sleep. A dumb love.

Decoy

We hold these truths to be self-evident:
That ostracism, both political and moral, has
Its place in the twentieth-century scheme of things;
That urban chaos is the problem we have been seeing into and seeing into,
For the factory, deadpanned by its very existence into a
Descending code of values, has moved right across the road from total
    financial upheaval
And caught regression head-on. The descending scale does not imply
A corresponding deterioration of moral values, punctuated
By acts of corporate vandalism every five years,
Like a bunch of violets pinned to a dress, that knows and ignores its own
    standing.
There is every reason to rejoice with those self-styled prophets of
    commercial disaster, those harbingers of gloom,
Over the imminent lateness of the denouement that, advancing slowly, never
    arrives,
At the same time keeping the door open to a tongue-and-cheek attitude on
    the part of the perpetrators,
The men who sit down to their vast desks on Monday to begin planning the
    week's notations, jotting memoranda that take
Invisible form in the air, like flocks of sparrows
Above the city pavements, turning and wheeling aimlessly
But on the average directed by discernible motives.

To sum up: We are fond of plotting itineraries
And our pyramiding memories, alert as dandelion fuzz, dart from one
    pretext to the next
Seeking in occasions new sources of memories, for memory is profit
Until the day it spreads out all its accumulation, delta-like, on the plain

For that day no good can come of remembering, and the anomalies cancel
    each other out.
But until then foreshortened memories will keep us going, alive, one to the
    other.

There was never any excuse for this and perhaps there need be none,
For kicking out into the morning, on the wide bed,
Waking far apart on the bed, the two of them:
Husband and wife
Man and wife

Evening in the Country

I am still completely happy.
My resolve to win further I have
Thrown out, and am charged by the thrill
Of the sun coming up. Birds and trees, houses,
These are but the stations for the new sign of being
In me that is to close late, long
After the sun has set and darkness come
To the surrounding fields and hills.
But if breath could kill, then there would not be
Such an easy time of it, with men locked back there
In the smokestacks and corruption of the city.
Now as my questioning but admiring gaze expands
To magnificent outposts, I am not so much at home
With these memorabilia of vision as on a tour
Of my remotest properties, and the eidolon
Sinks into the effective "being" of each thing,
Stump or shrub, and they carry me inside
On motionless explorations of how dense a thing can be,
How light, and these are finished before they have begun
Leaving me refreshed and somehow younger.
Night has deployed rather awesome forces
Against this state of affairs: ten thousand helmeted footsoldiers,
A Spanish armada stretching to the horizon, all
Absolutely motionless until the hour to strike
But I think there is not too much to be said or be done
And that these things eventually take care of themselves
With rest and fresh air and the outdoors, and a good view of things.
So we might pass over this to the real
Subject of our concern, and that is
Have you begun to be in the context you feel

Now that the danger has been removed?
Light falls on your shoulders, as is its way,
And the process of purification continues happily,
Unimpeded, but has the motion started
That is to quiver your head, send anxious beams
Into the dusty corners of the rooms
Eventually shoot out over the landscape
In stars and bursts? For other than this we know nothing
And space is a coffin, and the sky will put out the light.
I see you eager in your wishing it the way
We may join it, if it passes close enough:
This sets the seal of distinction on the success or failure of your attempt.
There is growing in that knowledge
We may perhaps remain here, cautious yet free
On the edge, as it rolls its unblinking chariot
Into the vast open, the incredible violence and yielding
Turmoil that is to be our route.

For John Clare

Kind of empty in the way it sees everything, the earth gets to its feet and salutes the sky. More of a success at it this time than most others it is. The feeling that the sky might be in the back of someone's mind. Then there is no telling how many there are. They grace everything—bush and tree—to take the roisterer's mind off his caroling—so it's like a smooth switch back. To what was aired in their previous conniption fit. There is so much to be seen everywhere that it's like not getting used to it, only there is so much it never feels new, never any different. You are standing looking at that building and you cannot take it all in, certain details are already hazy and the mind boggles. What will it all be like in five years' time when you try to remember? Will there have been boards in between the grass part and the edge of the street? As long as that couple is stopping to look in that window over there we cannot go. We feel like they have to tell us we can, but they never look our way and they are already gone, gone far into the future—the night of time. If we could look at a photograph of it and say there they are, they never really stopped but there they are. There is so much to be said, and on the surface of it very little gets said.

There ought to be room for more things, for a spreading out, like. Being immersed in the details of rock and field and slope—letting them come to you for once, and then meeting them halfway would be so much easier—if they took an ingenuous pride in being in one's blood. Alas, we perceive them if at all as those things that were meant to be put aside—costumes of the supporting actors or voice trilling at the end of a narrow enclosed street. You can do nothing with them. Not even offer to pay.

It is possible that finally, like coming to the end of a long, barely perceptible rise, there is mutual cohesion and interaction. The whole scene is fixed in your mind, the music all present, as though you could see each note as well as hear it. I say this because there is an uneasiness in things just now. Waiting for something to be over before you are forced to notice it. The pollarded trees scarcely bucking the wind—and yet it's keen, it makes you fall over. Clabbered sky. Seasons that pass with a rush. After all it's their time too—nothing says they aren't to make something of it. As for Jenny Wren, she cares, hopping about on her little twig like she was tryin' to tell us somethin', but that's just it, she couldn't even if she wanted to—dumb bird. But the others—and they in some way must know too—it would never occur to them to want to, even if they could take the first step of the terrible journey toward feeling somebody should act, that ends in utter confusion and hopelessness, east of the sun and west of the moon. So their comment is: "No comment." Meanwhile the whole history of probabilities is coming to life, starting in the upper left-hand corner, like a sail.

French Poems

for Anne and Rodrigo Moynihan

I.

The sources of these things being very distant
It is appropriate to find them, which is why mist
And night have "affixed the seals" to all the ardor
Of the secret of the search. Not to confound it
But to assure its living aeration.

And yet it is more in the mass
Of the mist that some day the same contacts
Will be able to unfold. I am thinking of the dance of the
Solid lightning-flashes under the cold and
Haughty sky all striated with invisible marblings.

And it does seem that all the force of
The cosmic temperature lives in the form of contacts
That no intervention could resolve,
Even that of a creator returned to the desolate
Scene of this first experiment: this microcosm.

2.

All kinds of things exist, and, what is more,
Specimens of these things, which do not make themselves known.
I am speaking of the laugh of the squire and the spur
Which are like a hole in the armor of the day.
It's annoying and then it's so natural

That we experience almost no feeling
Except a certain lightness which matches
The recent closed ambiance which is, besides,
Full of attentions for us. Thus, lightness and wealth.

But the existence of all these things and especially
The amazing fullness of their number must be
For us a source of unforgettable questions:
Such as: whence does all this come? and again:
Shall I some day be a part of all this fullness?

3.

For it does seem as though everything will once again become number and
    smile
And that no hope of completing the magnitude which surrounds us
Is permitted us. But this hope (which doesn't exist) is
Precisely a form of suspended birth,
Of that *invisible light* which spatters the silence
Of our everyday festivities. A glebe which has pursued
Its intentions of duration at the same time as reinforcing
Its basic position so that it is now
A boiling crater, form of everything that is beautiful for us.

4.

Simple, the trees placed on the landscape
Like sheaves of wheat that someone might have left there.
The manure of vanished horses, the stones that imitate it,
Everything speaks of the heavens, which created this scene
For our position alone.
Now, in associating oneself too strictly with the trajectories of things
One loses that sublime hope made of the light that sprinkles the trees.
For each progress is negation, of movement and in particular of number.
This number having lost its indescribable fineness,
Everything must be perceived as infinite quantities of things.

Everything is landscape:
Perspectives of cliffs beaten by innumerable waves,
More wheatfields than you can count, forests
With disappearing paths, stone towers
And finally and above all the great urban centers, with

Their office buildings and populations, at the center of which
We live our lives, made up of a great quantity of isolated instants
So as to be lost at the heart of a multitude of things.

5.

It is probably on one of the inside pages
That the history of his timidity will be written,
With all the libertine thoughts of a trajectory
Roughly in the shape of a heart, around a swamp
Which for many of us will be the ultimate voyage
In view of the small amount of grace which has been accorded us,

This banality which in the last analysis is our
Most precious possession, because allowing us to
Rise above ourselves, which would not be very much
Without the presence of a lot of friends and enemies, all

Willing to swear allegiance to us, entering thus
The factory of our lives. The greatest among us, counting little
On this last-minute ennoblement, remain
Colossal, our wide-brimmed hats representing
All the shame of glory, shutting us up in the idea of number:
The ether dividing our victories, past and future: teeth and blood.

The Double Dream of Spring

for Gerrit Henry

Mixed days, the mindless years, perceived
With half-parted lips
The way the breath of spring creeps up on you and floors you.
I had thought of all this years before
But now it was making no sense. And the song had finished:
This was the story.

Just as you find men with yellow hair and blue eyes
Among certain islands
The design is complete
And one keeps walking down to the shore
Footsteps searching it
Yet they can't have it can't not have the tune that way.
And we keep stepping . . . down . . .
The rowboat rocked as you stepped into it. How flat its bottom
The little poles pushed away from the small waves in the water
And so outward. Yet we turn
To examine each other in the dream. Was it sap
Coursing in the tree
That made the buds stand out, each with a peculiar coherency?
For certainly the sidewalk led
To a point somewhere beyond itself
Caught, lost in millions of tree-analogies
Being the furthest step one might find.

And now amid the churring of locomotives
Moving on the land the grass lies over passive

Beetling its "end of the journey" mentality into your forehead
Like so much blond hair awash
Sick starlight on the night
That is readying its defenses again
As day comes up

Rural Objects

Wasn't there some way in which you too understood
About being there in the time as it was then?
A golden moment, full of life and health?
Why can't this moment be enough for us as we have become?

Is it because it was mostly made up of understanding
How the future would behave when we had moved on
To other lands, other suns, to say all there is time for
Because time is just what this instant is?

Even at the beginning the manner of the hourglass
Was all-severing, weaning of that delicious thread
That comes down even to us, *"Bénédiction de Dieu dans la Solitude,"*
Sand shaper, whistler of affectionate destinies, flames and fruit.

And now you are this thing that is outside me,
And how I in token of it am like you is
In place. In between are the bits of information
That circulate around you, all that ancient stuff,

Brought here, reassembled, carted off again
Into the back yard of your dream. If we are closer
To anything, it is in this sense that doesn't count,
Like the last few blank pages of a book.

This is why I look at you
With the eyes you once liked so much in animals:
When, in that sense, is it to be?
An ultimate warm day of the year

With the light unapproachable on the beaches?
In which case you return to the fork in the road
Doubtless to take the same path again? The second-time knowledge
Gives it fluency, makes it less of a choice

As you are older and in a dream touch bottom.
The laburnum darkened, denser at the deserted lake;
Mountain ash mindlessly dropping berries: to whom is all this?
I tell you, we are being called back

For having forgotten these names
For forgetting our proper names, for falling like nameless things
On unfamiliar slopes. To be seen again, churlishly into life,
Returning, as to the scene of a crime.

That is how the singer spoke,
In vague terms, but with an eternity of thirst
To end with a small tumbler of water
Or a single pink, leaning against the window frame in the bubble evening,

The mind of our birth. It was all sad and real.
They slept together at the commercial school.
The binding of a book made a tall V, like undone hair,
"To say all there was never time for."

It is no triumph to point out
That no accounting was ever asked.
The land lies flat under the umbrella
Of anxiety perpetually smoothed over

As though some token were required of how each
Arrived early for the appointment in different cities.
The least suspicion would have crumbled,
Positive, but in the end you were right to

Pillage and obstruct. And she
Stared at her toes. The argument
Can be brought back intact to the point
Of summarizing how it's just a cheap way

Of letting you off, and finally
How blue objects protruded out of the
Potential, dying and recoiling, returning as you meet them
Touching forever, water lifted out of the sea.

Years of Indiscretion

Whatever your eye alights on this morning is yours:
Dotted rhythms of colors as they fade to the color,
A gray agate, translucent and firm, with nothing
Beyond its purifying reach. It's all there.
These are things offered to your participation.

These pebbles in a row are the seasons.
This is a house in which you may wish to live.
There are more than any of us to choose from
But each must live its own time.

And with the urging of the year each hastens onward separately
In strange sensations of emptiness, anguish, romantic
Outbursts, visions and wraiths. One meeting
Cancels another. "The seven-league boot
Gliding hither and thither of its own accord"
Salutes these forms for what they now are:

Fables that time invents
To explain its passing. They entertain
The very young and the very old, and not
One's standing up in them to shoulder
Task and vision, vision in the form of a task
So that the present seems like yesterday
And yesterday the place where we left off a little while ago.

Farm Implements and Rutabagas in a Landscape

The first of the undecoded messages read: "Popeye sits in thunder,
Unthought of. From that shoebox of an apartment,
From livid curtain's hue, a tangram emerges: a country."
Meanwhile the Sea Hag was relaxing on a green couch: "How pleasant
To spend one's vacation *en la casa de Popeye*," she scratched
Her cleft chin's solitary hair. She remembered spinach

And was going to ask Wimpy if he had bought any spinach.
"M'love," he intercepted, "the plains are decked out in thunder
Today, and it shall be as you wish." He scratched
The part of his head under his hat. The apartment
Seemed to grow smaller. "But what if no pleasant
Inspiration plunge us now to the stars? *For this is my country.*"

Suddenly they remembered how it was cheaper in the country.
Wimpy was thoughtfully cutting open a number 2 can of spinach
When the door opened and Swee'pea crept in. "How pleasant!"
But Swee'pea looked morose. A note was pinned to his bib. "Thunder
And tears are unavailing," it read. "Henceforth shall Popeye's apartment
Be but remembered space, toxic or salubrious, whole or scratched."

Olive came hurtling through the window; its geraniums scratched
Her long thigh. "I have news!" she gasped. "Popeye, forced as you know to
    flee the country
One musty gusty evening, by the schemes of his wizened, duplicate father,
    jealous of the apartment
And all that it contains, myself and spinach
In particular, heaves bolts of loving thunder
At his own astonished becoming, rupturing the pleasant

Arpeggio of our years. No more shall pleasant
Rays of the sun refresh your sense of growing old, nor the scratched
Tree-trunks and mossy foliage, only immaculate darkness and thunder."
She grabbed Swee'pea. "I'm taking the brat to the country."
"But you can't do that—he hasn't even finished his spinach,"
Urged the Sea Hag, looking fearfully around at the apartment.

But Olive was already out of earshot. Now the apartment
Succumbed to a strange new hush. "Actually it's quite pleasant
Here," thought the Sea Hag. "If this is all we need fear from spinach
Then I don't mind so much. Perhaps we could invite Alice the Goon over"—
    she scratched
One dug pensively—"but Wimpy is such a country
Bumpkin, always burping like that." Minute at first, the thunder

Soon filled the apartment. It was domestic thunder,
The color of spinach. Popeye chuckled and scratched
His balls: it sure was pleasant to spend a day in the country.

Sunrise in Suburbia

The tone is hard is heard
Is the coming of strength out of night: unfeared;
Still the colors are there and they
Ask the question of this what is to be
Out of a desert of chance in which being is life
But like a paradox, death reinforcing the life,
Sound under memory, as though our right to hear
Hid old unwillingness to continue
Or a style of turning to the window,
Hands directing the air, and no design sticks,
Only agreement not to let it die.

Others will bend these as it is possible
And a new mode will be sunning into the past:
Refreshment and ease to the statement
And back to the safe beginning, because it starts out
Once more, drawn to and fro in a warm current of breathing
As fires start in hope and cold and
Color those nearest and only warm the most distant.
The inflection is suspended,
Not to be thoroughly initiated, under a spell to continue;
Its articulate flatness, goal, barrier and climate.

Through the clutter of
The unbound year, the first dazed marks of waking
Stir on the cloud-face like texture of paper, breath at elbow
And the collapsed sign of yesterday afternoon, its
Variance put up like a shutter,
Taxing you into January of stomping, cursing and the breath-bite.
The entrance you need is

Sideways in pentagonal fields cursive in advance
Before the fathoming of spring and
Sound let deep into the flank of occurrence
As maps lean south and shrivel toward the north.

It is fine to be in on it, stone markings, always
And eventually at some limit with a high view
But cross-country skirtings were part of the next lesson
That sleep evades, and in him was no parking space
For looks dragged under windows next time, from boarded-up places
Speaking no mind into the center of the rout.

And as day followed day the plainer meaning of it
Became a constant projected on the emigration.
The tundra seemed elaborated.
Then a permanent falling back shapes, signs the residue
As a tiny wood fence's the signature of disgust and decay
On an otherwise concerned but unmoved, specially obtruded hill:
Flatness of what remains
And modelling of what fled,
Decisions for a proper ramble into known but unimaginable, dense
Fringe expecting night,
A light wilderness of spoken words not
Unkind for all their aimlessness,
A blank chart of each day moving into the premise of difficult visibility
And which is nowhere, the urge to nowhere,
To retract that statement, sharply, within the next few minutes.
For it is as though it turns you back,
Your eyes through the recent happenings as they advance through you,
Never satisfied on the way, but
There is reasonable assurance in the way it is not seen again,
Banging of the shuttle, repeated swipes of the wind,
For the afterthought coincides: much of it was intentional.
It is aloes to be remembered toward the place

Out of which it grew like forest out of mountain, when later someone says
     there was no mountain
Only roads, and stars hanging over them,
Only a flat stone over the place where it says there is more.

It is a low game, too tired to sleep,
Feeling through equipment to the less developed:
"You've gone and mixed me up
I was happy just bumming along,
Any old way, in and out, up and down."
The passion has left his head, and the head reports.

And then some morning there is a nuance:
Suddenly in the city dirt and varied
Ideas of rubbish, the blue day stands and
A sudden interest is there:
Lying on the cot, near the tree-shadow,
Out of the thirties having news of the true source:
Face to kiss and the wonderful hair curling down
Into margins that care and are swept up again like branches
Into actual closeness
And the little things that lighten the day
The kindness of acts long forgotten
Which give us history and faith
And parting at night, next to oceans, like the collapse of dying.
It is all noticed before it is too late
But its immobility gives no comfort, only chapter headings and folio
     numbers
And it can go on being divine in itself
Neither treasured nor cast down in anger
For we cannot imagine the truth of it.
This deaf rasping of branch against branch
Like a noncommittal sneer among many superimposed chimes
As we go separate ways
That have translated the foreground of paths into quoted spaces:

They are empty beyond consternation because
These are the droppings of all our lives
And they recall no past de luxe quarters
Only a last cube.
The thieves were not breaking in, the castle was not being stormed.
It was the holiness of the day that fed our notions
And released them, sly breath of Eros,
Anniversary on the woven city lament, that assures our arriving
In hours, seconds, breath, watching our salary
In the morning holocaust become one vast furnace, engaging all tears.

Definition of Blue

The rise of capitalism parallels the advance of romanticism
And the individual is dominant until the close of the nineteenth century.
In our own time, mass practices have sought to submerge the personality
By ignoring it, which has caused it instead to branch out in all directions
Far from the permanent tug that used to be its notion of "home."
These different impetuses are received from everywhere
And are as instantly snapped back, hitting through the cold atmosphere
In one steady, intense line.

There is no remedy for this "packaging" which has supplanted the old
    sensations.
Formerly there would have been architectural screens at the point where the
    action became most difficult
As a path trails off into shrubbery—confusing, forgotten, yet continuing to
    exist.
But today there is no point in looking to imaginative new methods
Since all of them are in constant use. The most that can be said for them
    further
Is that erosion produces a kind of dust or exaggerated pumice
Which fills space and transforms it, becoming a medium
In which it is possible to recognize oneself.

Each new diversion adds its accurate touch to the ensemble, and so
A portrait, smooth as glass, is built up out of multiple corrections
And it has no relation to the space or time in which it was lived.
Only its existence is a part of all being, and is therefore, I suppose, to be
    prized
Beyond chasms of night that fight us
By being hidden and present.

And yet it results in a downward motion, or rather a floating one
In which the blue surroundings drift slowly up and past you
To realize themselves some day, while, you, in this nether world that could
   not be better
Waken each morning to the exact value of what you did and said, which
   remains.

Parergon

We are happy in our way of life.
It doesn't make much sense to others. We sit about,
Read, and are restless. Occasionally it becomes time
To lower the dark shade over it all.
Our entity pivots on a self-induced trance
Like sleep. Noiseless our living stops
And one strays as in a dream
Into those respectable purlieus where life is motionless and alive
To utter the few words one knows:

"O woebegone people! Why so much crying,
Such desolation in the streets?
Is it the present of flesh, that each of you
At your jagged casement window should handle,
Nervous unto thirst and ultimate death?
Meanwhile the true way is sleeping;
Your lawful acts drink an unhealthy repose
From the upturned lip of this vessel, secretly,
But it is always time for a change.
That certain sins of omission go unpunished
Does not weaken your position
But this underbrush in which you are secure
Is its doing. Farewell then,
Until, under a better sky
We may meet expended, for just doing it
Is only an excuse. We need the tether
Of entering each other's lives, eyes wide apart, crying."

As one who moves forward from a dream
The stranger left that house on hastening feet

Leaving behind the woman with the face shaped like an arrowhead,
And all who gazed upon him wondered at
The strange activity around him.
How fast the faces kindled as he passed!
It was a marvel that no one spoke
To stem the river of his passing,
Now grown to flood proportions, as on the sunlit mall
Or in the enclosure of some court
He took his pleasure, savage
And mild with the contemplating.
Yet each knew he saw only aspects,
That the continuity was fierce beyond all dream of enduring,
And turned his head away, and so
The lesson eddied far into the night:
Joyful its beams, and in the blackness blacker still,
Though undying joyousness, caught in that trap.

The Hod Carrier

You have been declining the land's
Breakable extensions, median whose face is half my face.
Your curved visor's the supposition that unites us.

        I've been thinking about you

After a dry summer, fucking in the autumn,
Reflecting among arabesques of speech that arise
The certain anomaly, the wise smile
Of winter fitted over the land
And your activity disappears in mist, or translates too easily
Into a general puree, someone's aura or idea of games—
The stone you cannot perfect, the sharp iron blade you cannot prevent.

But this new way we are, the melon head
Half-mirrored, the way sentences suddenly spurt up like gas
Or sting and jab, is it that we accepted each complication
As it came along, and are therefore happy with the result?
Or was it as a condition of seeing
That we vouchsafed aid and comfort to the seasons

        As each came begging

And the present, so flat in its belief, so "outside it"
As it maintains, becomes the blind side of
The fulfillment of that condition; and work, ripeness
And tired but resolute standing up for one's rights
Mean leaning toward the stars

        The way a tree leans toward the sun

Not meaning to get close

And the bird walked right up that tree.

You have reached the point closest to your destination

O tired beacon
Dominating the plain
Yet all but invisible

To the mind surrounding your purpose
You are totally subsumed
The good abstracted, squandered, thrown away
As it was in the lean time.
Are these floorboards, to be stared at
In moments of guilt, as wallpaper can stream away and yet

You cannot declare it?

Then each breath is a redeeming feature
Resolving in alteration
The inanity of flowers into perfect conditions
That their mildness can only postpone, not change.

And surveying the hundredfold record of the summer
The shapely witness declares herself at last
Content with the result:
Whitecaps wincing at every point of the compass
The justified demands of commerce, difficult departures and all
Into a hemisphere where no credit is expected
And the shipping is rendered into its own terms.

It is what keeps itself
From going blind

All aging is perpetual chatter
On these buff planes, protuberances
And you are in the wind at night

        And so it is an even darker night

And death is the prevention of which the cure's
Metal polish and sawdust

        Light grinding into your heels.

An Outing

"These things . . . that you are going to have—
Are you paid specially for them?"

                    "Yes."

"And when it is over, do you insist,
Do you insist that the visitor leave the room?"
"My activity is as random as the wind.
Why should I insist? The visitor is free to go,
Or to stay, as he chooses."

Are you folks just going out for a walk
And if you are would you check the time
On your way back? It's too late to do anything today.
I would just take a pratfall if I stepped outside that door.

"I don't know whether I should apply or nothing."
"I think you should make your decision."

So it was by chance we found ourselves
Gumshod on the pebbled path, Denmark O Denmark
Flat, rounded eyes, Denmark Denmark
Gray parchment landscape Denmark O Denmark
Unmanageable sky, Denmark that cannot shift
The faucet drips, the minutes apply, Denmark.

Some Words

from the French of Arthur Cravan

Life is not at all what you might think it to be
A simple tale where each thing has its history
   It's much more than its scuffle and anything goes
Both evil and good, subject to the same laws.
   Each hour has its color and forever gives place
Leaving less than yon bird of itself a trace.
In vain does memory attempt to store away
The scent of its colors in a single bouquet
Memory can but shift cold ashes around
When the depths of time it endeavors to sound.
   Never think that you may be allowed, at the end,
To say to yourself, "I am of myself the friend,"
Or make with yourself a last reconciliation.
You will remain the victim of your hesitation
You will forget today before tomorrow is here
And disavow yourself while much is still far from clear.
   The defunct days will offer you their images
Only so that you may read of former outrages
And the days to come will mar with their complaints
The splendor that in your honor dejected evening paints.
   Wishing to collect in your heart the feelings
Scattered in the meadows of misfortune's hard dealings
You will be the shepherd whose dog has run away
You will know even less whence comes your dismay
Than you know the hour your boredom first saw the light.
   Weary of seeking day you will relish the night
In night's dim orchards you will find some rest
The counsels of the trees of night are best
Better than those of the tree of knowledge, which corrupts us at birth
And which you allowed to flourish in the accursèd earth.

When your most arduous labors grow pale as death
And you begin to inhale autumn's chilly breath
Winter will come soon to batter with his mace
Your precious moments, scattering them all over the place.

  You will always be having to get up from your chairs
To move on to other heartbreaks, be caught in other snares.

  The seasons will revolve on their scented course
Solar or devastated you will perforce
Be perfumed at their tepid passing, and not know
Whether their fragrance brings you joy or woe.

  At the moment when your life becomes a total shambles
You will have to resume your hopeless rambles
You have left everything behind and you still are eligible
And all alone, as the gulf becomes unbridgeable
You will have to earn your daily bread
Although you feel you'd be better off dead.

  They'll hurt you, and you'd like to put up some resistance
Because you know that your very existence
Depends on others as unworthy of you
As you are of God, and when it's time to review
Your wrongs, you will feel no pain, they will seem like a joke
For you will have ceased to suffer under their yoke.

  Whether you pass through fields, towns or across the sea
You will always retain your melancholy
And look after it; you will have to think of your career
Not live it, as in a game where the best player
Is he who forgets himself, and cannot say
What spurs him on, and makes him win the day.

  When weary henceforth of wishing to gaze
At the sinuous path of your spun-out days
You return to the place where your stables used to tower
You will find nothing left but some fetid manure
Your steeds beneath other horsemen will have fled
To autumn's far country, all rusted and red.

  Like an ardent rose in the September sun

You will feel the flesh sag from your limbs, one by one,
Less of you than of a pruned rosebush will remain,
That spring lies in wait for, to clothe once again.

If you wish to love you won't know whom to choose
There are none whose love you'd be sorry to lose
Not to love at all would be the better part
Lest another seize and confiscate your heart.

When evening descends on your deserted routes
You won't be afraid and will say, "What boots
It to worry and fret? To rail at my luck?
Since time my actions like an apple will pluck."

You would like of yourself to curtail certain features
That you dislike, making allowances for this creature,
Giving that other one a chance to show his fettle,
Confining yet another behind bars of metal:
That rebel will soon become an armèd titan.

Then let yourself love all that you take delight in
Accept yourself whole, accept the heritage
That shaped you and is passed on from age to age
Down to your entity. Remain mysterious;
Rather than be pure, accept yourself as numerous.
The wave of heredity will not be denied:
Best, then, on a lover's silken breast to abide
And be wafted by her to Nirvana's blue shoals
Where the self is abolished and renounces its goals.

In you all things must live and procreate
Forget about the harvest and its sheaves of wheat
You are the harvest and not the reaper
And of your domain another is the keeper.

When you see the lapsed dreams that childhood invents
Salute your adolescence and fold their tents
Virginal, tall and slim beside the jasmine tree
An adorable girl is plaiting tenderly
The bouquet of love, which will stick in your memory
As the final vision and the final story.

Henceforth you will burn with lascivious fire
Accursèd passion will strum its lyre
At the charming crossroads where day is on the wane
As the curve of a hill dissolves in a plain.

The tacit beauty of the sacred plateau
Will be spoiled for you and you will never know
Henceforth the peace a pious heart bestows
To the soul its gentle sister in whom it echoes;
Anxiety will have called everything into question
And you will be tempted to the wildest actions.

Then let all fade at the edge of our days!
No God emerges to dream our destinies.
The days depart, only boredom does not retreat
It's like a path that flies beneath one's feet
Whose horizon shifts while as we trudge
The dust and mud stick to us and do not budge.

In vain do we speak, provoke actions or think,
We are prisoners of the world's demented sink.

The soft enchantments of our years of innocence
Are harvested by accredited experience
Our fondest memories soon turn to poison
And only oblivion remains in season.

When, beside a window, one feels evening prevail
Who is there who can receive its slanting veil
And not regret day that bore it on its stream
Whether day was joy or under evil's regime
Drawing us to the one and deploring the other
Regretting the departure of all our brothers
And all that made the day, including its stains.

Whoever you may be O man who complains
Not at your destiny, can you then doubt,
When the moment arrives for you to stretch out,
That remorse, a stinking jackal with subtle nose,
Will come at the end to devour your repose?

. . . Something gentle and something sad eftsoons

In the flanks of our pale and realistic noons
Holds with our soul a discourse without end
The curtain rises on the afternoon wind
Day sheds its leaves and now will soon be gone
And already my adulthood seems to mourn
Beside the reddish sunsets of the hollow vase
As gently it starts to deepen and slowly to increase.

Young Man with Letter

Another feeble, wonderful creature is making the rounds again,
In this phraseology we become, as clouds like leaves
Fashion the internal structure of a season
From water into ice. Such an abstract can be
Dazed waking of the words with no memory of what happened before,
Waiting for the second click. We know them well enough now,
Forever, from living into them, tender, frivolous and puzzled
And we know that with them we will come out right.

But a new question poses itself:
Is it we who are being transformed?
The light in the hallway seems to indicate it
And the corrosive friends whose breath is so close
It whistles, are changed to tattered pretexts
As a sign, perhaps, that all's well with us.
Yet the quiet bickering on the edge of morning

That advances to a steady drone by noon
And to hollow rumblings by night: is there so much good then
Blushing beyond the sense of it, standing straight up for others to view?
Is it not more likely that such straining and puffing
As commas produce, this ferment
We take as suddenly our present
Is our waltzing somewhere else, down toward the view
But holding off? The spiked neon answers it
Up against the charged black of a full sky:
"We thought you knew, brothers not ancestors;
Your time has come, has come to stay;
The sieved dark can tell you about it."

Clouds

All this time he had only been waiting,
Not even thinking, as many had supposed.
Now sleep wound down to him its promise of dazzling peace
And he stood up to assume that imagination.

There were others in the forest as close as he
To caring about the silent outcome, but they had gotten lost
In the shadows of dreams so that the external look
Of the nearby world had become confused with the cobwebs inside.

Yet all would finish at the end, or go undreamed of.
It was a solid light in which a man and woman could kiss
Yet dark and ambiguous as a cloakroom.
No noise was to underline the notion of its being.

Thus the thing grew heavy with the mere curve of being,
As a fruit ripens through the long summer before falling
Out of the idea of existence into the fact of being received,
As many another guest. And the helloes and goodbyes are never stilled;

They stay in the foreground and look back on it.
It was still possible of course to imagine that an era had ended,
Yet this time was marked also by new ideas of progress and decay.
The old ideals had been cast aside and people were restless for the new,

In a wholly different mass, so there was no joining,
Only separate blocks of achievement and opinion
With no relation to the conducive ether
Which surrounded everything like the clear idea of a ruler.

And it was that these finally flattened out or banded together
Through forgetting, into one contemporaneous sea
With no explanations to give. And the small enclave
Of worried continuing began again, putting forth antennae into the night.

How do we explain the harm, feeling
We are always the effortless discoverers of our career,
With each day digging the grave of tomorrow and at the same time
Preparing its own redemption, constantly living and dying?

How can we outsmart the sense of continuity
That eludes our steps as it prepares us
For ultimate wishful thinking once the mind has ended
Since this last thought both confines and uplifts us?

He was like a lion tracking its prey
Through days and nights, forgetful
In the delirium of arrangements.
The birds fly up out of the underbrush,

The evening swoons out of contaminated dawns,
And now whatever goes farther must be
Alien and healthy, for death is here and knowable.
Out of touch with the basic unhappiness

He shoots forward like a malignant star.
The edges of the journey are ragged.
Only the face of night begins to grow distinct
As the fainter stars call to each other and are lost.

Day re-creates his image like a snapshot:
The family and the guests are there,
The talking over there, only now it will never end.
And so cities are arranged, and oceans traversed,

And farms tilled with especial care.
This year again the corn has grown ripe and tall.
It is a perfect rebuttal of the argument. And Semele
Moves away, puzzled at the brown light above the fields.

The Bungalows

Impatient as we were for all of them to join us,
The land had not yet risen into view: gulls had swept the gray steel towers
    away
So that it profited less to go searching, away over the humming earth
Than to stay in immediate relation to these other things—boxes, store parts,
    whatever you wanted to call them—
Whose installedness was the price of further revolutions, so you knew this
    combat was the last.
And still the relationship waxed, billowed like scenery on the breeze.

They are the same aren't they,
The presumed landscape and the dream of home
Because the people are all homesick today or desperately sleeping,
Trying to remember how those rectangular shapes
Became so extraneous and so near
To create a foreground of quiet knowledge
In which youth had grown old, chanting and singing wise hymns that
Will sign for old age
And so lift up the past to be persuaded, and be put down again.

The warning is nothing more than an aspirate "h";
The problem is sketched completely, like fireworks mounted on poles:
Complexion of evening, the accurate voices of the others.
During Coca-Cola lessons it becomes patent
Of noise on the left, and we had so skipped a stage that
The great wave of the past, compounded in derision,
Submerged idea and non-dreamer alike
In falsetto starlight like "purity"
Of design that had been the first danger sign
To wash the sticky, icky stuff down the drain—pfui!

How does it feel to be outside and inside at the same time,
The delicious feeling of the air contradicting and secretly abetting
The interior warmth? But the land curdles the dismay in which it's written
Bearing to a final point of folly and doom
The wisdom of these generations.
Look at what you've done to the landscape—
The ice cube, the olive—
There is a perfect tri-city mesh of things
Extending all the way along the river on both sides
With the end left for thoughts on construction
That are always turning to alps and thresholds
Above the tide of others, feeding a European moss rose without glory.

We shall very soon have the pleasure of recording
A period of unanimous tergiversation in this respect
And to make that pleasure the greater, it is worth while
At the risk of tedious iteration, to put first upon record a final protest:
Rather decaying art, genius, inspiration to hold to
An impossible "calque" of reality, than
"The new school of the trivial, rising up on the field of battle,
Something of sludge and leaf-mold," and life
Goes trickling out through the holes, like water through a sieve,
All in one direction.

You who were directionless, and thought it would solve everything if you
    found one,
What do you make of this? Just because a thing is immortal
Is that any reason to worship it? Death, after all, is immortal.
But you have gone into your houses and shut the doors, meaning
There can be no further discussion.
And the river pursues its lonely course
With the sky and the trees cast up from the landscape
For green brings unhappiness—*le vert porte malheur.*
"The chartreuse mountain on the absinthe plain
Makes the strong man's tears tumble down like rain."

284

All this came to pass eons ago.
Your program worked out perfectly. You even avoided
The monotony of perfection by leaving in certain flaws:
A backward way of becoming, a forced handshake,
An absent-minded smile, though in fact nothing was left to chance.
Each detail was startlingly clear, as though seen through a magnifying glass,
Or would have been to an ideal observer, namely yourself—
For only you could watch yourself so patiently from afar
The way God watches a sinner on the path to redemption,
Sometimes disappearing into valleys, but always *on the way*,
For it all builds up into something, meaningless or meaningful
As architecture, because planned and then abandoned when completed,
To live afterwards, in sunlight and shadow, a certain amount of years.
Who cares about what was there before? There is no going back,
For standing still means death, and life is moving on,
Moving on towards death. But sometimes standing still is also life.

The Chateau Hardware

It was always November there. The farms
Were a kind of precinct; a certain control
Had been exercised. The little birds
Used to collect along the fence.
It was the great "as though," the how the day went,
The excursions of the police
As I pursued my bodily functions, wanting
Neither fire nor water,
Vibrating to the distant pinch
And turning out the way I am, turning out to greet you.

Sortes Vergilianae

You have been living now for a long time and there is nothing you do not
 know.
Perhaps something you read in the newspaper influenced you and that was
 very frequently.
They have left you to think along these lines and you have gone your own
 way because you guessed that
Under their hiding was the secret, casual as breath, betrayed for the asking.
Then the sky opened up, revealing much more than any of you were
 intended to know.
It is a strange thing how fast the growth is, almost as fast as the light from
 polar regions
Reflected off the arctic ice-cap in summer. When you know where it is
 heading
You have to follow it, though at a sadly reduced rate of speed,
Hence folly and idleness, raging at the confines of some miserable sunlit
 alley or court.
It is the nature of these people to embrace each other, they know no other
 kind but themselves.
Things pass quickly out of sight and the best is to be forgotten quickly
For it is wretchedness that endures, shedding its cancerous light on all it
 approaches:
Words spoken in the heat of passion, that might have been retracted in good
 time,
All good intentions, all that was arguable. These are stilled now, as the
 embrace in the hollow of its flux
And can never be revived except as perverse notations on an indisputable
 state of things,
As conduct in the past, vanished from the reckoning long before it was time.
Lately you've found the dull fevers still inflict their round, only they are
 unassimilable

Now that newness or importance has worn away. It is with us like day and
   night,
The surge upward through the grade school positioning and bursting into
   soft gray blooms
Like vacuum-cleaner sweepings, the opulent fuzz of our cage, or like an
   excited insect
In nervous scrimmage for the head, etching its none-too-complex
   ordinances into the matter of the day.
Presently all will go off satisfied, leaving the millpond bare, a site for new
   picnics,
As they came, naked, to explore all the possible grounds on which exchanges
   could be set up.
It is "No Fishing" in modest capital letters, and getting out from under the
   major weight of the thing
As it was being indoctrinated and dropped, heavy as a branch with apples,
And as it started to sigh, just before tumbling into your lap, chagrined and
   satisfied at the same time,
Knowing its day over and your patience only beginning, toward what
   marvels of speculation, auscultation, world-view,
Satisfied with the entourage. It is this blank carcass of whims and tentative
   afterthoughts
Which is being delivered into your hand like a letter some forty-odd years
   after the day it was posted.
Strange, isn't it, that the message makes some sense, if only a relative one in
   the larger context of message-receiving
That you will be called to account for just as the purpose of it is becoming
   plain,
Being one and the same with the day it set out, though you cannot imagine
   this.
There was a time when the words dug in, and you laughed and joked,
   accomplice
Of all the possibilities of their journey through the night and the stars,
   creature
Who looked to the abandonment of such archaic forms as these, and
   meanwhile

Supported them as the tools that made you. The rub became apparent only
 later
And by then it was too late to check such expansive aspects as what to do
 while waiting
For the others to show: unfortunately no pile of tattered magazines was in
 evidence,
Such dramas sleeping below the surface of the everyday machinery; besides
Quality is not given to everybody, and who are you to have been supposing
 you had it?
So the journey grew ever slower; the battlements of the city could now be
 discerned from afar
But meanwhile the water was giving out and malaria had decimated their
 ranks and undermined their morale,
You know the story, so that if turning back was unthinkable, so was
 victorious conquest of the great brazen gates.
Best perhaps to fold up right here, but even that was not to be granted.
Some days later in the pulsating of orchestras someone asked for a drink:
The music stopped and those who had been confidently counting the
 rhythms grew pale.
This is just a footnote, though a microcosmic one perhaps, to the greater
 curve
Of the elaboration; it asks no place in it, only insertion *hors-texte* as the
 invisible notion of how that day grew
From planisphere to heaven, and what part in it all the "I" had, the insatiable
 researcher of learned trivia, bookworm,
And one who marched along with, "made common cause," yet had neither
 the gumption nor the desire to trick the thing into happening,
Only long patience, as the star climbs and sinks, leaving illumination to the
 setting sun.

Fragment

The last block is closed in April. You
See the intrusions clouding over her face
As in the memory given you of older
Permissiveness which dies in the
Falling back toward recondite ends,
The sympathy of yellow flowers.
Never mentioned in the signs of the oblong day
The saw-toothed flames and point of other
Space not given, and yet not withdrawn
And never yet imagined: a moment's commandment.

These last weeks teasing into providential
Reality: that your face, the only real beginning,
Beyond the gray of overcoat, that this first
Salutation plummet also to the end of friendship
With self alone. And in doing so open out
New passages of being among the correctness
Of familiar patterns. The stance to you
Is a fiction, to me a whole. I find
New options, white feathers, in a word what
You draw in around you to the protecting bone.

This page only is the end of nothing
To the top of that other. The purity
Of how hard it is to choose between others where
The event takes place and the outside setting.
Day covers all this with leaves, with laughter and tears.
But at night other sounds are heard
Propositions hitherto omitted in the heat
Of smoke. You can look at it all

Inside out for the emblem to become the statue
Of discipline that rode in out of the past.

Not forgetting either the chance that you
Might want to revise this version of what is
The only real one, it might be that
No real relation exists between my wish for you
To return and the movements of your arms and legs.
But my inability to accept this fact
Annihilates it. Thus
My power over you is absolute.
You exist only in me and on account of me
And my features reflect this proved compactness.

That coming together of masses coincides
With that stable emptiness, detaining
Where this energy, not yet or only partially
Distributed to the imagination creates
A claim to the sides of early autumn.
Suffocating, with remorse, and winking with it
To tablelands of disadumbrated feeling
Treetops whose mysterious hegemony concerns
Merely, by opening around factors of accident
So as to install miscellaneous control.

The part in which you read about yourself
Grew out of this. Your interpretation is
Extremely bitter and can serve no profitable end
Except continual development. Best to break off
All further choice. In
This way new symptoms of interest having a
Common source could produce their own ingenious
Way of watering into the past with its religious
Messages and burials. Out of this cold collapse
A warm and near unpolished entity could begin.

Although beyond more reacting
To this cut-and-dried symposium way of seeing things
To outflank next mediocre condition
Of storms. The hollow thus produced
A kind of cave of the winds; distribution center
Of subordinate notions to which the stag
Returns to die: the suppressed lovers.
Then ghosts of the streets
Crowding, propagating the feeling into furious
Waves from the perfunctory and debilitated sunset.

Yet no one has time for its preoccupation.
Our daily imaginings are swiftly tilted down to
Death in its various forms. We cannot keep the peace
At home, and at the same time be winning wars abroad.
And the great flower of what we have been twists
On its stem of earth, for not being
What we are to become, fated to live in
Intimidated solitude and isolation. No brother
Bearing the notion of responsibility of self
To the surrounding neighborhood lost out of being.

Slowly as from the center of some diamond
You begin to take in the world as it moves
In toward you, part of its own burden of thought, rather
Idle musing, afternoons listing toward some sullen
Unexpected end. Seen from inside all is
Abruptness. As though to get out your eye
Sharpens and sharpens these particulars; no
Longer visible, they breathe in multicolored
Parentheses, the way love in short periods
Puts everything out of focus, coming and going.

Thus your only world is an inside one
Ironically fashioned out of external phenomena

Having no rhyme or reason, and yet neither
An existence independent of foreboding and sly grief.
Nothing anybody says can make a difference; inversely
You are a victim of their lack of consequence
Buffeted by invisible winds, or yet a flame yourself
Without meaning, yet drawing satisfaction
From the crevices of that wind, living
In that flame's idealized shape and duration.

Whereas through an act of bunching this black kite
Webs all around you with coal light: wall and reef
Imbibe and the impossible saturation,
New kinds of fun, is an earnest
Of the certain future. Yet the spores of the
Difference as it's imagined flower
In complicated chains for the eyebrow, and pre-delineate
Phantom satisfaction as it would happen. This time
You get over the threshold of so much unmeaning, so much
Being, prepared for its event, the active memorial.

And more swiftly continually in evening, limpid
Storm winds, commas are dropped, the convention gapes,
Prostrated before a monument disappearing into the dark.
It would not be good to examine these ages
Except for sun flecks, little, on the golden sand
And coming to reappraisal of the distance.
The welcoming stuns the heart, iron bells
Crash through the transparent metal of the sky
Each day slowing the method of thought a little
Until oozing sap of touchable mortality, time lost and won.

Like the blood orange we have a single
Vocabulary all heart and all skin and can see
Through the dust of incisions the central perimeter
Our imaginations' orbit. Other words,

Old ways are but the trappings and appurtenances
Meant to install change around us like a grotto.
There is nothing laughable
In this. To isolate the kernel of
Our imbalance and at the same time back up carefully;
Its tulip head whole, an imagined good.

The sense of that day toward its center
Is perforated or crisscrossed with rewards
As though the stumbling that stranded me here were
The means of some spontaneity. But upper pressures
Lifted the direction of the prevailing winds
Allowing an awaited entrance down below.
Yet all is different metric system
Flapping from grace to intense surprise.
As in a tub. No candle is lit. No theory
Strap it to the maturity of surroundings.

Its landscape puts toward a pointed roof
Continuing inquiry and reappraisal of always new
Facts pushing past into bright cold
As from general spindles a waterfall of data
Is absorbed above by command. Whether construed
As lead or gold it leaves a ring
On the embellished, attendant time. The farms
Knew it, that is why they stood so still.
The gold might reverse them to fields
Of flowering sand or black, ancient and intimate.

The volcanic entrance to an antechamber
Was not what either of us meant.
More outside than before, but what is worse, outside
Within the periphery, we are confronted
With one another, and our meeting escapes through the dark
Like a well.

Our habits ask us for instructions.
The news is to return by stages
Of uncertainty, too early or too late. It is the invisible
Shapes, the bed's confusion and prattling. The late quiet. This is how it feels.

The pictures were really pictures
Of loving and small things. There was a winter scene
And half-hidden sketches of the other three seasons.
Autumn was a giant with a gray woollen cap.
Near him was spring, a girl in green draperies
Half sitting, half standing near the trunk of an old tree.
Summer was a band of nondescript children
Bordering the picture of winter, which was indistinct
And gray like the sky of a winter afternoon.
The other pictures told in an infinity of tiny ways

Stories of the past: separate incidents
Recounted in touching detail, or vast histories
Murmured confusingly, as though the speaker
Were choked by sighs and tears, and had forgotten
The reason why he was telling the story.
It was these finally that made the strongest
Impression, they shook you like wind
Roaring through branches with no leaves left on them.
The vagueness was bigger than life and its apotheosis
Of shining incidents, colored or dark, vivid or serious.

But now the tidings are dark in the
Expected late afternoon suddenly dipping into
Reserves of anxiety and restlessness which dutifully
Puff out these late, lax sails, pennants;
The vertical black-and-white-striped weather indicator's
One sign of triumph, a small one, to stand
For universal concessions, charters and deeds to
Wilderness or the forested sea, cord after cord

Equaling possession and possessiveness
Instantaneously extending your hesitation to an

Empire, back lands whose sparsely populated look is
Supreme dominion. It will be divided into tracks
And these be lived in the way now the lowered
Angles of this room. Waxed moustache against the impiety
Of so much air of change, but always and nowhere
A cave. Gradually old letters used as bookmarks
Inform the neighbors; an approximate version
Circulates and the incident is officially closed.
And I some joy of this have, returning to the throbbing
Mirror's stiff enclave, the sides of my face steep and overrun.

So many ways grew over to this
Mild decline. The grave of authority
Matches wits with upward-spinning lemon spirals
Telling of the influences of night, so many decisions
Not to act accruing to the outward stretches.
The civilities of day also creep
To extremities, fly on a windowpane, sweeping
The changed refuse under the rug. Just one step
Takes you into so much outside, the candor
Of what had been going on makes you pause momentarily,

A bag of October, without being able to tell it
To the others, so that it loses silence.
I haven't made clear that I want it all from you
In writing, so as to study your facial expressions
Simultaneously: hesitations, reverse darts, the sky
Of your plans run through with many sutured points.
Only in this way can a true basis for understanding be
Set up. But meanwhile if I try to turn away
Looking for my own shadow in the excess
Like quarreling jays our heads fall to in agreement.

It exposed us on a moving gangway.
Leaning from an upper story
We should not separate in misunderstanding.
Where you were going was the key to
Saturday afternoon spent in shopping and washing dishes
Just right so the newly strengthened land would
Disinter the music box what keeps happening to
The photo of a baby girl disguised as an old man
With a long white beard. What comes after
The purge, she not mentioning it yet.

This meant (and the tone voice, repeating
"He's hurt read bad" worked up the wall of celerity
To inaudible foam) all divers and all speechless
Apostrophes of solar unit stay on the bottom.
At last there was a chance to explore the forest,
Shadow of yawning magnetic poles, in which the castle
Had been inserted like an afterthought—bare walls
With somewhere a center and even further, a widening
To accommodate eventual reaction, such as ropes,
Pikes, chains of memory, of sleep, and an end of board.

The apotheosis had sunk away
As wind incarnates its glass cone
Aiming where further identifications should
Not be worked for, are reached. The whole
Is a mound of changing valors for some who
Live out as under a dome, are participated in
As the ordinary grandeur of a dome's the thing that
Keeps them living so that additional grace
Is eternal procrastination, not to be considered
Unless a description of the actual scene.

Shedding perennial beauty on angles
Of questions asked and often answered in a

Given period. It all moves more slowly, yet
The change is more complete than ever before:
A pessimistic lighting up as of autumn woods
Demanding more than ever to be considered, for full
Substance. For the calculable stutter of a laugh.
Returning late you were not surprised to meet
This gray visitor, perpendicular to the weather.
Quiet ambition of the note variously sounded.

All space was to be shut out. Now there was no
Earthly reason for living; solitude proceeded
From want of money, her quincunxes standing
To protect the stillness of the air. Darkness
Intruded everywhere. This was the first day
Of the new experience. The familiar brown trees
Stirred indifferent at their roots, deeply transformed.
Like a sail its question disappeared into
An ocean of newsprint. To be precipitated
In desire, as hats are handed. Awnings raised.

Coming in the phaeton to the end of the
Day that had served on previous occasions
An orchard diminishes the already tiny
Notion of abstract good and bad qualities
Pod of darkness which goes vociferating early
Unchangeables that in time's mire have hid weapons.
Past waterfall wooden huts open places
Assaulted by the wind, the usual surroundings chafed
Foreknowledge of the immense journey, as the sea
Flattens, uncritical, beyond wide docks.

To persist in the revision of very old
Studies, as though mounted on a charger,
With the door to the next room partly open
To the borrowed density, what keeps happening to

So much dead surprise, a weight of spring.
An odor of explosives hangs over the change,
Now at its apogee. This presupposes a will
To carry out all instructions, dotting the last i
Though cancelling with one stroke of a pen all
The provisions, revisions and so on made until now.

But why should the present seem so particularly urgent?
A time of spotted lakes and the whippoorwill
Sounding over everything? To release the importance
Of what will always remain invisible?
In spite of near and distant events, gladly
Built? To speak the plaits of argument,
Loosened? Vast shadows are pushed down toward
The hour. It is ideation, incrimination
Proceeding from necessity to find it at
A time of day, beside the creek, uncounted stars and buttons.

We talked, and after that went out.
It was nice. There was lots of time left
And we could always come back to it, and use it later
But the flowers dropped in the conservatory
For this was the last day of the year.
Conclusion of many ups and downs, it had begun
To be foreshadowed, leaning out into novelty
As into a bank of subtraction. The night
A dull varnish muffled the comic eagerness
Of those first steps, halted for all eternity.

Then the accounts must be reexamined,
Shifting ropes of figures. Expressions of hope
Too late, a few seconds before. Only normal
Transparent width separated them from the smaller,
Flame-colored phenomena of each settled day.
This information was like a road no one ever took

Perhaps because the end was widely known, a collection
Of ceiling fumes, inert curiosity, attacked
Rarely, and out of compunction, by millionaires
Bent on turning everyday affairs into something tragic.

Thus there was a time for all activity
As memory of regret not made known
Except as illegal pilfering on the furthest
Sketchy place of the course of a day
Which scarcely matters even for anxious
Gendarmes of these late, recent hours, now
So frequently referred to. Thus floods,
Surprising us, seem to subside
When scarcely begun. Yet so much in time for
What arrives, unnoticed our separate, parallel thought.

It is that the moment of sinking in
Is always past, yet always in question, on the surface
Of the goggles of memory. Nothing is stationary
Nor yet uncertain; a rhythm of standing still
Keeps us in continual equilibrium, like an arch
That frames swiftly receding clouds, never
Getting deeper. The shouts of children
Penetrate this motion toward, as a drop of water
Slides under a lens. Soon all is shining, mined,
Tears dissolving laughter, the isolated clouds spent.

It is appropriate that this extension is,
Has been, and always should be independent
Of elaborate misgivings concerning the future status
Of a hostile address toward each other.
Not being able to see one's way clear to
Approving ecstatic, past projects is
Equivalent to destruction of all these myths,
Wiped, like dust, from the lips. So

The weather of that day, and scalloped
Appearance of those who went by you

Are changed like mist. You see, it is
Not wrong to have nothing. But
It is important that the latter be not just
The points of disappearance, signs of the
Reduction of the little that was left, which
Disappeared all the faster because it was so little.
This part of the game keeps you for old ostracism
Long mixed with wrinkles of that horrible, blatant day
To be avoided at all costs because already known
And perhaps even more because, unlike carelessness, avoidable.

That hole, towering secret, familiar
If one is poking among the evening rubbish, yet how
Square behind you in the mirror, so much authority
And intelligence in such a miserable result.
Could it bind you because of the simplicity
Or could you in fact escape because of that limp frame,
Those conditions tumbling upward, like piles of smoke?
In that way any disorderly result is often seen
As the result of the general's fixed smile, calipers,
Moustache, and the other way was closed too.

Out of this intolerant swarm of freedom as it
Is called in your press, the future, an open
Structure, is rising even now, to be invaded by the present
As the past stands to one side, dark and theoretical
Yet most important of all, for his midnight interpretation
Is suddenly clasped to you with the force of a hand
But a clear moonlight night in which distant
Masses are traced with parental concern.
After silent, colored storms the reply quickly
Wakens, has already begun its life, its past, just whole and sunny.

Thus reasoned the ancestor, and everything
Happened as he had foretold, but in a funny kind of way.
There was no telling whether the thought had unrolled
Down to the heap of pebbles and golden sand now
Only one step ahead, and itself both a trial and
The possibility of turning aside forever. It was the front page
Of today, looming as white as
The furthest mountains, and oh, all kinds of things
Caught in that net and shaken, so often
The way people respond to things.

It had grown up without anybody's
Thinking or doing anything about it, so that now
It was the point of where you wanted it to go.
The fathers asked that it be made permanent,
A vessel cleaving the dungeon of the waves.
All the details had been worked out
And the decks were clear for sensations
Of joy and defeat, not so closely worked in
As to demolish the possibility of the game's ever
Becoming dangerous again, or of an eventual meeting.

But it was not easy to tell in what direction
The permanence tended, whether it was
Easy decline, like swallows after the rough
Business of the long day, or eternal suspension
Over emptiness, dangerous perhaps, in any case
Not the peaceful cawing of which so much had been
Made. I can tell you all
About freedom that has turned into a painting;
The other is more difficult, though prompt—in fact
A little too prompt: therein lies the difficulty.

And still not satisfied with the elder
Version, to see the painting as pitch black

Was no cause for happiness among those who surround
The young, and had expected peevish
Fires lit by the setting sun, and sunken boats.
It seemed the only honorable way, and fertile
If darkness is ever anything else. But the way
Of that song was to be consumed, corrosive;
A surprise dragging the signs
Of no peace after it, into the disquiet of early accidents.

The head notwithstanding. A narrow strip of land
Coinciding with the riders to where
Illusion mattered no more than the rest. Flat
Walls only surrounding only abating memory.
On this new area ideas kept the same
Distance, with profiles spent into the sparse
Immediacy of excavation, land and gulls to be explored.
It was time to compare all past sets of impressions
Slowly peeling these away so that the mastered
Impression of servitude and barbarism might shrink to allegorical human
    width.

A moment of addition, then one hidden look
At it all, but it is scattered, not the outline
Of your famous openness, but kind of the sleeves
In the weather time after the doubtful present saluted.
All that ever came of it was words
To indicate any kind of barrier, with the land
Lasting beyond hope or scruple, both cell and vortex.
Further on it is a forest of mud pillars. Determined
To live, so that you and your possessions
May be dealt with at last, you forgot the other previous station.

If there was no truth in it, only pleasure
In the telling, might not others set out
Across impossible oceans with this word whose power

Was the opposite reverence to secret deities
Of shame? Or absent-mindedness? Because the first memory
Now, like patches, was worn, only as the inadequate
Memento of all that was never going to be? Its
Allusion not even blasphemous, but truly insignificant
Beside that lake opening out broader than the sun!
This, then, was indifference: it was what it always had been.

The boat stood hieratically still
On the unread page of water. No moon punching
With ideas of the majesty of crowds. A universal infamy
Became the element of living, a breath
Beyond telling, because forgetful of the
Chaos whose expectancy had engendered it, and so on, through
Popular speech down to the externals of present
Continuing—incomplete, good-natured pictures that
Flatter us even when forgotten with dwarf speculations
About the insane, invigorating whole they don't represent.

The victims were chosen through lightness in obscurity.
A firm look of the land, old dismissals
And the affair was concluded in snow and also in
The satisfaction of the outline formulated against the sky.
People were delighted getting up in the morning
With the density that for once seemed the promise
Of everything forgotten, and the well-being
Grew, at the expense of whoever lay dying
In a small room watched only by the progression
Of hours in the tight new agreement.

And they now too seem invaded, though before it was
The dancers who anticipated making unnecessary
The curtailment of one to the other. And yet,
As though this were strict premonition, their chance
Is cancelled out by earlier claims, a victim perhaps

Of its earnestness. The dance continues, but darker, and
As if in a sudden lack of air. And as one figure
Supplants another, and dies, so the postulate of each
Tires the shuffling floor with slogans, present
Complements mindful of our absorbing interest.

One swallow does not make a summer, but are
What's called an opposite: a whole of raveling discontent,
The sum of all that will ever be deciphered
On this side of that vast drop of water.
They let you sleep without pain, having all that
Not in the lesson, not in the special way of telling
But back to one side of life, not especially
Immune to it, in the secret of what goes on:
The words sung in the next room are unavoidable
But their passionate intelligence will be studied in you.

But what could I make of this? Glaze
Of many identical foreclosures wrested from
The operative hand, like a judgment but still
The atmosphere of seeing? That two people could
Collide in this dusk means that the time of
Shapelessly foraging had come undone: the space was
Magnificent and dry. On flat evenings
In the months ahead, she would remember that that
Anomaly had spoken to her, words like disjointed beaches
Brown under the advancing signs of the air.

AUTHOR'S NOTES

"The Double Dream of Spring" is the title of a painting by Giorgio de Chirico in the collection of The Museum of Modern Art, New York.

I am grateful to Mrs. Fritz Benedict of Aspen, Colorado, daughter of Arthur Cravan, for permission to publish a translation of the latter's poem, "Des Paroles."

The title "Sortes Vergilianae" refers to the ancient practice of fortune-telling by choosing a passage from Virgil's poetry at random.

THREE POEMS

FOR DAVID

The New Spirit

I thought that if I could put it all down, that would be one way. And next the thought came to me that to leave all out would be another, and truer, way.

   clean-washed sea

                                        The flowers were.

These are examples of leaving out. But, forget as we will, something soon comes to stand in their place. Not the truth, perhaps, but—yourself. It is you who made this, therefore you are true. But the truth has passed on

                                        to divide all.

Have I awakened? Or is this sleep again? Another form of sleep? There is no profile in the massed days ahead. They are impersonal as mountains whose tops are hidden in cloud. The middle of the journey, before the sands are reversed: a place of ideal quiet.

You are my calm world. This is my happiness. To stand, to go forward into it. The cost is enormous. Too much for one life.

There are some old photographs which show the event. It makes sense to stand there, passing. The people who are there—few, against this side of the air. They made a sign, were making a sign. Turning on yourself as a leaf, you miss the third and last chance. They don't suffer the way people do. True. But it is your last chance, this time, the last chance to escape the ball

of contradictions, that is heavier than gravity bringing all down to the level. And nothing be undone.

It is the law to think now. To think becomes the law, the dream of young and old alike moving together where the dark masses grow confused. We must drink the confusion, sample that other, concerted, dark effort that pushes not to the light, but toward a draft of dank, clammy air. We have broken through into the meaning of the tomb. But the act is still proposed, before us,

it needs pronouncing. To formulate oneself around this hollow, empty sphere . . . To be your breath as it is taken in and shoved out. Then, quietly, it would be as objects placed along the top of a wall: a battery jar, a rusted pulley, shapeless wooden boxes, an open can of axle grease, two lengths of pipe. . . . We see this moment from outside as within. There is no need to offer proof. It's funny. . . . The cold, external factors are inside us at last, growing in us for our improvement, asking nothing, not even a commemorative thought. And what about what was there before?

This is shaped in the new merging, like ancestral smiles, common memories, remembering just how the light stood on the water that time. But it is also something new. Outside, can't you hear it, the traffic, the trees, everything getting nearer. To end up with, inside each other, moving upward like penance. For the continual pilgrimage has not stopped. It is only that you are both moving at the same rate of speed and cannot apprehend the motion. Which carries you beyond, alarmingly fast out into the confusion where the river pours into the sea. That place that seems even farther from shore. . . .

There is nothing to be done, you must grow up, the outer rhythm more and more accelerate, past the ideal rhythm of the spheres that seemed to dictate you, that seemed the establishment of your seed and the conditions of its growing, upward, someday into leaves and fruition and final sap. For it is to be transcended. . . . The pace is softening now, we can see why it had to be. Our older relatives told of this. It happened a long time ago but it had to happen, which is why we are here now telling about it. If you thought you received more than your share, you could tell about that too. It was a free forum where each one came to cast off these irksome memories, strip down for the night that had preceded us to this place. Surely this was, also, a time of doing, not harvesting, for nothing was ripe, nothing had then been planted. . . . An active time, tense at the forehead and nostrils before sleep, pushing into the near piles of sticks and leaves and being gently nudged by them in return. A segment, more, of reality. This must be remembered too, it is even very important, but will the memory call itself to the point of being? For it is more tired than anything else. And so it slips away, like the face on a deflated balloon, shifted into wrinkles, permanent and matter-of-fact, though a perversion of itself.

Because life is short
We must remember to keep asking it the same question
Until the repeated question and the same silence become answer
In words broken open and pressed to the mouth
And the last silence reveal the lining
Until at last this thing exist separately
At all levels of the landscape and in the sky
And in the people who timidly inhabit it
The locked name for which is open, to dust and to no thoughts
Even of dying, the fuzzy first thought that gets started in you and then
    there's no stopping it.
It is so much debris of living, and as such cannot be transmitted
Into another, usable substance, but is irreducible
From these glares and stony silences and sharp-elbowed protests.
But it is your landscape, the proof that you are there,
To deal with or be lost in
In which the silent changes might occur.

It's just beginning. Now it's started to work again. The visitation, was it more or less over. No, it had not yet begun, except as a preparatory dream which seemed to have the rough texture of life, but which dwindled into starshine like all the unwanted memories. There was no holding on to it. But for that we ought to be glad, no one really needed it, yet it was not utterly worthless, it taught us the forms of this our present waking life, the manners of the unreachable. And its judgments, though harmless and playful, were yet the form of utterance by which judgment shall come to be known. For we judge not, lest we be judged, yet we are judged all the same, without noticing, until one day we wake up a different color, the color of the filter of the opinions and ideas everyone has ever entertained about us. And in this form we must prepare, now, to try to live.

It is not easy at first. There are dark vacancies the light of the hunter's moon does little to attenuate. Ever thought about the moon, how well it fits what it has to light? And those lacquer blobs and rivers of daylight, shaken out of a canister—so unmanageable, so indigestible . . . Well, isn't that the point? No, but there comes a time when what is to be revealed actually conceals itself in casting off the mask of its identity, when the identity itself is revealed as another mask, and a lesser one, antecedent to that we had come to know and accept. You think of clean legends, of this waking as penetrating a solid block of day. But day is there to assure you that you can't have this in another way, as you could with the films and shadows of night, to tell you that your mutually amused half-acceptance is not the wrong way to start, at any rate, that any breathing is to be breathing into each other, and imperfect, like all apprehended things.

Nevertheless the winter wears on and death follows death. I've tried it, and know how the narrowing-down feeling conflicts with the feeling of life's coming to a point, not a climax but a point. At that point one must, yes, be selective, but not selective in one's choices if you see what I mean. Not choose this or that because it pleases, merely to assume the idea of choosing, so that some things can be left behind. It doesn't matter which ones. I could tell you about some of the things I've discarded but that wouldn't help you because you must choose your own, or rather not choose them but let them be inflicted on and off you. This is the point of the narrowing-down process. And gradually, as the air gets thinner as you climb a mountain, these things will stand forth in a relief all their own—the look of belonging. It is a marvelous job to do, and it is enough just to approximate it. Things will do the rest. Only then will the point of not having everything become apparent, and it will flash on you with such dexterity and such terribleness that you will wonder how you lived before—as though a valley hundreds of miles in length and full of orchards and all sorts of benevolent irregularities of landscape were suddenly to open at your feet, just as you told yourself you could not climb a step higher. This casual, poorly seen new environment (but how gladly you are aware of imperfect vision, this time!)

is to be the new kind of arbitrariness for you, one that protects and promotes without ever leaving the time-inflicted lesions of the old, toward which you struggled so hard without knowing it. These are vanished with the saw-toothed anomalies of time itself, and an open, moist, impregnable order of the day—kind, generous and protective—surrounds you as the artless gestures of a beautiful girl surround her with nobility which may never be detected, the fountain of one's life. And one never need wish to see it, for its truth does not matter, and is unimaginable.

You were always a living
But a secret person
As much into life
Yet not wanting to "presume"
Was the insurance
That life churned thick in the after-feeling
And so, even more, a sign of what happens today,
The glad mess, the idea of striking out.

Such particulars you mouthed, all leading back into the underlying question: was it you? Do these things between people partake of themselves, or are they a subtler kind of translucent matter carrying each to a compromise distance painfully outside the rings of authority? For we never knew, never knew what joined us together. Perhaps only a congealing of closeness, deserving of no special notice. But then the eyes directing out, living into their material and in that way somehow making more substance than before, and yet the outward languid motion, like girls hanging out of windows . . . Is this something to be guessed at, though? Can it be identified with some area in someone's mind? The answer is yes, if it is experienced, and it has only to be expected to be lived, suspended in the air all around us. As I was going to say, this outward-hanging, ledge over the pitfalls of mankind, proves that it is something you know, not just as the tree is aware of its bark, but as something left with you on consignment. And it need not just be, it can grow, with you though not part of you, if you are willing to see it as reverting back to nature and not as the ultimate realization of Roman engineers, a stone T-square.

But how does this work? And yet you see yourself growing up around the other, posited life, afraid for its inertness and afraid for yourself, intimidated and defensive. And you lacerate yourself so as to say, These wounds are me. I cannot let you live your life this way, and at the same time I am slurped into it, falling on top of you and falling with you. At this point it is again time for forgetting, not casually so as to repeal it delightedly later on, but with a true generous instinct for ending it all. This is the only way in which new lives—not ours—can ever begin again. But the thought haunts me—will they be defined in terms of what we never were? Will the negative outlines of our never doing define their being, a repoussoir, and so enmesh themselves even more disastrously with their wanting to become? If that were the case it would be better to stop right here, in this room, only to continue breathing so that life might pursue its unwanted course, far from temptations of the future, yes that's it, so that in getting to know you I renounce any right to ulterior commemoration even in the unconscious dreams of those mythical and probably nonexistent beings of whose creation I shall never be aware. I'm sorry—in staring too long out over this elaborate view one begins to forget that one is looking inside, taking in the familiar interior which has always been there, reciting the only alphabet one knows. To escape in either direction is impossible outside the frost of a dream, and it is just this major enchantment that gave us life to begin with, life for each other. Therefore I hold you. But life holds us, and is unknowable.

They told this tale long ago
The legend of the children, in which they get closer
To the darkness, but go on living.
The motion of the story is moving though not

getting nearer.

They told this throughout all times, in all cities. The shape-filled foreground: what distractions for the imagination, incitements to the copyist, yet nobody has the leisure to examine it closely. But the thinness behind, the vague air: this captivates every spectator. All eyes are riveted to its slowly unfolding expansiveness; it is the magnanimity that creates this urge to emulate, like life, to grow, and it is the shapeless modest tale, told in the cottage at twilight. Progress to be born.

You know that emptiness that was the only way you could express a thing? The awkwardness around what were necessary topics of discussion, amounting to total silence on all the most important issues? This was our way of doing. Your body could formulate these things, projecting them into me, as though I had thought of them. Everything drops in before getting sorted out. This is our going now. I as I seem to you, you as you are to me, an endless game in which the abraded memories are replaced progressively by the new empty-headed forms of greeting. Even as I say this I seem to hear you and see you wishing me well, your eyes taking in some rapid lateral development

reading without comprehension

and always taken up on the reel of what is happening in the wings. Which becomes a medium through which we address one another, the independent life we were hoping to create. This is your eyes noting the passing of telephone poles and the tops of trees. A permanent medium in which we are lost, since becoming robs it of its potential. Nothing is to be learned, only avoided, nor can the truth of this be avoided, but it lingers on like microorganisms in the crevices. In you I fall apart, and outwardly am a single fragment, a puzzle to itself. But we must learn to live in others, no matter how abortive or unfriendly their cold, piecemeal renderings of us: they create us.

To you:

I could still put everything in and have it come out even, that is have it come out so you and I would be equal at the end of our lives, which would have been lived fully and without strain. But each of us has more of the vital elements than the other needs, or less: to sort them out would be almost impossible inasmuch as we are kept, each from the other: only the thawing nerve reveals it is time when one has broken out of some stupor or afternoon dream, and by then one is picking up for the evening, far from the famous task, close to the meaningless but real snippets that are today's doing. You understand we cannot casually borrow elements of each other so that it all comes out right. Force and mastery are required, they are ready in fact, but to use them deeply without excuses is a way of intermittent life, and the point was that the moments of awareness have to be continuous if they are to exist at all. Thus the sadness as I look out over all this and realize that I can never have any of it, even though I have it all as I in fact do. To be living, in each other, the perfect life but without happiness.

Well, this is what I get for all my plotting and precautions. But you, living free beyond me, are still to be reckoned into your own account of how it happens with you. I am afraid that you will never see your way clear through the velleities of the excursion to that other shore, eternal despite its finite nature, of acquisitions, suggestions and hints, useful, irregular: the exposed living that is going on, and of which you are a part, so that it could be said to exist only for you. You are too close to this happy state for it to matter for you. But meanwhile I am to include everything: the furniture of this room, everyday expressions, as well as my rarest thoughts and dreams, so that you may never become aware of the scattered nature of it, and meanwhile you *are* it all, and my efforts are really directed toward keeping myself attached, however dimly, to it as it rolls from view, like a river which is never really there because of moving on someplace. And so the denser moments of awareness are yours, not the firm outline I believe to be mine and which is probably a hoax as well: it contains nothing after all, only a few notions of how life should be lived that are unusable because too general. Nothing applies to your strict handling of how the roots should be lived, without caring about the flowers and leaves that may tower over them, a subsidiary mass, someday. Only the day-to-day implications matter for you. You are right, I suppose, but there was this image as it once came to me, of its brightness being together—not hanging together, for this implies waiting to be seen—but existing as smoke up around the bright levels of incidence and so on up into the sky, purified from being breathed in and alive from having lost life at last. Leaving rolls of experience and they happen further down too, are filling space up as they create more space.

Is it correct for me to use you to demonstrate all this? Perhaps what I am saying is that it is I the subject, recoiling from you at ever-increasing speed just so as to be able to say I exist in that safe vacuum I had managed to define from my friends' disinterested turning away. As if I were only a flower after all and not the map of the country in which it grows. There is more to be said about this,

I guess, but it does not seem to alter anything that I am the spectator, you what is apprehended, and as such we both have our own satisfying reality, even each to the other, though in the end it falls apart, falls to the ground and sinks in. For I care nothing about apparitions, neither do you, scrutinizing the air only to ask, "Is it giving?" but not so dependent on the answer as not to have our hopes and dreams, our very personal idea of how to live and go on living. It does not matter, then,

but there always comes a time when the spectator needs reassurance, to be touched on the arm so he can be sure he is not dreaming.

We were just the other night leafing through some old declarations, nostalgic for the first crisp rendering of the difference, like an outcry, the difference between what separated us and what we were now going to do. How like children in the way of thinking that some beatific scrap may always fall and as time goes by and *nothing* ever happens one is not disappointed but secretly pleased and confirmed in one's superstition: the magic world really does exist. Its dumbness is the proof of this. Indeed any sign of activity on its part would be cause for alarm, since it does not need us, need to signal its clarion certainties into our abashed, timid, half-make-believe commerce of every day. So we grew up confident, in ourselves and in each other, confident that we would one day meet, strip ourselves of the real business of believing, preparing to live in the all-too-short night. And now these attitudes which were merely sketched on the air of the room have hardened into the official likeness of what we were doing there, the life has gone out of our acts and into the attitudes. So that we must despair of all realism now, because it is there, it is totally adequate for what was being represented, only we cannot feel it as such, but that is our tough luck. Indeed—is this really the end toward which everything was rotating? We wanted it to come out all right, and in the end that is what has happened. Others are sorry about other things. And we have the success of our gradual, growing belief in the importance of the universe as it came through to us to keep us going. Even the fact that there is no joy written into the ending, unless relief is the same thing, ought to be a comfort because it was recognized in the timid fairy-tale beginning that the happy ending was an artifice and that the happiness would be artificial, though real. Is it then that we wanted the whole thing to misfire? to be caught off-base? or any of those myriad other expressions for failure that now come to mind? Is there something intrinsically satisfying about not having the object of one's wishes, about having miscalculated?

I can only say that the wind of the change as it has happened has numbed me, to the point where the false way and the true way are confounded, where there is no way or rather where everything is a way, none more suitable nor more accurate than the last, oblivion rapidly absorbing their outline like snow filling footprints. This despite the demonstrable rightness of the way we took, of our emergence into a reality that is perfect. Despite the satisfaction, endless as a sea.

You private person.

To every thing there is a season:
Today is cooler or warmer than yesterday, and it all works itself out into a map, projects, placed over the other real like a sheet of tracing paper, and these two simultaneously become what is going on. They can join, but never touch: such is the etiquette of knowing what you're doing, but they can get along in this way and progress can be noted. Your hair is fairer and your eyes are fairer. There can be no doubt you have outlived that early confusion and that now the outlines of a somewhat less perfunctory maturity have been laid down. Too, those other eyes and your fragmentary awareness of what they observed have tended to merge with your own as the focus was adjusted, and now the target—empty but with a rush of promise of fulfillment—lies under you, wonderful, the air you drink in in great gulps, laughing too.

It is not enough that these go hand in hand, what is wanted is some secret feeling of an administrator beyond the bounds of satisfying intimacy, a sort of intendant to whom the important tasks may be entrusted so as to leave you free for the very necessary task of idleness that is a condition, the condition, of your being, being together. This is not so easy. And already something like envy is lurking there, ready to destroy the whole solid but fragile mass with just a push too much. The whole structure must be subtracted from harm's way. It is better to take in a third person as a confidant, but since there is nothing to confide . . . But how much more prudent to have begun the whole thing in a different spirit, manfully, crossing each bridge as you came to it, flattening obstacles. . . . But there is no help for it and it must be remembered that the half-hearted, seemingly lazy way of moving forward is both the impetus and the nature of the work. It could have happened differently in no other world. And so tomorrow coming up is still a feast of expectation, is moving fast into the caves of your soul and this is the only way to have had the refreshment and the reward intact, in the midst of it all happening around you. There was no possibility of a bargain's being struck; it is offered this way and resumes its continuing in this way, in the clues to your personality. You have to take this as it opens up. There must be nothing resembling nostalgia for a past which in any case never existed. It is like standing up because you've been sitting all day and are tired of it.

However,
the honesty of this approach is eased, not softened, by its situation in the self-propagating wind. The wind is now fresh and full, with leaves and other things flying. And to release it from its condition of hardness you will have to take apart the notion of you so as to reconstruct it from an intimate knowledge of its inner workings. How harmless and even helpful the painted wooden components of the Juggernaut look scattered around the yard, patiently waiting to be reassembled! So ends the first lesson: that the concave being, enfolding like air or spirit, does not dissolve when breathed upon but comes apart neatly, like a watch, and the parts may be stocked or stored, their potential does not leak away through inactivity but remains bright and firm, so that in a sense it is just as much *there* as if it were put back together again and even more so: with everything sorted and labeled you can keep an eye on it a lot better than if it were again free to assume protean shapes and senses, the genie once more let out of the bottle, and who can say where all these vacant premises should end? No, it is far better to keep this potential dry, even at the risk of having its immobility come to seem a reproach, the mute appeal of the saber hung up on the wall. If you don't start, you don't have to stop. But it is moving, though not moving satisfactorily, so that the reproach would be unjust. Why, its imperfections are just a token of how life moves along, halt-

ingly but somehow always getting there in time, in our time. A cloak of somnolence, heavy and sticky as moonlight, translucent but imperfectly so (there are almost-transparent patches and parts that go under into darkness or some kind of unexplained activity—the whole is irregular, shifting, but up to its aim of clothing, concealing yet revealing) becomes the state of present affairs—one of erect passivity, polarized through hesitation and love, the odd details resolved but nesting in their quirkiness, free to come and go within a limited area, a sort of house-arrest of the free agent intentionally cut off from the forces of renewal, obliged to spend a certain penitential time of drawing in and not utilizing those intuitions that gave wings, inspirations to fly abruptly out of the windows of the house to the stars. If the truncated halves could find each other again, and so on, and then the ideal parts line up, their order into disorder, strong and vertical in the spring night, the circuit could become perfect again. But their unevenness is precisely the snag in the realization of that perfect irregular order. They must disappear into their odd angularity for a while, drift like the confetti they are until the appropriate carnival mood opens and they take fire like a haze of stars, ready to assume the light. In this scheme of things what is merely pleasant has to die to be born again as pleasure, and although it seems unfair this includes your outside view, openness, your penetrability and force to penetrate through outside agents that are merely the logical extensions of your inner decision to act and to bring this action to bear on the constellation of everyday phenomena. And so a new you takes shape. You can stand it at first. If the beloved were an angel, then this you would be the nameless spirit that watches from afar, halfway between heaven's celestial light and dull Acheron. But it is not necessary to sanctify the gods in order to live in the suddenly vast surroundings that open out among your features like pools of quicksilver: hours that seem like minutes, invitations to spend time with strangers in unknown places, no more disappointing orgasms, intentional symbols, gestures a time's stand away, no more of the group's reluctance to fully celebrate anything new. Yet there is a narrowness too in this expansion that eternal waiting slops over into, helplessly, in which you see yourself as momentarily absorbed in some commonplace occupation, but then the late afternoon gushes in to support you, prop you up triumphantly in the narrow sector that forethought and carelessness combined have brought you to, monarch of all you survey and there is nothing mean or squalid in being deprived, the space is aerated, and just as the days get whittled down to more and more darkness at the end of the year without one's wishing to be back at midsummer, for this is somehow a higher ledge though a narrower and bleaker one, so time running out does not make this position less worthy or any of the individual instants of light darker. As in a novel the unmistakable truth of your character comes crashing through, having come to mean what it had been called on for, and meanwhile the tale itself, a bundle of incidents related to but separate and distinct from you, got up and did a dance and left. If a subconscious grievance persisted, a dream in which you try to catch up to me in the street, still with the same features, the glassy limpidity that both receives and projects the aura in which we bloomed and later shriveled (how could we know, any more than those insects whose life-span is a single day?), it is there only because it is natural, because "the public" expects it, to add in its own way a note of dignity to this wholesome, tear-jerking ending that is both a completion and the firm promise of a new beginning, first the ball of string as the kite jerks it across the field and then its shadow, fainter and fainter, with the idea of its all being continued somewhere, in some more fortunate time and place, but really: it's not a fairy tale, this time. It wasn't so as to play real characters in an age-old fantasy that we were combined: there is very little romanesque element, more the ugliness of waiting and the obscenities we think and speak, this is more like it, and somehow they give dignity and immobility to us in relation to one another. There are projections as we come to consider ourselves, but no vulgar forced entry or forced turning away: we remain separate forever, and this confers an admittedly somewhat wistful beauty on the polarity that is our firm contact and uneven stage of development at this moment which threatens to be the last, unless the bottle with the genie squealing inside be again miraculously stumbled on, or a roc, its abrasive eye scouring the endless expanses of the plateau, appear at first like a black dot in the distance that little by little gets larger, beating its wings in purposeful and level flight. I urge you one last time to reconsider. You can feel the wind in the room, the curtains are moving in the draft and a door slowly closes. Think of what it must be outside. Since time will in any case be reckoned into the final addition, it is not as though you need concern yourself. This is always taken care of. The whole thing is calibrated according to time's way of walking sideways out of the event, at the same time proceeding in a straight line toward an actual vanishing point. Already it has moved us, toward and away from each other, farther than we expected: the everyday glamor of a "personal life," keeping a diary and so forth, is the outward sign of this progression that is built into us like the chain of breathing. So there is no need to wait to be transformed: you are already. I am aware of it because I see you like a star, that mild, friendly and warming presence so many trillion miles away, and this suits me because I would have you only in this way: as you are, as you are to me. Therefore the major turn—third and last fateful step in the triad, already moving into something else—cannot be postponed, therefore there is no need to anticipate it, and it would be impossible to do this. But I know that my reasoning falls on the ear like "special" pleading, it too is in due season, and though all I really want to do is to call attention to principles, it is part of growing up to accept this new projection forward, and therefore we are to travel abreast, twin riders dazzled and disintegrating under the kaleidoscopic performance of the night sky this time, we too projected sideways in advancing like waves pushed away from the keel of a ship, rejoining in this way the secret of the movement forward that made possible this full-circle absorption of the voyage and its brilliant phenomena—each distinct and, however modest, of a certain importance in the hierarchy. Nevertheless storms do occur. It would be inconceivable for the progression to pursue its course unmolested, since it is a progression, for it not to be narrowed down to that single moment of grabbing you and shaking you mercilessly, nor that this moment become the practical meaning of the pattern of events, thus to be terminated "sadder and wiser," drawing the rueful lesson from experience, and yet it was an accident, wasn't it? Not just the part where everything went haywire but the whole thing, a series of accidents complete in themselves and as components fitting into one big accident? There would be nothing very encouraging about this either except that our shared apprehending of the course as plotted turns it into a way, something like an old country road. We can stop, we have stopped, we are stopping now, turning to look into the fulfillment that each unconsciously exhibits to the other, without wanting to especially or knowing too much about it. This possibility of fulfillment creates the appetite for itself, with the result that the dislocations come through to us as romantic episodes or chapters: "There's the one in which I fell away gradually, without even realizing it until we were already far apart, separated by new habits and preoccupations that had arisen even as we sat close to each other, talking about the weather and so on." To have the whole outline in mind yet not notice the individual changes as they occur, and then one day it dawns on you that you are the change, so naturally you could have seen it coming. A subtle corrosion has taken over this branching out, on a higher plane because the totality of its gradations had been breathed into the start, yet sinking deeper than that other that is cast aside because, whatever you might say of it, in the pattern of base voluptuousness it was perfect, a luminary, and things that are perfect of their kind are better than the flawed, interrupted spiral of that other narration whose purpose was to instruct and entertain, but which succeeded in doing neither because it was too turned in upon itself, and therefore suffered a shameful destiny, a chariot going down kicking and struggling at the first brush with the sun's deleterious rays. Quick thinking on your part saved us from such a melodramatic end, though: you merely restored the dimension of the exploratory dialogue, conducted in the general interest, and we resumed our roles of progressive thinkers and builders of the art of love. Not that such a thing could exist, or if it did it would certainly not be anything like an art, which can only exist by coming into existence, and then the rules may be drawn up, though it makes very little difference since no one will ever play that game again. It lay there in our already clouded vision as we looked at each other, some dark beginning force that made it clear that the time for action was past and the time for making speeches had come. So, somewhat stimulated at the idea of not turning back but going forward, making virtue of necessity, no doubt, we proceeded to actually examine what there was left for us. Not really, of course, but we could feel it as one feels the temperature dropping even though one senses only separate instances and not the movement of the fall. It was waiting for us: the sense that we must now put our ideas together and use them as steps for attaining some kind of rational beauty within the limits of possibility, that would not offend everyday experience, even of the coarsest or most monotonous kind. A prison, in sum, but disguised as a school, built on the false premise of education, that the boredom now would necessarily result in some ultimate note of improvement, though nothing resembling that magnificent but empty structure we had started to build incorrectly and had even begun to get used to despite its having remained largely at the blueprint stage. This was hell or worse, since there was no disproportion, no juxtapositions to distract, nothing but the day-to-day growth without change, no kind of manner in the sullen sunlight that trickled in, illuminating everything equally: a moral universe which the present had transcended but which was able to reassert its authority during the confusion that followed on its inevitable downfall and had now emerged stronger than before: strong as iron. In the very act of contemplating such a state of affairs prior to rejecting it one is caught up on the wheel, there is no alternative, and one finds oneself liking oneself and whatever it is quite as much as ever, more in fact now that a sure sense of purpose implements the drive into a definite thingness, virtue still from necessity, mother of invention, but its own reward. Remnants of the old atrocity subsist, but they are converted into ingenious shifts in scenery, a sort of "English garden" effect, to give the required air of naturalness, pathos and hope. Are you sad about something today? On days like this the old flanking motion almost seems to be possible again. Certainly the whiff of nostalgia in the air is more than a hint, a glaring proof that the old irregular way of doing is not only some piece of furniture of the memory but is ours, if we had the initiative to use it. I have lost mine. It has been replaced by a strange kind of happiness within the limitations. The way is narrow but it is not hard, it seems almost to propel or push one along. One gets the narrowness into one's seeing, which also seems an inducement to moving forward into what one has already caught a glimpse of and which quickly becomes vision, in the visionary sense, except that in place of the panorama that used to be our customary setting and which we never made much use of, a limited but infinitely free space has established itself, useful as everyday life but transfigured so that its signs of wear no longer appear as a reproach but as indications of how beautiful a thing must have been to have been so much prized, and its noble aspect which must have been irksome before has now become interesting, you are fascinated and keep on studying it. We have broken through into the consequences of the grey, sagging flesh that was our due, and it is surface enchantment, healing to the eye and to the touch. But there is no celebration of sensuality—there never could be, now—only of its counterpart, a temporary dignity for the mind, and waiting, that is satisfying anyway because it is a kind of a way of being, any old kind but belonging to itself, in and of itself and our-

324

selves. The "luxury" of details that coagulated into the old sad excitement told us so little, really: at most the secret of choosing the most significant ones to be put together into something to play that takes up time, a scansion of that tough anxiety, ordering without analyzing it. The rewards and punishments remain the same, each accepted in a spirit of weary gratitude regardless of its nature. Take them away and the lived space will not have altered, but will have drawn enough initiative from the drop in tension produced by the sudden removal of competition to expand its spark into a glow, suffusing but not illuminating it, and the mind's suburbs too are suddenly infected with the new spirit, commenting on it in their accustomed lilting or droning vernacular; in some cases it will take the form of clumsy removal of the barriers by force—a slow but probably useful process; in others, getting used to inhabiting the ruins and artfully adapting them to present needs; in still others, standing up in the space certain that it is the right one, and feeling the sense of its proportions leave your mind like rays, striking out to the antipodes and polishing them, perfecting them through use. One can then go about one's business unencumbered by nostalgia but still feeling the habit of this place where one has accomplished things before; it will change and you will go on thinking about it to your mutual satisfaction and joy. The fact that you did all this—cleared away all the debris so that the created vacuum would expel you forward into an exact set of conditions replying to exact demands—fertilizes each instant as it is born, increases and dies, spontaneously generating the light that flushes through the silver-outlined mask of your face—baleful silver and black, the enchanter's colors—so that the lines gradually become invisible and disappear in the total modest radiance that builds up on its surface and finally blends with the ordinary daylight outside. And gradually the whirring and catcalls, rumbles and high-pitched screeches, the daily turnips and radishes, the *Kraut und Rüben* take over and are as if they had never ceased to be. I alone know that you were here before, even though nothing here any longer bears your imprint.

The problem becomes more definite. Smiling as though for the photographer, pleased to be here since it was promised you and has now made up for the lag in getting around to you, you overlap once again with the one that thought you, sent you speeding like an arrow into this pleasant desert where everything happens agreeably at a sign from you, in which you are still solitary despite the magnanimous currents in the air around you like a humming of wings. Safe, out in the open, and ready to start again,

only this time toward no special goal, its sense having become generalized in the environment, so that you are already part of it, a little, as you prepare to try to fathom its warpless and woofless subtleties. But it is hard, this not knowing which direction to take, only knowing that you are moving in one, not because no rest was decreed for you but because the force that shot you here remains through inertia, and even while contemplating the globe of seeming contradictions that grow out of your present standing you have begun to evolve in that other direction not included by the archer, a present time draped backward over the past, the appetites no longer chided, full in the expectation of becoming belief but just as surely periled by the negative of premature ripeness that haunts the joyous wilderness like the shadow of the grave.

At a sign from you these spirits could be set free from their tunnels in the earth to complete the circle of the act which you would have begun in this way, giving ideas to local deities of place and river gods to whom it might never have occurred otherwise that they might break open the one physical act they know and reveal the kernel like a picture that is taking place before them in order to proceed definitely into the future, sweeping aside all ifs and buts at the stately pace of a caravan disappearing into an undivided somewhere, all its secrets locked, swaying with the progressive movement toward and away from. But what is needed is some act other than pressing a button and having it all happen, some way of living into the layers as they occur and not losing momentum in order to strike,

except that in your night no knowledge can be present without your knowing it, and hence can never inflict itself on anything else. The various segments of knowledge are by definition divided up and distributed in an equilibrium guaranteed by the nature of their existence, yet it can all be grasped and used quite handily when an occasion presents itself. In among the trees that occasion may be growing, be ready to pounce on it holding the muzzle to its temple as the veins bulge, but there is a sickness built into this act of moving: it can never take place, only approach a buffer area where negotiations may be undertaken; in this way it prepares its own downfall while never quite beginning.

There is probably more than one way of proceeding but of course you want only the one way that is denied you, the leaves over that barrier will never turn the sorrowful agate hue of the rest but only burnish perpetually in a colorless, livid explosion that is a chant of praise for your having remained behind to think rather than act. Meditation rains down on you to be sucked up in turn by the sun like steam, making it all the more difficult to know where the branching out should occur. It is like approaching a river at night, uncertain of the direction of the current. But the pulsating of it leads to further certainties because, bouncing off the vortexes to be joined, the cyclical force succeeds in defining its negative outline. For the moment uncertainty is banished at the same time that growing is introduced almost surreptitiously, under the guise of an invitation to learn all about these multiple phenomena which are our being here, since a knowledge of them is after all vital to our survival in this place of provocative but baffling commonplace events.

What was it we said to each other? We must have spoken to each other many times, but of these only the trace of the words remains, and the expressions of your face and your body

as you spoke or listened. Perhaps they are the most important after all, like a writer's style. But now only the sound of the truth as it is broken off from your mouth can kindle this apathetic valley that wants nothing better than to lapse back into the scenery of its dull vegetation. It wants to surround, because this way you will accept yourself as being here, in a place, any place, content to make the rounds you know so well, the philosopher's daily walk that the neighbors set their watches by.

You could then ignore the equal but opposed forces again building up in you, though not forever since their paths are not quite parallel and must eventually join in conflict, a tormented sphere of cloud you carry in you like a blind lantern. For the time being you can go on pretending that it is enough to listen to those inner promptings, the voice of the soul, until that fatal day when the look of the beloved flashes on you with its intensity of fixed lightning. That day you will realize that just having a soul was not enough: you must yield it up, vanish into the oblivion prepared for you by your years of waiting that all your practice of stoicism was not enough to seal off. And you know at last the condition of weightlessness and everything it implies: for the future, the present and most of all for the past into which you now slip helplessly, no longer prevented by the grid of everyday language, remaining in suspension in that greenish aquarium light which is your new element, compelled to re-enact the same scene in the old park, with snow on the ground and the waiting look on the faces of the nearest buildings, some distance away. All this in the interests of getting at the truth.

Little by little
You are the mascot of that time
You have your own life too
But are circumscribed by the time's growing concern
So that your activities are diminished
Or simplified, like a dog's.

Yet it was almost enough to be growing up in that city.
The taste of it, rationed through a medicine dropper,
Filled up the day.
In the evening the newspaper was delivered, ready to be read.
Darkness glossed over the imbalances
And the last irregularities dissolved in sleep.
That metropolis was like the kitchen of the world
And we were like servants, setting out on the task of life
As on a tour of duty.

In summer our desires crossed
And were gradually veiled by foliage
Into a solid, bluish shadow
Yet one was aware of the living structure underneath
And sensed its pulsations at a distance
Imbibing the love as was meant

For it must be consumed
As surely as the appetite dies on the lips
And the guests move away in a chain.

So this meaning came to arise
Towering above the rest
With a place for each member of the family
And further up in the hierarchy
For every thought and feeling that had passed or would come to pass
In the finite universe defined by flocks of birds.
Simultaneously it was penetrable
And was being saturated by the direction of the journey we must take
Since it is before us helplessly waiting:
It must exist once the idea of it exists.
And so the meaning is brought down
To be with us together, never the same again.
We have passed through.

The aftermath of sunny days was a period so much like the first, newly joined-
together one that one might have mistaken it for part of an alternating pattern
of planned growth if the signal hadn't been given right away in the form of a
kind of fanfare of lucky accidents that drained the succeeding weeks of any
suspense. There could be no doubt now that this continuing was merely an-
other stone added to the haphazard masonry of assorted beliefs that was far
from threatening to shut out the sun. And afterward as the calm illumination
persisted one could even go back to believing that this was the miracle, just as
it had been in the past. Oh, nothing so very miraculous, just a feeling of being
installed, as in a ship while it still rides at anchor on the bay, of having been led
to the starting point and then proceeding a short distance, enough to erase any
serious doubts about the nature of the rest of the trajectory. And yet it wasn't
the same, since I was a very different person by now and even recognized it.
For starting out, even just a very few steps, completely changes the nature of
the journey as it was when it lay intact and folded. That first step ignites the
endless cycle of rising and falling; it is born; and one is aware of the still-invis-
ible future as of a sudden pause in the conversation that one could have pre-

dicted but didn't: sure enough, it's twenty minutes to the hour or twenty minutes past, you say, and they all smile, thinking obscurely of how this pause might have been scheduled and where it has brought us. The days are getting shorter, in fact quite a lot shorter. And suddenly you have been occupied for some time with unlearning their rhythm, drawing sleep about you like a blanket, but the dotted rhythms persist and waking is somehow divided up among them. You forget the salty and slightly bitter taste of those morning dreams whose aim was both to mislead and instruct. For a while they can be put away and it is as though they disappear, and, faced with your satisfaction at being awake and free, you admit that there never was a day like this for getting things done, and action pursues its peaceful advance on the lethargic, malarial badlands of the day, draining swamps, clearing scrub forests, putting the hygienic torch to the villages, planting ground cover crops such as clover, alfalfa, colza, buckwheat and cowpeas. This is so. Yet there are other books, stories of how it might happen: merely to imagine them is enough to set one's head spinning, and swearing never to open any of them does no good of course, it sets the hydra in furious motion, pullulating beyond the limits of the imagination. But to have one person's affirmation of the way it happens for him . . . Yes, but you do not know this person.

He exists, but he is as a stranger for you in your own home. Just his being there beside you makes him a stranger because you can't tell how he got there. Nor can he, or at least he never seems to feel the urge to do so. So you are left with your blurred version slipping into mindlessness, but somehow merely being forced to focus on it brings it back, just for a while, but long enough to remind you that this happened before, and so on until a new occurrence important enough to eclipse all procedural questions and even to join you both in your singularity, reflecting each other's concerns for the first time and at the same moment seeing them vanish like Rumpelstiltskin, furious that you guessed the name.

At this point an event of such glamor and such radiance occurred that you forgot the name all over again. It could be compared to arriving in an unknown city at night, intoxicated by the strange lighting and the ambiguities of the streets. The person sitting next to you turned to you, her voice broke and a kind of golden exuberance flooded over you just as you were lifting your arm to the luggage rack. At once the weight of the other years and above all the weight of distinguishing among them slipped away. You found yourself not wanting to care. Everything was guaranteed, it always had been, there would be no future, no end, no development except this steady wavering like a breeze that gently lifted the tired curtains day had let fall. And all the possibilities of civilization, such as travel, study, gastronomy, sexual fulfillment—these no longer lay around on the cankered earth like reproaches, hideous in their reminder of what never could be, but were possibilities that had always existed, had been created just for both of us to bring us to the summit of the dark way we had been traveling without ever expecting to find it ending. Indeed, without them nothing could have happened. Which is why the intervening space now came to advance toward us separately, a wave of music which we were, unable to grasp it as it unfolded but living it. That space was transfigured as though by hundreds and hundreds of tiny points of light like flares seen from a distance, gradually merging into one wall of even radiance like the sum of all their possible positions, plotted by coordinates, yet open to the movements and suggestions of this new life of action without development, a fixed flame.

It was only much later that the qualities of the incandescent period became apparent, and by then it had been dead for many years. But in recalling itself it assumed its first real life. That time was for living without the reflection that gives things and objects a certain relief, or weight; one drank the rapture of un-lived moments and it blinded one to how it looked from outside, and—well, that is what would have been necessary to give it the illusion of duration that would have rounded out those other essential qualities and given them a reason to live for each other. Otherwise their intensity evaporates from sheer effervescence, leaving you pleasantly dazed and sleepy—that feeling that comes after all great periods in history, whose isolation is such that they seem to promise more than even possibilities can give.

Behind this weather of indifference is of course a concern for the real qualities that inform our continuing to see each other about a lot of things. Luckily they are already there, maybe they are what it is all about, though probably we tend to overesteem them because we had to dig them out of the earth and clean them off and shine them up. But they offer a pretext for looking into ourselves, examining the achievements of that easy time when an invisible agency caused the meals to appear smoking hot on the table, and afterward you could take home the gold and silver dishes on condition that everything next day would have assumed its slightly guilty air of naturalness, for sheepishness and a little feigned stumbling were always the note by which regular progression could be recognized and furthered in secret, and its achievements, through exercising those atrophied muscles of content and disbelief, had readied them for new accomplishments next to which those of the lunar phase would pale. It's true that a lot of grumbling had to accompany this and even an occasional bursting into tears, but that is the cost that reality, as opposed to naturalness, exacts. The wheels, constantly getting mired, have to presage a complete breakdown which must even occur over and over again in order to lead back to the quiet but superior normalities of life in eternity. What have we done? We cannot see through each other, the way is closed. Each has to go his own separate way, comforted only by the thought that it could never have been otherwise, and that this way as we understood it was the true one, leading to pitfalls of self-defiance and to our ultimate downfall as individuals with a concern for each other and for the welfare of the group.

The change is not complete.
The new morals have altered the original data
Which have again outstripped the message deduced from them.
The phenomena have not changed
But a new way of being seen convinces them they have.
We must live in the way of their gradually getting out of date
In order to plot the new change at the risk of predicting it this time.
Hence, diminished strength from paying too close attention to the curve of
    events,
Trying to imagine in advance what we were never intended to know
Even as children, when knowledge was free.

And things decay into the pit left for them
By that greater happening as it is imagined:
Shorn of duration.

Just to be aware of the discrepancy isn't enough:
Knowledge does not make us happy.
It ought to be enough since
We sat to receive it
Passive and mutually shy
But this was the way we had chosen,
The way that leads to understanding.

Condemned to stand still
We now understood what had happened, not actively,
Which would have been to live again, but we understood it
As motionless, having no live projection
Beyond the fact of the words in which it was written down
And these took on special meanings,
Rigid, but beautiful, like a stained-glass window
As the light begins to improve and sharpen it
Until finally we had grown up in that region without ever having left it.
Still, it was possible to imagine everything that existed elsewhere.

We were ideally happy. We had reached that stage in our perennial evolution where holy thoughts no longer exist and one can speak one's mind freely, and the night shot back an answering fragrance: too far to the stars, but it was here in its intimacy that wraps you in permissiveness, leaving you free as it wanes to learn more about your special thoughts or any ideas you might have. It is never too late to mend. When one is in one's late thirties, ordinary things—like a pebble or a glass of water—take on an expressive sheen. One wants to know more about them, and one is in turn lived by them. Young people might not envy this kind of situation, perhaps rightly so, yet there is now interleaving the pages of suffering and indifference to suffering a prismatic space that cannot be seen, merely felt as the result of an angularity that must have existed from earliest times and is only now succeeding in making its presence felt through the mists of helpless acceptance of everything else projected on our miserable, dank span of days. One is aware of it as an open field of narrative possibilities. Not in the edifying sense of the tales of the past that we are still (however) chained to, but as stories that tell only of themselves, so that one realizes one's

self has dwindled and now at last vanished in the diamond light of pure spec-
ulation. Collar up, you are lighter than air. The only slightly damaged bundle
of receptive nerves is humming again, receiving the colorless emanations from
outer space and dispatching dense, precisely worded messages. There is room
to move around in it, which is all that matters. The pain that drained the blood
from your cheeks when you were young and turned you into a whitened spec-
ter before your time is converted back into a source of energy that peoples this
new world of perceived phenomena with wonder. You wish you could shake
hands with your lovers and enemies, forgive and love them, but they too are
occupied as you are, though they greet you with friendly, half-distracted smiles
and nods. The Hermit has passed on, slowly and haltingly, the light streaming
from under his cloak, and in his place the Hanged Man points his toe at the
stars, at ease at last in comfortably assuming that age-old attitude of sacrifice;
the gold coins slither out of his pockets and fall to earth which they fertilize
with many ideas, some harebrained, others daringly original. In the sky a note
of fashionable melancholy has begun to prevail: it is the quick-witted devotion
of Sagittarius, the healer, caustic but kind, sweeping away the cobwebs of intu-
itive idealism that still lingered here and there in pockets of darkness. The
Archer takes careful aim, his arrow flies to the nearest card, the Five of Cups:
"Trouble from a loved one. Trouble introduced into the midst of an already re-
alized state. Amorous dangers. Perils through a woman." And also rectitude,
for the aim was just. From the tiny trickle of blood from the wounded card a
green stain grows; soon leaves shoot up and then tiny white odorless flowers,
the promise of what still remains to be fulfilled. But of course since this was no
shot in the dark it is an already realized state in its potential. The note is struck,
the development of its resonances ready to snap into place. For the moment we
know nothing more than this.

But the light continues to grow, the eternal disarray of sunrise, and one can
now distinguish certain shapes such as haystacks and a clocktower. So it was
true, everything was holding its breath because a surprise was on the way. It
has already installed itself and begun to give orders: workmen are struggling to
raise the main pole that supports the tent while over there others are watering
the elephants, dressing down the horses; one is pretending to box with a tame
bear. Everything is being lifted or locked into place all over the vast plain,

without fuss or worry it slowly nears completion thanks to exceptional team-work on the part of the crew of roustabouts and saltimbanques whose job this was anyway, and whose ardor need never have excited any jealousy on your part: they are being paid, after all. And one moves closer, drawn first by the aura of the spectacle, to come to examine the merit of its individual parts so as to enjoy even more connecting them up to the whole.

All this happened in April as the sun was entering the house of Aries, the Ram, the agent of Mars and fire and the first of the twelve signs of the Zodiac, bringing a spirit of reconciliation and amnesty amid the wars and horror that choked the earth; a feeling of sacrifice too and bloodletting in the annual per-formance of the rites of spring. The pure in heart rejoiced for they were sure now that something terrific was going to happen. And as a matter of fact in places all over the earth where the ephemeral sexing was going on, the indiffer-ent glances of adolescents scarcely accosted their elders, who were themselves too caught up in the excitement of the eternal tragedy to pay much mind. The Ram is imbued with tremendous force which can easily turn into shouted ob-scenities if he doesn't get his way, as sometimes happens. He wants to go it alone, but at this time of year the populations emerge again into the arena of life after the death of winter, and one is newly conscious of the multitudes that swarm past one in the street; there is something of death here too in the way they plunge past toward some unknown destination, leaving one a little shaken up on the edge of the sidewalk. Who are all these people? What does it mean that there are so many? Is it possible that the desires of one might not conflict with the desires of all the others, and vice versa, or is it precisely this imbroglio of defeated desires that is coming up now, a sort of Thirty Years' War of the human will, terrible in its destructive surging that threatens to completely an-nihilate the life which it so ebulliently manifests? One stays like this on the edge of the throng, trying to think these things out. It may become necessary to shut them all out, with the light of the sun and the other planets, to retreat again into the hard, dark recesses of yourself where you know no comfort is to be found, but which are preferable nevertheless to this perilous position on the edge of the flood, looking down awestruck into the coiling waters that some-times strike out and ensnare a parcel of land that had seemed secure. Surely there are things to be thought out, for the renewal of life poses terrible problems, no matter how fortunate in the context. At last there is the sense of destiny, the one thing that never could have happened, but even as its word fills your mouth you realize the terrible things that are left unsaid: what happens after that?

Something *is* happening. The new casualness had been introducing itself, casually of course, but suddenly its credentials lay everywhere. It was a new time of being born, looking ahead almost fiercely enough to be the ripe ear, and still keeping discreetly in the early stage of noncommittal promises. It wasn't the lily-pad stage yet, but there was buzzing everywhere as though the news had already broken out and was flooding the city and the whole country. The next day he rose up from that bed of reflective voluptuousness, determined never again to fall into the richly human excesses that his horizontal state had left him vulnerable to, having decided to grant a personal interview to each member of the enemy that blackened the plain as far as one could see in all directions. And the rumor strengthened with the night. In the morning they had all vanished at least as far as the nearest mountains and probably from the face of the earth.

Meanwhile he had taken the universal emotional crisis on his own shoulders, not from altruism but through a mistaken notion that things could be no other way, that riches would automatically result from the world's following its preordained course. And alas, to be releasing the prey for the shadow at this late date was, no doubt, to fall in with the plans of the cosmos, but how faintly it echoed, how pallid the evening glare that was supposed to strike fear into the hearts of nations! There was no getting around it, the Moon had triumphed easily once again, Hecate and her brood of snarling mutts were always around messing up the place, and in the meantime the crayfish had glided unnoticed out of the water and begun its upward course, drawn by some baffling magnetism toward its mother, the moon, who places everything in a false and puzzling light from which a fraction of the truth is not altogether absent, for the moon does illuminate, though erratically.

Thus summed up, he felt sickened at the wholeness. Better it should evaporate into the almost palpable clouds of the night than sit around as a reproach for all that was never going to be, now, since it included everything. Begone! But the solid block just sat there. Little by little its mass began to grow transparent, like clouds just before dawn. It was noticed that this transparency was the same as emptiness. There were no further alterations, none being necessary. Men went about their business as they had before, a little more disenchanted perhaps, but on the whole not unhappy; there was a lot of life to look forward to and a whole new assortment of celestial phenomena as well. But the one of whom this is written remained motionless. Anguish had pierced his soul, like the lead point of an arrowhead. Everything had stopped for him. There were no new stories. Nobody invented things for him any more. He tried to remember what it had been like before everything had been canceled out, before the great Common Denominator had proved beyond the shadow of a doubt that $ax^2 = ay^2$, but the difference between now and the other hard times was that now there was no comfort in remembering scenes of past unhappiness, indeed he was quite sure there had never been any, and was therefore quite content to remain as he had been, staring uncertainly into the fire as though looking for a sign, a portent, but in reality thinking of nothing at all.

It is very early.
The heavens only seem to be in a state of ferment.
If one might choose to see them differently there would be
Peace at the outer fringes
For their reluctance is never far away
And harmony, by the same token, is never ruled out completely.

One can accomplish the thing quite quickly
And turn toward the ruled outside space
That defines our hesitations so majestically
Though negatively.

It is necessary to go forward completing
The gesture from the beginning of life
That was worrying its shape into the trees
All this time, as though that shape were responsible
For the many fluctuating situations that fill the air.

Ultimately only one continuous bell sound
Exemplifies the crowding around of
All the things that need getting done.
They fall away like memories of the seasons.

There is no staying here
Except a pause for breath on the peak
That night fences in
As though the spark might not be extinguished.

He thought he had never seen anything quite so beautiful as that crystalliza-
tion into a mountain of statistics: out of the rapid movement to and fro that
abraded individual personalities into a channel of possibilities, remote from
each other and even remoter from the eye that tried to contain them: out of
that river of humanity comprised of individuals each no better than he should
be and doubtless more solicitous of his own personal welfare than of the gen-
eral good, a tonal quality detached itself that partook of the motley intense
hues of the whole gathering but yet remained itself, firm and all-inclusive,
scrupulously fixed equidistant between earth and heaven, as far above the tall-
est point on the earth's surface as it was beneath the lowest outcropping of cu-
mulus in the cornflower-blue empyrean. Thus everything and everybody were
included after all, and any thought that might ever be entertained about them;
the irritating drawbacks each possessed along with certain good qualities were
dissolved in the enthusiasm of the whole, yet individuality was not lost for all
that, but persisted in the definition of the urge to proceed higher and further as
well as in the counter-urge to amalgamate into the broadest and widest kind of
uniform continuum. The effect was as magnificent as it was unexpected, not
even beyond his wildest dreams since he had never had any, content as he had
been to let the process reason itself out. "You born today," he could not resist
murmuring although there was no one within earshot, "a life of incredulity and
magnanimity opens out around you, incredulity at the greatness of your de-
signs and magnanimity that turns back to support these projects as they flag
and fail, as inevitably happens. But draw comfort meanwhile from the fact that
the planets have congregated to haruspicate at your birth; they can no longer
disentangle themselves but are fixed over you, showering down material and

immaterial advantages on whoever has the patience to remain immobile for a while, mindless of the efforts of his coevals to better themselves at the expense of humankind in general." Nothing appeared to give ear to these rantings and again light sank quickly into the low-lying mountains on the horizon like water into pumice stone, as night again erected with exact brilliance the very configurations he had been invoking, so that it might have seemed a sardonic construction put upon his words to anyone who had been there to notice. But the whole of mankind lay stupefied in dreams of toil and drudgery; their miserable condition offered no chance to glimpse how things were proceeding, no inkling that the fatal hour of liberation was advancing swiftly on measured and silent steps.

One day the thought occurred to him that it was still early, if you were to judge by how few events had actually taken place and how many others seemed to be waiting around half-prepared to come into existence if the demand arose. It wasn't that any of the previous forms of life he had taken: the animalistic one, the aristocratic one in which sex and knowledge fitted together to screen out the intriguing darkness, or the others in which idealism—child-love or sibling-love—gradually twisted the earth's barrenness into a sense from which both libertinage and liberty in its highest, most intellectual sense were subtly excluded, culminating in the (for him) highest form of love, which recognizes only its own generosity—it was not that these seemed no longer viable, stages in a progression whose end is still unseen and unimaginable. They had not merely served their purpose but were the purpose—what population is to the world, that explains as it uses it. But it dawned on him all of a sudden that there was another way, that this horrible vision of the completed Tower of Babel, flushed in the sunset as the last ceramic brick was triumphantly fitted into place, perfect in its vulgarity, an eternal reminder of the advantages of industry and cleverness—that the terror could be shut out—and really shut out—simply by turning one's back on it. As soon as it was not looked at it ceased to exist. In the other direction one saw the desert and drooping above it the constellations that had presided impassively over the building of the metaphor that seemed about to erase them from the skies. Yet they were in no way implicated in the success or the failure, depending on your viewpoint, of the project, as became clear the minute you caught sight of the Archer, languidly stretching his bow, aiming at a still higher and smaller portion of the heavens, no longer a figure of speech but an act, even if all the life had been temporarily drained out of it. It was obvious that a new journey would have to be undertaken, perhaps not the last but certainly an unavoidable one, into an area of an easier life, "where the lemons bloom," so that the last trials could be administered in an ambiance of relaxed understanding. You welcome these as an opportunity of definitively clearing your name, but are no less enthusiastic about the carefree, even frivolous atmosphere in which it all takes place—the sum total of all the good influences and friendly overtures in your direction, from which you have benefited intermittently all these years and which after periods of mutual discord have now banded together to create the impression of a climate in which nothing can go wrong, including the major question that revolves around you, your being here. And this is again affirmed in the stars: just their presence, mild and unquestioning, is proof that you have got to begin in the way of choosing some one of the forms of answering that question, since if they were not there the question would not exist to be answered, but only as a rhetorical question in the impassive grammar of cosmic unravelings of all kinds, to be proposed but never formulated.

The System

The system was breaking down. The one who had wandered alone past so many happenings and events began to feel, backing up along the primal vein that led to his center, the beginning of a hiccup that would, if left to gather, explode the center to the extremities of life, the suburbs through which one makes one's way to where the country is.

At this time of life whatever being there is is doing a lot of listening, as though to the feeling of the wind before it starts, and it slides down this anticipation of itself, already full-fledged, a lightning existence that has come into our own. The trees and the streets are there merely to divide it up, to prevent it from getting all over itself, from retreating into itself instead of logically unshuffling into this morning that had to be, of the day of temptation. It is with some playfulness that we actually sit down to the business of mastering the many pauses and the abrupt, sharp accretions of regular being in the clotted sphere of to-day's activities. As though this were just any old day. There is no need for setting out, to advertise one's destination. All the facts are here and it remains only to use them in the right combinations, but that building will be the size of today, the rooms habitable and leading into one another in a lasting sequence, eternal and of the greatest timeliness.

It is all that. But there was time for others, that were to have got under way, sequences that now can exist only in memory, for there were other times for them. Yet they really existed. For instance a jagged kind of mood that comes at the end of the day, lifting life into the truth of real pain for a few moments before subsiding in the usual irregular way, as things do. These were as much there as anything, things to be fumbled with, cringed before: dry churrings of no timbre, hysterical staccato passages that one cannot master or turn away from. These things led into life. Now they are gone but it remains, calm, lucid, but weightless, drifting above everything and everybody like a light in the sky, no more to be surmised, only remembered as so many things that remain at equal distances from us are remembered. The light drinks the dark and sinks down, not on top of us as we had expected but far, far from us in some other, unrelated sphere. This was not even the life that was going to happen to us.

It was different in those days, though. Men felt things differently and their reactions were different. It was all life, this truth, you forgot about it and it was there. No need to collect your thoughts at every moment before putting forth a hesitant feeler into the rank and file of their sensations: the truth was obstinately itself, so much so that it always seemed about to harden and shrink, to grow hard and dark and vanish into itself anxiously but stubbornly, but this was just the other side of the coin of its intense conviction. It really knew what it *was*. Meanwhile the life uncurled around it in calm waves, unimpressed by the severity and yet not paying much mind, also very much itself. It seemed as though innumerable transparent tissues hovered around these two entities and joined them in some way, and yet when one looked there was nothing special to be seen, only miles and miles of buoyancy, the way the mild blue sky of a summer afternoon seems to support a distant soaring bird. This was the outside reality. Inside there was like a bare room, or an alphabet, an alphabet of clemency. Now at last you knew what you were supposed to know. The words formed from it and the sentences formed from them were dry and clear, as though made of wood. There wasn't too much of any one thing. The feelings never wandered off into a private song or tried to present the procession of straightforward facts as something like a pageant: the gorgeous was still unknown. There was, however, a residue, a kind of fiction that developed parallel to the classic truths of daily life (as it was in that heroic but commonplace age) as they unfolded with the foreseeable majesty of a holocaust, an unfrightening one, and went unrecognized, drawing force and grandeur from this like the illegitimate offspring of a king. It is this "other tradition" which we propose to explore. The facts of history have been too well rehearsed (I'm speaking needless to say not of written history but the oral kind that goes on in you without your having to do anything about it) to require further elucidation here. But the other, unrelated happenings that form a kind of sequence of fantastic reflections as they succeed each other at a pace and according to an inner necessity of their own—these, I say, have hardly ever been looked at from a vantage point other than the historian's and an arcane historian's at that. The living aspect of these obscure phenomena has never to my knowledge been examined from a point of view like the painter's: in the round, bathed in a sufficient flow of overhead light, with "all its imperfections on its head" and yet without prejudice of the exaggerations either of the anathematist or the eulogist: quietly, in short, and I hope succinctly. Judged from this angle the whole affair will, I think, partake of and benefit from the enthusiasm not of the religious fanatic but of the average, open-minded, intelligent person who has never interested himself before in these matters either from not having had the leisure to do so or from ignorance of their existence.

From the outset it was apparent that someone had played a colossal trick on something. The switches had been tripped, as it were; the entire world or one's limited but accurate idea of it was bathed in glowing love, of a sort that need never have come into being but was now indispensable as air is to living creatures. It filled up the whole universe, raising the temperature of all things. Not an atom but did not feel obscurely compelled to set out in search of a mate; not a living creature, no insect or rodent, that didn't feel the obscure twitchings of dormant love, that didn't ache to join in the universal turmoil and hullabaloo that fell over the earth, roiling the clear waters of the reflective intellect, getting it into all kinds of messes that could have been avoided if only, as Pascal says, we had the sense to stay in our room, but the individual will condemns this notion and sallies forth full of ardor and *hubris,* bent on self-discovery in the guise of an attractive partner who is *the* heaven-sent one, the convex one with whom he has had the urge to mate all these seasons without realizing it. Thus a state of positively sinful disquiet began to prevail wherein men's eyes could be averted from the truth by the passing of a romantic stranger whose perfume set in motion all kinds of idle and frivolous trains of thought leading who knows where—to hell, most likely, or at very best to a position of blankness and ill-conceived repose on the edge of the flood, so that looking down into it one no longer saw the comforting reflection of one's own face and felt secure in the knowledge that, whatever the outcome, the struggle was going on in the arena of one's own breast. The bases for true reflective thinking had been annihilated by the scourge, and at the same time there was the undeniable fact of exaltation on many fronts, of a sense of holiness growing up through the many kinds of passion like a tree with branches bearing candelabra higher and higher up until they almost vanish from sight and are confused with the stars whose earthly avatars they are: the celestial promise of delights to come in another world and still lovely to look at in this one. Thus, in a half-baked kind of way, this cosmic welter of attractions was coming to stand for the real thing, which has to be colorless and featureless if it is to be the true reflection of the primeval energy from which it issued forth, once a salient force capable of assuming the shape of any of the great impulses struggling to accomplish the universal task, but now bogged down in a single aspect of these to the detriment of the others, which begin to dwindle, jejeune, etiolated, as though not really essential, as though someone had devised them for the mere pleasure of complicating the already complicated texture of the byways and torments through which we have to stray, plagued by thorns, chased by wild beasts, as though it were not commonly known from the beginning that not one of these tendrils of the tree of humanity could be bruised without endangering the whole vast waving mass; that that gorgeous, motley organism would tumble or die out unless each particle of its well-being were conserved as preciously as the idea of the whole. For universal love is as special an aspect as carnal love or any of the other kinds: all forms of mental and spiritual activity must be practiced and encouraged equally if the whole affair is to prosper. There is no cutting corners where the life of the soul is concerned, even if a too modest approximation of the wish that caused it to begin to want to flower be the result—a result that could look like overpruning to the untrained eye. Thus it was that a kind of blight fell on these early forms of going forth and being together, an anarchy of the affections sprung from too much universal cohesion.

Yet so blind are we to the true nature of reality at any given moment that this chaos—bathed, it is true, in the iridescent hues of the rainbow and clothed in an endless confusion of fair and variegated forms which did their best to stifle any burgeoning notions of the formlessness of the whole, the muddle really as ugly as sin, which at every moment shone through the colored masses, bringing a telltale finger squarely down on the addition line, beneath which these self-important and self-convoluted shapes added disconcertingly up to zero—this chaos began to seem like the normal way of being, so that some time later even very sensitive and perceptive souls had been taken in: it was for them life's rolling river, with its calm eddies and shallows as well as its more swiftly moving parts and ahead of these the rapids, with an awful roar somewhere in the distance; and yet, or so it seemed to these more sensible than average folk, a certain amount of hardship has to be accepted if we want the river-journey to continue; life cannot be a series of totally pleasant events, and we must accept the bad if we also wish the good; indeed a certain amount of evil is necessary to set it in the proper relief: how could we know the good without some experience of its opposite? And so these souls took over and dictated to the obscurer masses that follow in the wake of the discoverers. The way was picturesque and even came to seem carefully thought out; controls were waiting, in case things got out of hand, to restore the inevitable balance of happiness and woe; meanwhile the latter kept gradually diminishing whenever its turn came round and one really felt that one had set one's foot on the upward path, the spiral leading from the motley darkened and lightened landscape here below to the transparent veils of heaven. All that was necessary were patience and humbleness in recognizing one's errors, so as to be sure of starting out from the right place the next time, and so a sense of steady advancement came to reward one's efforts each time it seemed that one had been traveling too long without a view of the sun. And even in darkest night this sense of advancement came to whisper at one's side like a fellow traveler pointing the way.

Things had endured this way for some time, so that it began to seem as though some permanent way of life had installed itself, a stability immune to the fluctuations of other eras: the pendulum that throughout eternity has swung successively toward joy and grief had been stilled by a magic hand. Thus for the first time it seemed possible to consider ways toward a more fruitful and harmonious manner of living, without the fear of an adverse fate's coming to reduce one's efforts to nothing so soon as undertaken. And yet it seemed to those living as though even this state had endured for a considerable length of time. No one had anything against it, and most reveled in the creative possibilities its freedom offered, yet to all it seemed as though a major development had been holding off for quite a while and that its effects were on the verge of being felt, if only the present could give a slight push into the haphazard field of potentiality that lay stretched all around like a meadow full of wild flowers whose delightful promise lies so apparent that all question of entry into it and enjoyment is suspended for the moment. Hence certain younger spectators felt that all had already come to an end, that the progress toward infinity had crystallized in them, that they in fact were the other they had been awaiting, and that any look outward over the mild shoals of possibilities that lay strewn about as far as the eye could see was as gazing into a mirror reflecting the innermost depths of the soul.

Who has seen the wind? Yet it was precisely this that these enterprising but deluded young people were asking themselves. They were correct in assuming that the whole question of behavior in life has to be rethought each second; that not a breath can be drawn nor a footstep taken without our being forced in some way to reassess the age-old problem of what we are to do here and how did we get here, taking into account our relations with those about us and with ourselves, and the ever-present issue of our eternal salvation, which looms larger at every moment—even when forgotten it seems to grow like the outline of a mountain as one approaches it. To be always conscious of these multiple facets is to incarnate a dimensionless organism like the wind's, a living concern that can know no rest, by definition: it *is* restlessness. But this condition of eternal vigilance had been accepted with the understanding that somehow it would also mirror the peace that all awaited so impatiently: it could not proceed unless the generalized shape of this nirvana-like state could impose its form on the continually active atoms of the moving forward which was the price it exacted: hence a dilemma for any but the unrepentant hedonists or on the contrary those who chose to remain all day on the dung-heap, rending their hair and clothing and speaking of sackcloth and ashes: these, by far the noisiest group, made the least impression as usual, yet the very fact that they existed pointed to what seemed to be a tragic flaw in the system's structure; for among penance or perpetual feasting or the draconian requirements of a conscience eternally mobilized against itself, feeding on itself in order to re-create itself in a shape that the next instant would destroy, how was one to choose? So that those who assumed that they had reached the end of an elaborate but basically simple progression, the logical last step of history, came more and more to be the dominant party: a motley group but with many level heads among them, whose voices chanting the wise maxims of regular power gradually approached the point of submerging the other cacophony of tinkling cymbals and wailing and individual voices raised in solemn but unreal debate. This was the logical cutting-off place, then: ahead might lie new forms of life, some of them beautiful perhaps, but the point was that the effort of establishing them or anything else that was to come had ended here: a permanent now had taken over and was free to recast the old forms, riddles that had been expected to last until the Day of Judgment, as it saw fit, in whatever shape seemed expedient for living the next few crucial moments into a future without controls.

It seemed, just for a moment, that a new point had now been reached. It was not the time for digressions yet it made them inevitable, like a curtain at the end of an act. It brought you to a pass where turning back was unthinkable, and where further progress was possible only after it had been discussed at length, but which also outlawed discussion. Life became a pregnant silence, but it was understood that the silence was to lead nowhere. It became impossible to breathe easily in this constricted atmosphere. We ate little, for it seemed that in this way we could produce the inner emptiness from which alone understanding can spring up, the tree of contradictions, joyous and living, investing that hollow void with its complicated material self. At this time we were surrounded by old things, such as need not be questioned but which distill the meek information that is within them like a perfume on the air, to be used and disposed of; and also by certain new things which wear their newness like a quality, perhaps as an endorsement of the present, in all events as a vote of confidence in the currency of the just-created as a common language available to all men of good will, however disturbing the times themselves might turn out to be. Gradually one grew less aware of the idea of not turning back imposed as a condition for progress, as one imbibed the magic present that drew everything—the old and the new—along in the net of its infectious charm. Surely it would be possible to profit from the options of this cooperative new climate as though they were a charter instead of a vague sense of well-being, like a mild day in early spring, ready to be dashed to pieces by the first seasonable drop in temperature. And meanwhile there was a great sense of each one's going about his business, quiet in the elation of that accomplishment, as though it were enough to set one's foot on a certain path to be guaranteed of arriving at some destination. Yet the destinations were few. What actually was *wanted* from this constructive feeling? A "house by the side of the road" in which one could stay indefinitely, arranging new opportunities and fixing up old ones so that they mingled in a harmonious mass that could be called living with a sense of purpose? No, what was wanted and was precisely lacking in this gay and salubrious desert was an end to the "end" theory whereby each man was both an idol and the humblest of idolaters, in other words the antipodes of his own universe, his own redemption or his own damnation, with the rest of the world as a painted backdrop to his own monodrama of becoming of which he was the lone impassioned spectator. But the world avenges itself on those who would lose it by skipping over the due process of elimination, from whatever altruistic motive, by incrusting itself so thoroughly in these efforts at self-renewal that no amount of wriggling can dislodge its positive or negative image from all that is contemplated of present potentialities or the great sane simplifications to come. So that it was all lost, or rather all in the shade that instills weariness and sickness into the limbs under the guise of enraptured satiety. There was, again, no place to go, that is, no place that would not make a mockery of the place already left, casting all progress forward into the confusion of an eternally misapplied present. This was the stage to which reason and intuition working so well together had brought us, but it was scarcely their fault if now fear at the longest shadows of approaching darkness began to prompt thoughts of stopping somewhere for the night, as well as a serious doubt that any such place existed on the face of the earth.

On this Sunday which is also the last day of January let us pause for a moment to take note of where we are. A new year has just begun and now a new month is coming up, charged with its weight of promise and probable disappointments, standing in the wings like an actor who is conscious of nothing but the anticipated cue, totally absorbed, a pillar of waiting. And now there is no help for it but to be cast adrift in the new month. One is plucked from one month to the next; the year is like a fast-moving Ferris wheel; tomorrow all the riders will be under the sign of February and there is no appeal, one will have to get used to living with its qualities and perhaps one will even adjust to them successfully before the next month arrives with a whole string of new implications in its wake. Just to live this way is impossibly difficult, but the strange thing is that no one seems to notice it; people sail along quite comfortably and actually seem to enjoy the way the year progresses, and they manage to fill its widening space with multiple activities which apparently mean a lot to them. Of course some are sadder than the others but it doesn't seem to be because of the dictatorship of the months and years, and it goes away after a while. But the few who want order in their lives and a sense of growing and progression toward a fixed end suffer terribly. Sometimes they try to dope their consciousness of the shifting but ineluctable grid of time that has been arbitrarily imposed on them with alcohol or drugs, but these lead merely to mornings after whose waking is ten times more painful than before, bringing with it a new and more terrible realization of the impossibility of reconciling their own ends with those of the cosmos. If by chance you should be diverted or distracted for a moment from awareness of your imprisonment by some pleasant or interesting occurrence, there is always the shape of the individual day to remind you. It is a microcosm of man's life as it gently wanes, its long morning shadows getting shorter with the approach of noon, the high point of the day which could be likened to that sudden tremendous moment of intuition that comes only once in a lifetime, and then the fuller, more rounded shapes of early afternoon as the sun imperceptibly sinks in the sky and the shadows start to lengthen, until all are blotted in the stealthy coming of twilight, merciful in one sense that it hides the differences, blemishes as well as beauty marks, that gave the day its character and in so doing caused it to be another day in our limited span of days, the reminder that time is moving on and we are getting older, not older enough to make any difference on this particular occasion, but older all the same. Even now the sun is dropping below the horizon; a few moments ago it was still light enough to read but now it is no more, the printed characters swarm over the page to create an impressionistic blur. Soon the page itself will be invisible. Yet one has no urge to get up and put on a light; it is enough to be sitting here, grateful for the reminder that yet another day has come and gone, and you have done nothing about it. What about the morning resolutions to convert all the confused details in the air about you into a column of intelligible figures? To draw up a balance sheet? This naturally went undone, and you are perhaps grateful also for your laziness, glad that it has brought you to this pass where you must now face up to the day's inexorable end as indeed we must all face up to death some day, and put our faith in some superior power which will carry us beyond into a region of light and timelessness. Even if we had done the things we ought to have done it probably wouldn't have mattered anyway as everyone always leaves something undone and this can be just as ruinous as a whole life of crime or dissipation. Yes, in the long run there is something to be said for these shift-less days, each distilling its drop of poison until the cup is full; there is something to be said for them because there is no escaping them.

On the streets, in private places, they have no idea of the importance of these things. This exists only in our own minds, that is not in any place, nowhere. Possibly then it does not exist. Even its details are hazardous to consider. Most people would not consider it in its details, because (a) they would argue that details, no matter how complete, can give no adequate idea of the whole, and (b), because the details can too easily become fetishes, i.e., become prized for themselves, with no notion of the whole of which they were a part, with only an idolatrous understanding of the qualities of the particular detail. Certainly even this limited understanding can lead to a conception of beauty, insofar as any detail is a microcosm of the whole, as is so often the case. Thus you find people whose perfect understanding of love is deduced from lust, as the description of a flower can generate an idea of what it looks like. It is even possible that this irregular but satisfying understanding is the only one really allotted to us; that knowledge of the whole is impossible or at least so impractical as to be rarely or never feasible; that as we are born among imperfections we are indeed obligated to use them toward an assimilation of the imperfections that we are and the greater ones that we are to become; that not to do so would be to sin against nature, that is to end up with nothing, not even the reassuring knowledge that we have sinned to some purpose, but are instead empty and blameless as an inanimate object. Yet we know not what we are to become, therefore we can never completely rule out the possibility of intellectual understanding, even though it seems nothing but a snare and a delusion; we might miss out on everything by ignoring its call to order, which is in fact audible to each of us; therefore how can we decide? It is no solution either to combine the two approaches, to borrow from right reason or sensory data as the case seems to warrant, for an amalgam is not completeness either, and indeed is far less likely to be so through an error in dosage. So of the three methods: reason, sense, or a knowing combination of both, the last seems the least like a winner, the second problematic; only the first has some slim chance of succeeding through sheer perversity, which is possibly the only way to succeed at all. Thus we may be spared at least the agonizing wading through a slew of details of theories of action at the risk of getting hopelessly bogged down in them: better the erratic approach, which wins all or at least loses nothing, than the cautious semifailure; better Don Quixote and his windmills than all the Sancho Panzas in the world; and may it not eventually turn out that to risk all is to win all, even at the expense of intimate, visceral knowledge of the truth, of its graininess and contours, even though this approach leads despite its physicality to no practical understanding of the truth, no grasp of how to use it toward ends it never dreams of? This, then, is surely the way; but discovery of where it begins is another matter.

The great careers are like that: a slow burst that narrows to a final release, pointed but not acute, a life of suffering redeemed and annihilated at the end, and for what? For a casual moment of knowing that is here one minute and gone the next, almost before you were aware of it? Whole tribes of seekers of phenomena who mattered very much to themselves have gone up in smoke in the space of a few seconds, with less fuss than a shooting star. Is it then that our bodies combined in such a way as to show others that we really mean it to each other—is this really all we ever intended to do? Having been born with knowledge or at least with the capacity to judge, to spend all our time working toward a way to show off that knowledge, so as to be able to return to it at the end for what it is? Besides the obvious question of who knows whether it will still be there, there is the even more urgent one of whose life are we taking into our hands? Is there no way in which these things may be done for themselves, so that others may enjoy them? Already we have wandered far from the track and, as always happens in such cases, darkness has fallen and it would be impossible to find one's way back without getting lost. Is this a reason to stay where we are, on the false assumption that we are less lost right here, and thus to complete the cycle of inertia that we began wrongly supposing that it would lead to knowledge? No, it is far better to continue on our way, even at the risk of getting more lost (an impossibility, of course). We might at least wind up with a knowledge of who *they* are, with whom we began, and at the very least with a new respect toward the others, reached through a more perfect understanding of ourselves and the true way. But still the "career" notion intervenes. It is impossible for us at the present time not to think of these people as separate entities, each with his development and aim to be achieved, careers which will "peak" after a while and then go back to being ordinary lives that fade quite naturally into air as they are used up, and are as though they never were, except for the "lesson" which has added an iota to the sum of all human understanding. And this way of speaking has trapped each one of us.

An alternative way would be the "life-as-ritual" concept. According to this theory no looking back is possible, in itself a considerable advantage, and the stages of the ritual are each considered in themselves, for themselves, but here no danger of fetishism is possible because all contact with the past has been severed. Fetishism comes into being only when there is a past that may seem more or less attractive when compared with the present; the resulting inequality causes a rush toward the immediate object of contemplation, hardens it into a husk around its own being, which promptly ceases. But the ritual approach provides some bad moments too. All its links severed with the worldly matrix from which it sprang, the soul feels that it is propelling itself forward at an ever-increasing speed. This very speed becomes a source of intoxication and of more gradually accruing speed; in the end the soul cannot recognize itself and is as one lost, though it imagines it has found eternal rest. But the true harmony which would render this peace interesting is lacking. There is only a cold knowledge of goodness and nakedness radiating out in every direction like the spines of the horse chestnut; mere knowledge and experience without the visual irregularities, those celestial motes in the eye that alone can transform ecstasy into a particular state beyond the dearly won generality. Here again, if backward looks were possible, not nostalgia but a series of carefully selected views, hieratic as icons, the difficulty would be eased and self could merge with selflessness, in a true appreciation of the tremendous volumes of eternity. But this is impossible because the ritual is by definition something impersonal, and can only move further in that direction. It was born without a knowledge of the past. And any attempt to hybridize it can only result in destruction and even death.

In addition to these twin notions of growth, two kinds of happiness are possible: the frontal and the latent. The first occurs naturally throughout life; it is experienced as a kind of sense of immediacy, even urgency; often we first become aware of it at a moment when we feel we need outside help. Its sudden balm suffuses the soul without warning, as a kind of bloom or grace. We suppose that souls "in glory" feel this way permanently, as a day-to-day condition of being: yes, as a condition, for it is both more and less than a state; it exacts certain prerequisites and then it builds on these, but the foundation is never forgotten; it is the foundation that is happiness. And as it exacts, so it bestows. There is not the mindlessness, no idea of eternal lassitude permeated with the light of the firmament or whatever; there are only the value judgments of truth, exposed one after another like colored slides on the white wall that is the naked soul, or a kind of hard glaze that definitively transforms the ordinary clay of the soul into an object of beauty by obliterating the knowledge of what lies underneath. This is what we are all hoping for, yet we know that very few among us will ever achieve it; those who do will succeed less through their own efforts than through the obscure workings of grace as chance, so that although we would be very glad to have the experience of this sudden opening up, this inundation which shall last an eternity, we do not bother our heads too much about it, so distant and far away it seems, like those beautiful mosaic ceilings representing heaven which we crane up at from below, knowing that we cannot get near enough for it to be legible but liking all the same the vastness and aura of the conception, glad to have seen it and to know it's there but nevertheless firmly passing outward into the sunlight after two or three turns around the majestic dim interior. This kind of beauty is almost too abstract to be experienced as beauty, and yet we must realize that it is not an abstract notion, that it really can happen at times and that life at these times seems marvelous. Indeed this is truly what we were brought into creation for, if not to experience it, at least to have the knowledge of it as an ideal toward which the whole universe tends and which therefore confers a shape on the random movements outside us—these are all straining in the same direction, toward the same goal, though it is certain that few if any of those we see now will attain it.

The second kind, the latent or dormant kind, is harder to understand. We all know those periods of balmy weather in early spring, sometimes even before spring has officially begun: days or even a few hours when the air seems suffused with an unearthly tenderness, as though love were about to start, now, at this moment, on an endless journey put off since the beginning of time. Just to walk a few steps in this romantic atmosphere is to experience a magical but quiescent bliss, as though the torch of life were about to be placed in one's hands: after having anticipated it for so long, what is one now to do? And so the happiness withholds itself, perhaps even indefinitely; it realizes that the vessel has not yet been fully prepared to receive it; it is afraid it will destroy the order of things by precipitating itself too soon. But this in turn quickens the dismay of the vessel or recipient; it, or we, have been waiting all our lives for this sign of fulfillment, now to be abruptly snatched away so soon as barely perceived. And a kind of panic develops, which for many becomes a permanent state of being, with all the appearances of a calm, purposeful, reflective life. These people are awaiting the sign of their felicity without hope; its *nearness* is there, tingeing the air around them, in suspension, in escrow as it were, but they cannot get at it. Yet so great is their eagerness that they believe that they have already absorbed it, that they have attained that plane of final realization which we are all striving for, that they have achieved a state of permanent grace. Hence the air of joyful resignation, the beatific upturned eyelids, the paralyzed stance of these castaways of the eternal voyage, who imagine they have reached the promised land when in reality the ship is sinking under them. The great fright has turned their gaze upward, to the stars, to the heavens; they see nothing of the disarray around them, their ears are closed to the cries of their fellow passengers; they can think only of themselves when all the time they believe that they are thinking of nothing but God. Yet in their innermost minds they know too that all is not well; that if it were there would not be this rigidity, with the eye and the mind focused on a nonexistent center, a fixed point, when the common sense of even an idiot would be enough to make him realize that nothing has stopped, that we and everything around us are moving forward continually, and that we are being modified constantly by the speed at which we travel and the regions through which we pass, so that merely to think of ourselves as having arrived at some final resting place is a contradiction of fundamental logic, since even the dullest of us knows enough to realize that he is ignorant of everything, including the basic issue of whether we are in fact moving at all or whether the concept of motion is something that can even be spoken of in connection with such ignorant beings as we, for whom the term ignorant is indeed perhaps an overstatement, implying as it does that something is known somewhere, whereas in reality we are not even sure of this: we in fact cannot aver with any degree of certainty that we *are* ignorant.

Yet this is not so bad; we have at any rate kept our open-mindedness—*that,* at least, we may be sure that we have—and are not in any danger, or so it seems, of freezing into the pious attitudes of those true spiritual bigots whose faces are turned toward eternity and who therefore can see nothing. We know that we are en route in a certain sense, and also that there has been a hitch somewhere: we have as it were boarded the train but for some unexplained reason it has not yet started. But there is in this as yet only slight delay matter for concern even for the likes of us, intelligent and only modestly expectant as we are, patient, meek without any overtones of ironic resignation before a situation we are powerless to change and secretly believe is likely to go from bad to worse. There is nothing of that in us, we are not bigots and we have kept an open mind, we have all our mobility in a word, yet we too sense a danger and we do not quite know how we are going to react. Those first few steps, in the prematurely mild air that a blizzard is surely destined to dash from living memory before tomorrow comes—aren't we in danger of accepting these only for what they are, of being thankful for them and letting our gratitude take the place of further inquiry into what they were like, of letting it stand both for our attitude as eternity will view it and also for the fulfillment of which this was just the promise? That surely is the danger we run in our state of sophisticated but innocent enlightenment: that of not *demanding* and getting a hearing, of not finding out where these steps were leading even in the teeth of an almost dead certainty that it was nowhere, even of doubting that they ever took place, that any kind of structure or fabric in which they would assume being could ever have existed. So that in our way we are worse off or at least in worse danger than those others who imagine themselves already delivered from the chain of rebirth. *They* have their illusions to sustain them, even though these are full of holes and sometimes don't prevent their possessors from feeling the chilly drafts of doubt, while we can be brought to doubt that any of this, which we know in our heart of hearts to be a real thing, an event of the highest spiritual magnitude, ever happened. Here it is that our sensuality can save us *in extremis:* the atmosphere of the day that event took place, the way the trees and buildings looked, what we said to the person who was both the bearer and fellow recipient of that message and what that person replied, words that were not words but sounds out of time, taken out of any eternal context in which their content would be recognizable—these facts have entered our consciousness once and for all, have spread through us even into our pores like a marvelous antidote to the cup that the next moment had already prepared and which, whether hemlock or nectar, could only have proved fatal because it *was* the next, bringing with it the unspoken message that motion could be accomplished only in time, that is in a preordained succession of moments which must carry us far from here, far from this impassive but real moment of understanding which may be the only one we shall ever know, even if it is merely the first of an implied infinite series. But what if this were all? What if it were true that "once is enough"? That all consequences, all resonances of this singular event were to be cut off by virtue of its very singularity; nay, that even for memory, insofar as it can profit anyone, this instant were to be as though it had never existed, expunged from the chronicles of recorded time, fallen lower than the last circle of hell into a pit of total negation, and all this in our own best interests, so that we might not be led astray into imagining its goodness infinitely extendible, a thing that could never happen given the absolute and all-pervading nature of that goodness, destined to occur only once in the not-to-be-repeated cycle of eternity? Yet this seems not quite right, a little too pat perhaps, and here again it is our senses that are of some use to us in distinguishing verity from falsehood. For they never would have been able to capture the emanations from that special point of life if they were not meant to do something with them, weave them into the pattern of the days that come after, sunlit or plunged in shadow as they may be, but each with the identifying scarlet thread that runs through the whole warp and woof of the design, sometimes almost disappearing in its dark accretions, but at others emerging as the full inspiration of the plan of the whole, grandly organizing its repeated vibrations and imposing its stamp on these until the meaning of it all suddenly flashes out of the shimmering pools of scarlet like a vast and diaphanous though indestructible framework, not to be lost sight of again? And here we may say that even if the uniqueness were meant to last only the duration of its unique instant, which I don't for a moment believe, but let us assume so for the sake of argument—even if this were the case, its aura would still be meant to linger on in our days, informing us of and gently prodding us toward the right path, even though we might correctly consider ourselves shut off from the main source, never to be in a position to contemplate its rightness again, yet despite this able to consider its traces in the memory as a supreme good, as a god come down to earth to instruct us in the ways of the other kingdom, for he sees that we have not progressed very far on our own—no farther than those first few steps in the suddenly mild open air. And we are lucky that he chooses so to deal with us, for as of this moment our worries are over, we have only to step forward to be in the right path, we are all walking in it and we always have been, only we never knew it. The end is still shrouded in mystery, but the mystery diminishes without exactly becoming clearer the more we advance, like a city whose plan begins to take shape on the horizon as we approach it, yet that is not exactly the case here because we certainly perceive no more of the divine enigma as we progress, it is just that its mystery lessens and comes to seem, whenever we stop to think of it which is not very often, the least important feature of the whole. What does matter is our growing sense of certainty, whether deduced by the intellect or the sensual intelligence (this is immaterial): it is there, and this is all we need bother about, just as there is no need to examine a man's ancestry or antecedents in evaluating his personal qualities. But, after the question of how did it get there, which we now perceive to be futile, another question remains: how are we to use it? Not only by what means, which is an important enough consideration, but toward what end? Toward our own betterment and by extension that of the world around us or conversely toward the improvement of the world, which we might believe would incidentally render us as its citizens better people, even though this were just a side effect? The answer is in our morning waking. For just as we begin our lives as mere babes with the imprint of nothing in our heads, except lingering traces of a previous existence which grow fainter and fainter as we progress until we have forgotten them entirely, only by this time other notions have imposed themselves so that our infant minds are never a complete *tabula rasa*, but there is always something fading out or just coming into focus, and this whatever-it-is is always projecting itself on us, escalating its troops, prying open the shut gates of our sensibility and pouring in to augment its forces that have begun to take over our naked consciousness and driving away those shreds of another consciousness (although not, perhaps, forever—nothing is permanent—but perhaps until our last days when their forces shall again mass on the borders of our field of perception to remind us of that other old existence which we are now called to rejoin) so that for a moment, between the fleeing and the pursuing armies there is almost a moment of peace, of purity in which what we are meant to perceive could almost take shape in the empty air, if only there were time enough, and yet in the time it takes to perceive the dimness of its outline we can if we are quick enough seize the meaning of that assurance, before returning to the business at hand—just, I say, as we begin each day in this state of threatened blankness which is wiped away so soon, but which leaves certain illegible traces, like chalk dust on a blackboard after it has been erased, so we must learn to recognize it as the form—the only one—in which such fragments of the true learning as we are destined to receive will be vouchsafed to us, if at all. The unsatisfactoriness, the frowns and squinting, the itching and scratching as you listen without taking in what is being said to you, or only in part, so that you cannot piece the argument together, should not be dismissed as signs of our chronic all-too-human weakness but welcomed and examined as signs of life in which part of the whole truth lies buried. And as the discourse continues and you think you are not getting anything out of it, as you yawn and rub your eyes and pick your nose or scratch your head, or nudge your neighbor on the hard wooden bench, this knowledge is getting through to you, and taking just the forms it needs to impress itself upon you, the forms of your inattention and incapacity or unwillingness to understand. For it is certain that you will rise from the bench a new person, and even before you have emerged into the full daylight of the street you will feel that a change has begun to operate in you, within your very fibers and sinews, and when the light of the street floods over you it will have become real at last, all traces of doubt will have been pulverized by the influx of light slowly mounting to bury those crass seamarks of egocentricity and warped self-esteem you were able to navigate by but which you no longer need now that the rudder has been swept out of your hands, and this whole surface of daylight has become one with that other remembered picture of light, when you were setting out, and which you feared would disappear because of its uniqueness, only now realizing that this singleness was the other side of the coin of its many-faceted diversity and interest, and that it may be simultaneously cherished for the former and lived in thanks to the versatility of the latter. It may be eaten, and breathed, and it would indeed have no reason to exist if this were not the case. So I think that the question of how we are going to use the reality of our revelation, as well as to what end, has now been resolved. First of all we see that these two aspects of our question are actually one and the same, that there is only one aspect as well as only one question, that to wonder how is the same as beginning to know why. For no choice is possible. In the early moments of wondering after the revelation had been received it could have been that this way of doing seemed to promise more, that that one had already realized its potential, that therefore there was matter for hesitation and the possibility of loss between a way that had already proved itself and another, less sure one that could lead to greener pastures, to cloud-cuckoo land and even farther, just because the implied risk seemed to posit a greater virtue in the acceptance. But it is certain now that these two ways are the same, that we *have* them both, the risk and the security, merely through being human creatures subject to the vicissitudes of time, our earthly lot. So that this second kind of happiness is merely a fleshed-out, realized version of that ideal first kind, and more to be prized because its now ripe contours enfold both the promise and the shame of our human state, which they therefore proceed to transmute into something that is an amalgam of both, the faithful reflection of the idealistic concept that got us started along this path, but a reflection which is truer than the original because more suited to us, and whose shining perspectives we can feel and hold, clenching the journey to us like the bread and meat left by the wayside for the fatigued traveler by an anonymous Good Samaritan—ourselves, perhaps, just as Hop-o'-My-Thumb distributed crumbs along the way to guide him back in the dark, only these the birds have miraculously spared: they are ours. To know this is to be able to relax without any danger of becoming stagnant. Thus the difficulty of living with the unfolding of the year is erased, the preparing for spring and then for the elusive peace of summer, followed by the invigorating readjustments of autumn and the difficult and never very successful business of adapting to winter and the approach of another year. This way we are automatically attuned to these progressions and can forget about them; what matters is us and not what time makes of us, or rather it is what we make of ourselves that matters. What is this? Just the absorption of ourselves seen from the outside, when it is really what is going on inside us—all this overheard chatter and speculation and the noises of the day as it wears on into the calm of night, joyful or abysmal as it may be: this doesn't matter once we have accepted it and taken it inside us to be the interior walls of our chamber, the place where we live. And so all these conflicting meaningless details are transformed into something peaceful that surrounds, like wallpaper that could be decorated with scenes of shipwrecks or military attributes or yawning crevasses in the earth and which doesn't matter, which indeed can paradoxically heighten the feeling of a peaceful domestic interior. Yet this space wasn't made just for the uses of peace, but also for action, for planned assaults on the iniquity and terror outside, though this doesn't mean either that we shall have at some point to go outside or on the contrary that our plans will remain at the stage of dreams or armies in the fire: we carry both inside and outside around with us as we move purposefully toward an operation that is going to change us on every level, and is also going to alter the balance of power of happiness in the world in our favor and that of all the human beings in the world. And how is this to become possible? Let us assume for the sake of argument that the blizzard I spoke of earlier has occurred, shattering the frail décor of your happiness like a straw house, replunging you and your world into the grey oblivion you had been floundering in all your life until the day your happiness was given to you as a gift, a reward or so it seemed for the stale unprofitable journey you called your life, only now it seemed that it was just beginning, and at the same moment you had an impression of stopping or ending. Apparently then happiness was to be a fixed state, but then you perceived that it was both fixed and mobile at the same time, like a fixed source of light with rays running out from and connecting back to it. This suited you very well, because it replied to your twin urges to act and to remain at peace with yourself and with the warring elements outside. And now these have again taken over and crushed your fragile dream of happiness, so that it all seems meaningless. Gazing out at the distraught but inanimate world you feel that you have lapsed back into the normal way things are, that what you were feeling just now was a novelty and hence destined to disappear quickly, its sole purpose if any being to light up the gloom around you sufficiently for you to become aware of its awesome extent, more than the eye and the mind can take in. The temptation here is to resume the stoic pose, tinged with irony and self-mockery, of times before. There was no point in arriving at this place, but neither, you suppose, would there have been any in avoiding it. It is all the same to you. And you turn away from the window almost with a sense of relief, to bury yourself again in the task of sorting out the jumbled scrap basket of your recent days, without any hope of completing it or even caring whether it gets done or not. But you find that you are unable to pick up the threads where you left off; the details of things shift and their edges swim before your tired eyes; it is impossible to make even the rudimentary sense of them that you once could. You see that you cannot do without it, that singular isolated moment that has now already slipped so far into the past that it seems a mere spark. You cannot do without it and you cannot have it. At this point a drowsiness overtakes you as of total fatigue and indifference; in this unnatural, dreamy state the objects you have been contemplating take on a life of their own, in and for themselves. It seems to you that you are eavesdropping and can understand their private language. They are not talking about you at all, but are telling each other curious private stories about things you can only half comprehend, and other things that have a meaning only for themselves and are beyond any kind of understanding. And these in turn would know other sets of objects, limited to their own perceptions and at the limit of the scope of visibility of those that discuss them and dream about them. It could be that time and space are filled up with these to infinity and beyond; that there is no such thing as a void, only endless lists of things that may or may not be aware of one another, the "sad variety of woe." And this pointless diversity plunges you into a numbing despair and blankness. The whole world seems dyed the same melancholy hue. Nothing in it can arouse your feelings. Even the sun seems dead. And all because you succumbed to what seemed an innocent and perfectly natural craving, to have your cake and eat it too, forgetting that, widespread as it is, it cannot be excused on any human grounds because it cannot be realized. Therefore even to contemplate it is a sin. But, you say, in those first moments . . . Never mind that now. You must forget them. The dream that was fleetingly revealed to you was a paradox, and for this reason must be forgotten as quickly as possible. But, you continue to argue, it mattered precisely because it was a paradox and about to be realized here on earth, in human terms; otherwise one would have forgotten it as quickly as any morning dream that clings to you in the first few waking moments, until its incongruities become blatant in the reasonable daylight that seeps back into your consciousness. It was not a case of a spoiled child asking its mother for something for the nth time or of wishing on a star; it was a *new arrangement* that existed and was on the point of working. And now it is all the same; any miracles, if there ever are any again, will be partial ones, mere virtuosic exhibitions beside the incontrovertible reality of that other, as amazingly real as a new element or a new dimension. And so it goes. But if it was indeed as real as all that, then it *was* real, and therefore it *is* real. Just as matter cannot be added to or subtracted from the universe, or energy destroyed, so with something real, that is, real in the sense you understood it and understand it. When will you realize that your dreams have eternal life? I of course don't mean that you are a moonstruck dreamer, but that they do exist, outside of you, without your having to do anything about it. Even if you do something it won't matter. And it is possible that you will always remain unaware of their existence; this won't matter either, to them, that is. But you must try to seize the truth of this: whatever was, is, and must be. The darkness that surrounds you now does not exist, because it never had any independent existence: you created it out of the spleen and torment you felt. It looks real enough to hide you from the light of the sun, but its reality is as specious as that of a mirage. The clouds are dispersing. And nothing comes to take their place, to interpose itself between you and the reality which you dreamed and which is therefore real. This new arrangement is already guiding your steps and indicating the direction you should take without your realizing it, for it is invisible now; it still seems that it is lost for there is of course no tangible evidence of it: *that* happens only once, it is true. But now to have absorbed the lesson, to have recovered from the shock of not being able to remember it, to again be setting out from the beginning—is this not something good to you? You no longer have to remember the principles, they seem to come to you like fragments of a buried language you once knew. You are like the prince in the fairy tale before whom the impenetrable forest opened and then the gates of the castle, without his knowing why. The one thing you want is to pause so as to puzzle all this out, but that is impossible; you are moving much too quickly for your momentum to be halted. How will it all turn out? What will the end be? But these are questions of the ignorant novice which you have forgotten about already. You think now only in terms of the speed with which you advance, and which you drink in like oxygen; it has become the element in which you live and which is you. Nothing else matters.

And so, not bothering about anything, you again took things into your own hands. You were a little incredulous as to the outcome, but you decided to try it anyway. Who could tell what would happen? It didn't do to dwell too much on those ideal forms of happiness that had haunted you ever since the cradle and had now defined themselves almost in a paroxysm; they could be assigned to the corners and cubbyholes of your mind since it didn't matter whether they were in evidence as long as you never actually lost sight of them. What did matter now was getting down to business, or back to the business of day-to-day living with all the tiresome mechanical problems that this implies. And it was just here that philosophy broke down completely and was of no use. How to deal with the new situations that arise each day in bunches or clusters, and which resist categorization to the point where any rational attempt to deal with them is doomed from the start? And in particular how to deal with this one that faces you now, which has probably been with you always; now it has a different name and a different curriculum vitae; its qualities are combined in such a way as to seem different from all that has gone before, but actually it is the same old surprise that you have always lived with. Forget about the details of name and place, forget also the concepts and archetypes that haunt you and which are as much a part of the typical earthbound situation you find yourself in as those others: neither the concept nor the state of affairs logically deduced from it is going to be of much help to you now. What is required is the ability to enter into the complexities of the situation as though it really weren't new at all, which it isn't, as one takes the first few steps into a labyrinth. Here one abruptly finds one's intuition tailored to the needs of the new demanding syndrome; each test is passed flawlessly, as though in a dream, and the complex climate that is formed by the vacillating wills and energies of the many who surround you becomes as easy as pie for you. You take on all comers but you do not advertise your presence. Right now it is important to slip as quickly as possible into the Gordian contours of the dank, barren morass (or so it seems at present) without uttering so much as a syllable; to live in that labyrinth that seems to be directing your steps but in reality it is you who are creating its pattern, embarked on a new, fantastically difficult tactic whose success is nevertheless guaranteed. You know this. But it will be a long time before the ordinary assurances will be able to make themselves felt in the strange, closed-off state you are in now. You may as well forget them and abandon yourself to the secret growing that has taken over. Nothing can stop it, so there is no point in worrying about it or even thinking about it.

How we move around in our little ventilated situation, how roomy it seems! There is so much to do after all, so many people to be with, and we like them all. But meanwhile it seems as if our little space were moving counter to us, dragging us backward. We have reached this far point of where we are by following someone's advice and at times it seems as though it might have been the wrong advice. If this were the case, to become aware of it would be no help because we have refined the baser elements out of our present situation and are technically on the same footing with others of different origins who meet and socialize with us. One sign of this is that no one remarks on the lateness of the hour, for we have reached a point where such details no longer count; we believe that we are immune to time because we are "out of" it. Yet we know dimly that the stillness we have attained is racing forward faster than ever toward its rendezvous with the encroaching past; we know this and we turn from it, to take refuge in dreams where all is not exactly well either, in which we reach the summit of our aspirations to find the mass below riddled and honeycombed with vacancy, yet there is room on the crest to move around in; it might almost qualify as an oasis. But as we all know, the thing about an oasis is that the whole desert has to become one before its exotic theories can benefit us, and even that would not be enough because then there would be too much of a contrast with the ordinary temperate climate leading up to it. Yet one can very well live and enjoy the fruits of one's considerable labors in arriving at this place which could be the end of the world in no unfavorable sense; there are the same things to look at and be surrounded by although in lesser numbers; what it is is quality as opposed to quantity. But can the one exist without the other? These thoughts oppress one in the social world one has built around oneself, especially the thought of these other infinite worlds upon worlds; and when one really examines one's own world in the harsher light of its happiness-potential one sees that it is a shambles indeed. Yet there is air to breathe. One may at least stay here a while hoping for more and better things to come.

That's the way it goes. For many weeks you have been exploring what seemed to be a profitable way of doing. You discovered that there was a fork in the road, so first you followed what seemed to be the less promising, or at any rate the more obvious, of the two branches until you felt you had a good idea of where it led. Then you returned to investigate the more tangled way, and for a time its intricacies seemed to promise a more complex and therefore a more practical goal for you, one that could be picked up in any number of ways so that all its faces or applications could be thoroughly scrutinized. And in so doing you began to realize that the two branches were joined together again, farther ahead; that this place of joining was indeed the end, and that it was the very place you set out from, whose intolerable mixture of reality and fantasy had started you on the road which has now come full circle. It has been an absorbing puzzle, but in the end all the pieces fit together like a ghost story that turns out to have a perfectly rational explanation. Nothing remains but to begin living with this discovery, that is, without the hope mentioned above. Even this is not so easy, for the reduced mode or scope must itself be nourished by a form of hope, or hope that doesn't take itself seriously. One must move very fast in order to stay in the same place, as the Red Queen said, the reason being that once you have decided there is no alternative to remaining motionless you must still learn to cope with the onrushing tide of time and all the confusing phenomena it bears in its wake, some of which perfectly resemble the unfinished but seemingly salvageable states of reality at cross-purposes with itself that first caused you to grow restless, to begin fidgeting with various impractical schemes that were in the end, we have seen, finally reduced to zero. Yet they cannot be banished from the system any more than physical matter can, and their nature, which is part and parcel of their existence, is to remain incomplete, clamoring for wholeness. So that now two quite other and grimmer alternatives present themselves: that of staying where you are and risking eventual destruction at the hands of those dishonest counselors of many aspects, or of being swept back by them into a past drenched in nostalgia whose sweetness burns like gall. And it is a choice that we have to make.

As a lost dog on the edge of a sidewalk timidly approaches first one passerby and then another, uncertain of what to ask for, taking a few embarrassed steps in one direction and then suddenly veering to another before being able to ascertain what reception his mute entreaty might have met with, lost, puzzled, ashamed, ready to slink back into his inner confusion at the first brush with the outside world, so your aspirations, my soul, on this busy thoroughfare that is the great highway of life. What do you think to gain from merely standing there looking worried, while the tide of humanity sweeps ever onward, toward some goal it gives every sign of being as intimately acquainted with as you are with the sharp-edged problems that beset you from every angle? Do you really think that if you succeed in looking pathetic enough some kindly stranger will stop to ask your name and address and then steer you safely to your very door? No, I do not think you are afflicted with that kind of presumption, and yet your pitiable waif's stance, that inquiring look that darts uneasily from side to side as though to ward off a blow—these do not argue in your favor, even though we both know you to be a strong upright character, far above such cheap attempts to play on the emotions of others. And there is no use trying to tell them that the touching melancholy of your stare is the product not of self-pity but of a lucid attempt to find out just where you stand in the fast-moving stream of traffic that flows endlessly from horizon to horizon like a dark river. *We* know that the pose you happen to be striking for the world to see matters nothing to you, it could just as easily be some other one, joyous-looking or haughty and overbearing, or whatever. It is only that you happened to be wearing this look as you arrived at the end of your perusal of the way left open to you, and it "froze" on you, just as your mother warned you it would when you were little. And now it is the face you show to the world, the face of expectancy, strange as it seems. Perhaps Childe Roland wore such a look as he drew nearer to the Dark Tower, every energy concentrated toward the encounter with the King of Elfland, reasonably certain of the victorious outcome, yet not so much as to erase the premature lines of care from his pale and tear-stained face. Maybe it is just that you don't want to outrage anyone, especially now that the moment of your own encounter seems to be getting closer. You can feel it in every pore, in the sudden hush that falls over the din of the busy street and the unusual darkness in the sky even though no clouds are apparent. Your miserable premature spring has finally turned into the real thing, confirmed by the calendar, but what a sad look it wears, especially after its promising beginnings that now seem so far back in the past. The air is moist and almost black, and sharp with the chill; the magnolia petals flatten and fall off one after the other onto the half-frozen mud of the ground where only a few spears of sickly green grass have managed to lift their heads. All this comes as no surprise, it is even somewhat of a relief, and better than the dire sequel that those precocious moments seemed to promise, cataclysms instead of the ominous hush that now lies over everything. And who is to say whether or not this silence isn't the very one you requested so as to be able to speak? Perhaps it seems ominous only because it is concentrating so intensely on you and what you have to say.

"Whatever was, is, and must be"—these words occur again to you now, though in a different register, transposed from a major into a minor key. Yet they are the same words as before. Their meaning is the same, only you have changed: you are viewing it all from a different angle, perhaps not more nor less accurate than the previous one, but in any case a necessary one no doubt for the in-the-round effect to be achieved. We see it all now. The thing that our actions have accomplished, and its results for us. And it is no longer a nameless thing, but something colorful and full of interest, a chronicle play of our lives, with the last act still in the dim future, so that we can't tell yet whether it is a comedy or a tragedy, all we know is that it is crammed with action and the substance of life. Surely all this living that has gone on that is ours is good in some way, though we cannot tell why: we know only that our sympathy has deepened, quickened by the onrushing spectacle, to the point where we are like spectators swarming up onto the stage to be absorbed into the play, though always aware this is an impossibility, and that the actors continue to recite their lines as if we weren't there. Yet in the end, we think, this may become possible; that is the time when audience and actor and writer and director all mingle joyously together as one, as the curtain descends a last time to separate them from the half-empty theater. When this happens—yet there is no point in looking to that either. The apotheosis never attracted you, only those few moments in the next-to-last act where everything suddenly becomes momentarily clear, to sink again into semiobscurity before the final blaze which merely confirms the truth of what had been succinctly stated long before. But there does not seem to be any indication that this moment is approaching.

Except that the silence continues to focus on you. Who am I after all, you say despairingly once again, to have merited so much attention on the part of the universe; what does it think to get from me that it doesn't have already? I know too that my solipsistic approach is totally wrongheaded and foolish, that the universe isn't listening to me any more than the sea can be heard inside conch shells. But I'm just a mute observer—it isn't my fault that I can really notice how everything around me is waiting just for me to get up and say the word, whatever that is. And surely even the eyes of the beloved are fixed on you as though wondering, "What is he going to do *this* time?" And those eyes as well as the trees and skies that surround you are full of apprehension, waiting for this word that must come from you and that you have not in you. "What am I going to say?" But as you continue gazing embarrassedly into the eyes of the beloved, talking about extraneous matters, you become aware of an invisible web that connects those eyes to you, and both of you to the atmosphere of this room which is leading up to you after the vagaries of the space outside. Suddenly you realize that you have been talking for a long time without listening to yourself; you must have said *it* a long way back without knowing it, for everything in the room has fallen back into its familiar place, only this time organized according to the invisible guidelines that radiate out from both of you like the laws that govern a kingdom. Now there is so much to talk about that it seems neither of you will ever get done talking. And the word that everything hinged on is buried back there; by mutual consent neither of you examined it when it was pronounced and rushed to its final resting place. It is doing the organizing, the guidelines radiate from its control; therefore it is good not to know what it is since its results can be known so intimately, appreciated for what they are; it is best then that the buried word remain buried for we were intended to appreciate only its fruits and not the secret principle activating them—to know this would be to know too much. Meanwhile it is possible to know just enough, and this is all we were supposed to know, toward which we have been straining all our lives. We are to read this in outward things: the spoons and greasy tables in this room, the wooden shelves, the flyspecked ceiling merging into gloom—good and happy things, nevertheless, that tell us little of themselves and more about ourselves than we had ever imagined it was possible to know. They have become the fabric of life.

Until, accustomed to disappointments, you can let yourself rule and be ruled by these strings or emanations that connect everything together, you haven't fully exorcised the demon of doubt that sets you in motion like a rocking horse that cannot stop rocking. You may have scored a few points there where you first took those few steps (no more than three, in all likelihood) when you first realized the enormity of the choice between two kinds of mutually exclusive universal happiness. And you also realized the error of forever ruminating on

and repeating those fatal steps, like a broken movie projector that keeps show-
ing the same strip of film—you realized this when you were already far from
that experience which had indeed begun to take on the unearthly weirdness of
an old photograph. You cried out in the desert and you collapsed into yourself,
indifferent to the progress of the seasons and the planets in their orbits, and
you died for the first time. And now that you have been raised from the tomb
like Lazarus by obscure miraculous forces you are surprised that the earth isn't
better than the one you left behind, that all things haven't yet perfected them-
selves as you believe you have done by dying and being resuscitated to the un-
certain glory of this day in early spring. You can't get over the fact that
conversations still sound the same, that clouds of unhappiness still persist in
the unseen mesh that draws around everything, uniting it in a firm purpose as
it causes each individual thing to bulge more brightly and more darkly at the
same time, drawing out the nature of its real being. But that is the wonder of it:
that you have returned not to the supernatural glow of heaven but to the ordi-
nary daylight you knew so well before it passed from your view, and which
continues to enrich you as it steeps you and your ageless chattels of mind,
imagination, timid first love and quiet acceptance of experience in its revitaliz-
ing tide. And the miracle is not that you have returned—you always knew you
would—but that things have remained the same. The day is not far advanced:
it still half-seriously offers with one hand the promise that it pockets with the
other, and it is still up to you to seize the occasion, jump into the fray, not be
ruled by its cruel if only human whims. The person sitting opposite you who
asked you a question is still waiting for the answer; he has not yet found your
hesitation unusual, but it is up to you to grasp it with both hands, wrenching it
from the web of connectives to rub off the grime that has obscured its bril-
liance so as to restore it to him, that pause which is the answer you have both
been expecting. When it was new everybody could tell this, but years of inac-
tivity and your own inattention have tarnished it beyond recognition. It needs
a new voice to tell it, otherwise it will seem just another awkward pause in a
conversation largely made up of similar ones, and will never be able to realize
its potential as a catalyst, turning you both in on yourself and outward to that
crystalline gaze that has been the backing of your days and nights for so long
now. For the time being only you know it for what it is, but as you continue to
hold on to it others will begin to realize its true nature, until finally it stands as

the shortest distance between your aims and those of the beloved, the only human ground that can nurture your hopes and fears into the tree of life that is as big as the universe and entirely fills it up with its positive idea of growth and gaining control. So it is permissible to rest here awhile in this pause you alone discovered: a little repose can do no harm at this stage; meanwhile do not fear that when you next speak the whole scene will come to life again, as though triggered by invisible machines. There is not much for you to do except wait in the anticipation of your inevitable reply.

Inevitable, but so often postponed. Whole eras of history have sprung up in the gaps left by these pauses, dynasties, barbarian invasions and so on until the grass and shards stage, and still the answer is temporarily delayed. During these periods one thought enclosed everything like the blue sky of history: that it really was this one and no other. As long as this is the case everything else can take its course, time can flow into eternity leaving a huge deltalike deposit whose fan broadens and broadens and is my life, the time I am taking; we get up in the morning and blow on some half-dead coals, maybe for the last time; my hair is white and straggly and I hardly recognize my face any more, yet none of this matters so long as your reply twists it all together, the transparent axle of this particular chapter in history. It seems that the blue of the sky is a little paler each morning, as happens toward the end of each epoch, yet one doesn't want to move hastily, but to continue at this half-savage, half-pastoral existence, until one day the unmistakable dry but deep accent is heard:

"You waited too long. And now you are going to be rewarded by my attention. Make no mistake: it will probably seem to you as though nothing has changed; nothing will show in the outward details of your life and each night you will creep tired and enraged into bed. Know however that I am listening. From now on the invisible bounty of my concern will be there to keep you company, and as you mature it will unlock more of the same space for you so that eventually all your territory will have become rightfully yours again."

I know now that I am no longer waiting, and that the previous part of my life in which I thought I was waiting and therefore only half-alive was not waiting, although it was tinged with expectancy, but living under and into this reply which has suddenly caused everything in my world to take on new meaning. It is as though I had picked up a thread which I had merely mislaid but which for a long time seemed lost. And all because I am certain now, albeit for no very good reason, that it was this one and no other. The sadness that infected us as children and stayed on through adulthood has healed, and there can be no other way except this way of health we are taking, silent as it is. But it lets us look back on those other, seemingly spoiled days and re-evaluate them: actually they were too well-rounded, each bore its share of happiness and grief and finished its tale just as twilight was descending; those days are now an inseparable part of our story despite their air of immaturity and tentativeness; they have the freshness of early works which may be wrongly discarded later. Nor is today really any different: we are as childish as ever, it turns out, only perhaps a little better at disguising it, but we still want what we want when we want it and no power on earth is strong enough to deny it to us. But at least we see now that this is how things are, and so we have the sense to stop insisting every so often under the guise of some apparently unrelated activity, because we think we shall be better satisfied this way; underneath the discreet behavior the desire is as imperious as ever, but after so many postponements we now realize that a little delay won't hurt and we can relax in the assurance of eventual satisfaction. This was the message of that day in the street, when you first perceived that conventional happiness would not do for you and decided to opt for the erratic kind despite the dangers that its need for continual growth and expansion exposed it to. This started you on your way, although it often seemed as though your feet had struck roots into the ground and you are doomed to grow and decay like a tree. Nevertheless you were aware of moving, whether it was you who were moving or the landscape moving forward toward you, and you could remain patient with the idea of growth as long as the concept of uniqueness—that one and no other—shone like a star in the sky above you.

Today your wanderings have come full circle. Having begun by rejecting the idea of oneness in favor of a plurality of experiences, earthly and spiritual, in fact a plurality of different lives that you lived out to your liking while time proceeded at another, imperturbable rate, you gradually became aware that the very diversity of these experiences was endangered by its own inner nature, for variety implies parallelism, and all these highly individualistic ways of thinking and doing were actually moving in the same direction and constantly threatening to merge with one another in a single one-way motion toward that invisible goal of concrete diversity. For just as all kinds of people spring up on earth and imagine themselves very different from each other though they are basically the same, so all these ideas had arisen in the same head and were merely aspects of a single organism: yourself, or perhaps your desire to be different. So that now in order to avoid extinction it again became necessary to invoke the idea of oneness, only this time if possible on a higher plane, in order for the similarities in your various lives to cancel each other out and the differences to remain, but under the aegis of singleness, separateness, so that each difference might be taken as the type of all the others and yet remain intrinsically itself, unlike anything in the world. Which brings us to you and the scene in the little restaurant. You are still there, far above me like the polestar and enclosing me like the dome of the heavens; your singularity has become oneness, that is your various traits and distinguishing marks have flattened out into a cloudlike protective covering whose irregularities are all functions of its uniformity, and which constitutes an arbitrary but definitive boundary line between the new informal, almost haphazard way of life that is to be mine permanently and the monolithic samenesses of the world that exists to be shut out. For it has been measured once and for all. It would be wrong to look back at it, and luckily we are so constructed that the urge to do so can never waken in us. We are both alive and free.

If you could see a movie of yourself you would realize that this is true. Movies show us ourselves as we had not yet learned to recognize us—something in the nature of daily being or happening that quickly gets folded over into ancient history like yesterday's newspaper, but in so doing a new face has been revealed, a surface on which a new phrase may be written before it rejoins history, or it may remain blank and do so anyway: it doesn't matter because each thing is coming up in its time and receding into the past, and this is what we all expect and want. What does matter is what becomes of it once it has entered the past's sacred precincts; when, bending under the weight of an all-powerful nostalgia, its every contour is at last revealed for what it was, but this can be known only in the past. It isn't wrong to look at things in this way—how else could we live in the present knowing it was the present except in the context of the important things that have already happened? No, one must treasure each moment of the past, get the same thrill from it that one gets from watching each moment of an old movie. These windows on the past enable us to see enough to stay on an even keel in the razor's-edge present which is really a no-time, continually straying over the border into the positive past and the negative future whose movements alone define it. Unfortunately we have to live in it. We are appalled at this. Because its no-time, no-space dimensions offer us no signposts, nothing to be guided by. In this dimensionless area a single step can be leagues or inches; the flame of a match can seem like an explosion on the sun or it can make no dent in the matte-grey, uniform night. The jolting and loss of gravity produce a permanent condition of nausea, always buzzing faintly at the blurred edge where life is hinged to the future and to the past. But only focus on the past through the clear movie-theater dark and you are a changed person, and can begin to live again. That is why we, snatched from sudden freedom, are able to communicate only through this celluloid vehicle that has immortalized and given a definitive shape to our formless gestures; we can live as though we had caught up with time and avoid the sickness of the present, a shapeless blur as meaningless as a carelessly exposed roll of film. There is hardness and density now, and our story takes on the clear, compact shape of the plot of a novel, with all its edges and inner passages laid bare for the reader, to be resumed and resumed over and over, that is taken up and put aside and taken up again.

What place is there in the continuing story for all the adventures, the wayward pleasures, the medium-size experiences that somehow don't fit in but which loom larger and more interesting as they begin to retreat into the past? There were so many things held back, kept back, because they didn't fit into the plot or because their tone wasn't in keeping with the whole. So many of these things have been discarded, and they now tower on the brink of the continuity, hemming it in like dark crags above a valley stream. One sometimes forgets that to be all one way may be preferable to eclectic diversity in the interests of verisimilitude, even for those of the opposite persuasion; the most powerful preachers are those persuaded in advance and their unalterable lessons are deeply moving just because of this rigidity, having none of the tepidness of the meandering stream of our narration with its well-chosen and typical episodes, which now seems to be trying to bury itself in the landscape. The rejected chapters have taken over. For a long time it was as though only the most patient scholar or the recording angel himself would ever interest himself in them. Now it seems as though that angel had begun to dominate the whole story: he who was supposed only to copy it all down has joined forces with the misshapen, misfit pieces that were never meant to go into it but at best to stay on the sidelines so as to point up how everything else belonged together, and the resulting mountain of data threatens us; one can almost hear the beginning of the lyric crash in which everything will be lost and pulverized, changed back into atoms ready to resume new combinations and shapes again, new wilder tendencies, as foreign to what we have carefully put in and kept out as a new chart of elements or another planet—unimaginable, in a word. And would you believe that this word could possibly be our salvation? For we are rescued by what we cannot imagine: it is what finally takes us up and shuts our story, replacing it among the millions of similar volumes that by no means menace its uniqueness but on the contrary situate it in the proper depth and perspective. At last we have that rightness that is rightfully ours. But we do not know what brought it about.

It could be anything, you say. But it could not have been an exercise in defining the present when our position, our very lives depend on those fixed loci of past and future that leave no room for the nominal existence of anything else. But it turns out you have been pursuing the discussion in a leisurely way throughout January and February and now to a point farther into the wilderness of this new year which makes such a commotion and goes by so quickly. These ample digressions of yours have carried you ahead to a distant and seemingly remote place, and it is here that you stop to give emphasis to all the way you have traveled and to your present silence. And it is here that I am quite ready to admit that I am alone, that the film I have been watching all this time may be only a mirror, with all the characters including that of the old aunt played by me in different disguises. If you need a certain vitality you can only supply it yourself, or there comes a point, anyway, when no one's actions but your own seem dramatically convincing and justifiable in the plot that the number of your days concocts. I have been watching this film, therefore, and now I have seen enough; as I leave the theater I am surprised to find that it is still daylight outside (the darkness of the film as well as its specks of light were so intense); I am forced to squint; in this way I gradually get an idea of where I am. Only this world is not as light as the other one; it is made grey with shadows like cobwebs that deepen as the memory of the film begins to fade. This is the way all movies are meant to end, but how is it possible to go on living just now except by plunging into the middle of some other one that you have doubtless seen before? It seems truly impossible, but invariably at this point we are walking together along a street in some well-known city. The allegory is ended, its coils absorbed into the past, and this afternoon is as wide as an ocean. It is the time we have now, and all our wasted time sinks into the sea and is swallowed up without a trace. The past is dust and ashes, and this incommensurably wide way leads to the pragmatic and kinetic future.

The Recital

All right. The problem is that there is no new problem. It must awaken from the sleep of being part of some other, old problem, and by that time its new problematical existence will have already begun, carrying it forward into situations with which it cannot cope, since no one recognizes it and it does not even recognize itself yet, or know what it is. It is like the beginning of a beautiful day, with all the birds singing in the trees, reading their joy and excitement into its record as it progresses, and yet the progress of any day, good or bad, brings with it all kinds of difficulties that should have been foreseen but never are, so that it finally seems as though they are what stifles it, in the majesty of a sunset or merely in gradual dullness that gets dimmer and dimmer until it finally sinks into flat, sour darkness. Why is this? Because not one-tenth or even one one-hundredth of the ravishing possibilities the birds sing about at dawn could ever be realized in the course of a single day, no matter how crammed with fortunate events it might turn out to be. And this brings on inevitable reproaches, unmerited of course, for we are all like children sulking because they cannot have the moon; and very soon the unreasonableness of these demands is forgotten and overwhelmed in a wave of melancholy of which it is the sole cause. Finally we know only that we are unhappy but we cannot tell why. We forget that it is our own childishness that is to blame.

That this is true is of course beyond argument. But we ought to look into the nature of that childishness a little more, try to figure out where it came from and how, if at all, we can uproot it. And when we first start to examine it, biased as we are, it seems as though we are not entirely to blame. We have all or most of us had unhappy childhoods; later on we tried to patch things up and as we entered the years of adulthood it was a relief, for a while, that everything was succeeding: we had finally left that long suffocating tunnel and emerged into an open place. We could not yet see very well due to the abrupt change from darkness to daylight, but we were beginning to make out things. We embarked on a series of adult relationships from which the sting and malignancy of childhood were absent, or so it seemed: no more hiding behind bushes to get a secret glimpse of the others; no more unspeakable rages of jealousy or the suffocation of unrequited and unrealizable love. Or at least these things retreated into their proper perspective as new things advanced into the foreground: new feelings as yet too complex to be named or closely inspected, but in which the breathless urgency of those black-and-white situations of childhood happily played no part. It became a delight to enumerate all the things in the new world our maturity had opened up for us, as inexhaustible in pleasures and fertile pursuits as some more down-to-earth Eden, from which the utopian joys as well as the torments of that older fantasy-world had been banished by a more reasonable deity.

But as the days and years sped by it became apparent that the naming of all the new things we now possessed had become our chief occupation; that very little time for the mere tasting and having of them was left over, and that even these simple, tangible experiences were themselves subject to description and enumeration, or else they too became fleeting and transient as the song of a bird that is uttered only once and disappears into the backlog of vague memories where it becomes as a dried, pressed flower, a wistful parody of itself. Meanwhile all our energies are being absorbed by the task of trying to revive those memories, make them real, as if to live again were the only reality; and the overwhelming variety of the situations we have to deal with begins to submerge our efforts. It becomes plain that we cannot interpret everything, we must be selective, and so the tale we are telling begins little by little to leave reality behind. It is no longer so much our description of the way things happen to us as our private song, sung in the wilderness, nor can we leave off singing, for that would be to retreat to the death of childhood, to the mere acceptance and dull living of all that is thrust upon us, a living death in a word; we must register our appraisal of the moving world that is around us, but our song is leading us on now, farther and farther into that wilderness and away from the shrouded but familiar forms that were its first inspiration. On and on into the gathering darkness—is there no remedy for this? It is as though a day which had begun brilliantly in the blaze of a new sunrise had become transfixed as a certain subtle change in the light can cast a chill over your heart, or the sight of a distant thin ribbon of cirrus ebbing into space can alter everything you have been feeling, dropping you back years and years into another world in which its fragile reminder of inexorable change was also the law, as it is here today.

You know now the sorrow of continually doing something that you cannot name, of producing automatically as an apple tree produces apples this thing there is no name for. And you continue to hum as you move forward, but your heart is pounding.

All right. Then this new problem is the same one, and that is the problem: that our apathy can always renew itself, drawing energy from the circumstances that fill our lives, but emotional happiness blooms only once, like an annual, leaving not even roots or foliage behind when its flower withers and dies. We are forced to recognize that we are still living in the same old state of affairs and that it never really went away even when it seemed to. Well, but what can we do about it? Because even though the hydraheaded monster of apathy can grow a new head each day to slash back at us with, more fearsome than the one we just succeeded in cutting off, so too nothing says that we aren't to fight back at it, using the sword that our condition of reasoning beings has placed in our hands. Although the task seems hopeless and there is no end to the heads in sight, we are within our rights in fighting back, the weapon is ours to wield, and it is possible that by dint of continually doing so we might at length gain a slight foothold or edge, for the enemy's powers though superhuman are not inexhaustible: we are basically certain that nothing is except the capacity for struggle that unites us, foe to foe, on the vast plain of life. We are like sparrows fluttering and jabbering around a seemingly indifferent prowling cat; we know that the cat is stronger and therefore we forget that we have wings, and too often we fall in with the cat's plans for us, afraid and therefore unable to use the wings that could have saved us by bearing us aloft if only for a little distance, not the boundless leagues we had been hoping for and insisting on, but enough to make a crucial difference, the difference between life and death.

"It almost seems—" How often this locution has been forced on us when we were merely trying to find words for a more human expression of our difficulty, something closer to home. And with this formula our effort flies off again, having found no place to land. As though there were something criminal in trying to understand a little this uneasiness that is undermining our health, causing us to think crazy thoughts and behave erratically. We can no longer live our lives properly. Every good impulse is distorted into something like its opposite; the people we see are like parodies of reasonable human beings. There is no spiritual model for our aspirations; no *vademecum* beckons in the light around us. There is only the urge to get on with it all. It is like the difference between someone who is in love and someone who is merely "good in bed": there is no vital remnant which would transform one's entire effort into an image somewhat resembling oneself. Meanwhile everything conspires to protect the business-as-usual attitude of the diurnal scenery—no leaf or brick must be found out of place, no timbre ring false lest the sickening fakery of the whole wormy apparatus, the dry rot behind the correct façade suddenly become glaringly and universally apparent, its shame at last real for all to see. Appearances must be kept up at whatever cost until the Day of Judgment and afterward if possible.

We are trying with mortal hands to paint a landscape which would be a faithful reproduction of the exquisite and terrible scene that stretches around us. No longer is there any question of adjusting a better light on things, to show them ideally as they may never have existed, of taking them out from under the sun to place them in the clean light that meditation surrounds them with. Youth and happiness, the glory of first love—all are viewed naturally now, with all their blemishes and imperfections. Even the wonderful poetry of growing a little older and realizing the important role fantasy played in the *Sturm und Drang* of our earlier maturity is placed in its proper perspective, so as not to exaggerate the importance in the general pattern of living of the disabused intellect, whose nature it is to travel from illusion to reality and on to some seemingly superior vision, it being the quality of this ebbing and flowing motion rather than the relevance of any of its isolated component moments that infuses a life with its special character. Until, accustomed to disappointments, it seemed as though we had triumphed over the limitations of logic and blindfold passion alike; the masterpiece we were on the point of achieving was classic in the sense of the Greeks and simultaneously informed by a Romantic ardor minus the eccentricity, and this all-but-terminated work was the reflection of the ideal shape of ourselves, as we might have lived had we been gifted with foreknowledge and also the ability to go back and retrace our steps. And so, pleased with it and with ourselves, we stepped back a few paces to get the proper focus.

Any reckoning of the sum total of the things we are is of course doomed to failure from the start, that is if it intends to present a true, wholly objective picture from which both artifice and artfulness are banished: no art can exist without at least traces of these, and there was never any question but that this rendering was to be made in strict conformity with the rules of art—only in this way could it approximate most closely the thing it was intended to reflect and illuminate and which was its inspiration, by achieving the rounded feeling almost of the forms of flesh and the light of nature, and being thus equipped for the maximum number of contingencies which, in its capacity as an aid and tool for understanding, it must know how to deal with. Perhaps this was where we made our mistake. Perhaps no art, however gifted and well-intentioned, can supply what we were demanding of it: not only the figured representation of our days but the justification of them, the reckoning and its application, so close to the reality being lived that it vanishes suddenly in a thunderclap, with a loud cry.

The days fly by; they do not cease. By night rain pelted the dark planet; in the morning all was wreathed in false smiles and admiration, but the daylight had gone out of the day and it knew it. All the pine trees seemed to be dying of a mysterious blight. There was no one to care. The sky was still that nauseatingly cloying shade of blue, with the thin ribbon of cirrus about to disappear and materialize over other, alien lands, far from here. If only, one thought, one had begun by having the courage of one's convictions instead of finishing this way, but "once burned, twice shy"; one proceeds along one's path murmuring idiotic formulas like this to give oneself courage, noticing too late that the landscape isn't making sense any more; it is not merely that you have misapplied certain precepts not meant for the situation in which you find yourself, which is always a new one that cannot be decoded with reference to an existing corpus of moral principles, but there is even a doubt as to our own existence. Why, after all, were we not destroyed in the conflagration of the moment our real and imaginary lives coincided, unless it was because we never had a separate existence beyond that of those two static and highly artificial concepts whose fusion was nevertheless the cause of death and destruction not only for ourselves but in the world around us? But perhaps the explanation lies precisely here: what we were witnessing was merely the reverse side of an event of cosmic beatitude for all except us, who were blind to it because it took place inside us. Meanwhile the shape of life has changed definitively for the better for everyone on the outside. They are bathed in the light of this tremendous surprise as in the light of a new sun from which only healing and not corrosive rays emanate; they comment on the miraculous change as people comment on the dazzling beauty of a day in early autumn, forgetting that for the blind man in their midst it is a day like any other, so that its beauty cannot be said to have universal validity but must remain fundamentally in doubt.

This single source of so much pleasure and pain is therefore a thing that one can never cease wondering upon. On the one hand, such boundless happiness for so many; on the other so much pain concentrated in the heart of one. And it is true that each of us is this multitude as well as that isolated individual; we experience the energy and beauty of the others as a miraculous manna from heaven; at the same time our eyes are turned inward to the darkness and emptiness within. All records of how we came here have been effaced, so there is no chance of working backward to some more primitive human level: the spiritual dichotomy exists once and for all time, like the mind of creation, which has neither beginning nor end. And the proof of this is that we cannot even imagine another way of being. We are stuck here for eternity and we are not even aware that we are stuck, so natural and even normal does our quandary seem. The situation of Prometheus, bound to the crags for endless ages and visited daily by an eagle, must have seemed so to him. We were surprised once, long ago; and now we can never be surprised again.

What is it for you then, the insistent now that baffles and surrounds you in its loose-knit embrace that always seems to be falling away and yet remains behind, stubbornly drawing you, the unwilling spectator who had thought to stop only just for a moment, into the sphere of its solemn and suddenly utterly vast activities, on a new scale as it were, that you have neither the time nor the wish to unravel? It always presents itself as the turning point, the bridge leading from prudence to "a timorous capacity," in Wordsworth's phrase, but the bridge is a Bridge of Sighs the next moment, leading back into the tired regions from whence it sprang. It seems as though every day is arranged this way. The movement is the majestic plodding one of a boat crossing a harbor, certain of its goal and upheld by its own dignity on the waves, a symbol of patient, fruitful activity, but the voyage always ends in a new key, although at the appointed place; a note has been added that destroys the whole fabric and the sense of the old as it was intended. The day ends in the darkness of sleep.

Therefore since today, a day that is really quite cool despite the deceptive appearance of the sunlight on things, is to really be the point when everything changes for better or for worse, it might be good to examine it, see how far it goes, since the far reaches of sleep are to be delayed indefinitely. It is not even a question of them any more. What matters is how you are going to figure your way out of this new problem which has again come home to roost. Will the answer be another delay, prolonged beyond the end of time, and disguised once again as an active life intelligently pursued? Or is it to be a definite break with the past—either the no of death shutting you up in a small cell-like space or a yes whose vibrations you cannot even begin to qualify or imagine?

As I thought about these things dusk began to invade my room. Soon the outlines of things began to grow blurred and I continued to think along well-rehearsed lines like something out of the past. Was there really nothing new under the sun? Or was this novelty—the ability to take up these tattered enigmas again and play with them until something like a solution emerged from them, only to grow dim at once and fade like an ignis fatuus, a specter mocking the very reality it had so convincingly assumed? No, but this time something real did seem to be left over—some more solid remnant of the light as the shadows continued to pile up. At first it seemed to be made merely of bits and pieces of the old, haggard situations, rearranged perhaps to give a wan impersonation of modernity and fecundity. Then it became apparent that certain new elements had been incorporated, though perhaps not enough of them to change matters very much. Finally—these proportions remaining the same—something like a different light began to dawn, to make itself felt: just as the first glimmers of day are often mistaken for a "false dawn," and one waits a long time to see whether they will go away before gradually becoming convinced of their authority, even after it has been obvious for some time, so these tremors slowly took on the solidity, the robustness of an object. And by that time everything else had gone away, or retreated so far into the sidelines that one was no longer conscious of those ephemera that had once seemed the very structure, the beams and girders defining the limits of the ambiguous situation one had come to know and even to tolerate, if not to love.

The point was the synthesis of very simple elements in a new and strong, as opposed to old and weak, relation to one another. Why hadn't this been possible in the earlier days of experimentation, of bleak, barren living that didn't seem to be leading anywhere and it couldn't have mattered less? Probably because not enough of what made it up had taken on that look of worn familiarity, like pebbles polished over and over again by the sea, that made it possible for the old to blend inconspicuously with the new in a union too subtle to cause any comment that would have shattered its purpose forever. But already it was hard to distinguish the new elements from the old, so calculated and easygoing was the fusion, the partnership that was the only element now, and which was even now fading rapidly from memory, so perfect was its assimilation by the bystanders and décor that in other times would have filled up the view, and that now were becoming as transparent as the substance that was giving them back to life.

A vast wetness as of sea and air combined, a single smooth, anonymous matrix without surface or depth was the product of these new changes. It no longer mattered very much whether prayers were answered with concrete events or the oracle gave a convincing reply, for there was no longer anyone to care in the old sense of caring. There were new people watching and waiting, conjugating in this way the distance and emptiness, transforming the scarcely noticeable bleakness into something both intimate and noble. The performance had ended, the audience streamed out; the applause still echoed in the empty hall. But the idea of the spectacle as something to be acted out and absorbed still hung in the air long after the last spectator had gone home to sleep.

TITLE INDEX

385

▬▬▬

ABOUT THE AUTHOR

JOHN ASHBERY is the author of sixteen books of poetry, including *Can You Hear, Bird* (Farrar, Straus & Giroux, 1995), and a volume of art criticism, *Reported Sightings*. His *Self-Portrait in a Convex Mirror* received the Pulitzer Prize, the National Book Critics Circle Award, and the National Book Award. He is now Charles P. Stevenson, Jr., Professor of Languages and Literature at Bard College. He has been named a Guggenheim Fellow, a MacArthur Fellow, and a chancellor of the Academy of American Poets. In 1995, he received the Poetry Society of America's Robert Frost Medal, the highest honor awarded by that institution.